Who's Driving

THE

PURPOSE
DRIVEN
CHURCH

Printed in the United States of America

ISBN 0-9744764-5-5

Who's Driving

THE

PURPOSE
DRIVEN
CHURCH

*A Documentary on the
Teachings of Rick Warren*

by James Sundquist

Dedicated to the saints throughout the ages
who endured hardships, were persecuted and martyred,
who were destitute and naked, who were beaten, mistreated,
who were stoned, sawed in two, were put to death by the sword,
who were burned at the stake, who loved their lives not unto death,
who overcame by the Blood of the Lamb
and the word of their testimony,
yet somehow found their purpose in life through Scripture alone
(Sola Scriptura) —
this world is not worthy of them.

(See Hebrews 11; Ephesians 3:4, 11; and Revelation 12:11)

"Take heed therefore that the light which is in thee be not darkness."

—Jesus Christ
Luke 11:35

"Now the Spirit speaketh expressly, that in the latter times some shall depart from the faith, giving heed to seducing spirits, and doctrines of devils; . . . If thou put the brethren in remembrance of these things, thou shalt be a good minister of Jesus Christ, nourished up in the words of faith and of good doctrine, whereunto thou hast attained."

—The Apostle Paul
1 Timothy 4:1,6

Contents

Appendices

Foreword and Acknowledgments

I would like to personally thank Rev. Noah Hutchings and Dr. Larry Spargimino for reading my documentary and sharing the urgency for publishing this book through Southwest Radio Church Ministries.

I also wish to extend my profound gratitude to my wife Karen and all of my brothers and sisters in the Lord who have been telling me for years that I needed to write a book. But the time has had to be the Lord's. I believe now is that time. And though there are a number of great subjects in the field of biblical discernment and the end times (about which I have personally written articles), and many other topics I would love to address, it is the subject of post-modernism in the form of the Church Growth Movement and the Purpose Driven Church that I believe poses the greatest clear and present danger to the church because of both its magnitude and its subtlety.

Upon reviewing Rick Warren's *Purpose Driven Life* book, his web sites, and follow-up programs, I am now more convinced than ever that light must be brought to his teachings. I am also very grateful to the many pastors, discernment scholars, and many other brothers and sisters around the world who have reviewed my manuscript to help ensure accuracy, as iron sharpens iron.

Some of those whom I would like to personally acknowledge are: Pastor Bob DeWaay, Twin City Fellowship, Minneapolis, MN; Pastor Gary Gilley, Southern View Chapel, Springfield, IL; Dr. Carl Laney, Professor, Western Seminary, Portland, OR; Susan Anderson for all of your help and encouragement; Dusty Peterson and Elizabeth McDonald, both of Bayith Ministries, United Kingdom; Ryan and Lisa Bazler, authors of *Psychology Debunked*; Mike and Christine Narloch,

Jr.; Jacob Prasch, Moriel Ministries; Art Pfeiffer; Chris Carmichael; Dennis Hyde; Jeannette Haley; Jo Reaves, *Midnight Herald;* Mike Oppenheimer, Let Us Reason Ministry; Sandy Simpson, Apologetics Coordination Team; Dr. Opal Reddin; Wendy B. Howard, Editor, *Despatch Magazine*, Australia; Jewel Grewe, Discernment Ministries; Ned Collingridge; Rita Williams, Cephas Ministry; Dr. Kent Hovind; Matt Costella, Fundamental Evangelistic Association; Paul Proctor; Reverend Ed Hird, Past National Chair, ARM Canada; and Simon Altaf and Walid Shoebat, *Abrahamic-faith.com.* I would also like to thank my parents who raised me in the ways of the Lord. Finally, and most importantly, I would like to thank the Lord for giving me a hunger for the truth.

It is my fervent prayer that because you too love the truth and are good Bereans, that you will read this documentary with an open mind.

> —James Sundquist
> Founder
> Rock Salt Publishing
> *www.abrahamic-faith.com/False-Teachers.html*

Preface

Many of our readers and listeners of Southwest Church Radio Ministries have been very disturbed by the introduction of the *Purpose Driven Life* and *40 Days of Purpose* books and programs by Rick Warren into their churches and individual lives. You have indicated that you would just love to go before your congregations, and appeal to your pastors and elders to reconsider introducing this campaign and teaching, as well as warn them to change course and remove his teachings from pulpit and small group Bible studies. But you have lamented, "We need facts. . . . We need proof. . . . Please equip us with something we can use to convince them!" We have heard your plea! And the Lord hears your cries.

In this regard, we are pleased to introduce you to James Sundquist, who has spent several years researching the Church Growth Movement and the Purpose Driven Church teachings, and had just completed his documentary on Rick Warren's *Purpose Driven Life* and sent it to us, not even knowing of our desire to address this very important issue. So this book could not come at a better time. We hope and pray that it will both encourage you and equip you to challenge the biblical foundations and teachings of Rick Warren.

> In Christ,
> Rev. Noah Hutchings
> President
> Southwest Radio Church Ministries
> *and*
> Dr. Larry Spargimino
> Associate Pastor and Editor
> Southwest Radio Church Ministries

Introduction

The Purpose Driven Life by Rick Warren has become a Number 1 best-seller in both Christian as well as secular bookstores, and has been distributed to over 180,000 pastors worldwide according Rick Warren's own web site, *www.purposedriven.com,* having sold 20 million copies as of April 2004. Rick Warren's theology and book have infiltrated almost every Christian denomination, including private label versions such as "We Build People" in the Assembly of God church. Just some of the denominations incorporating Rick Warren's book include Conservative Baptist, American Baptist, Southern Baptist, Reformed, Lutheran, Episcopal, Nazarene, Methodist, Christian and Missionary Alliance, Foursquare church, Presbyterian, Vineyard, Seventh-Day Adventist, and United Pentecostal church, Church of God, Evangelical Free, Calvary Chapel, and a host of community and non-denominational churches throughout the United States and the rest of the world. Because of this, I believe it is more imperative than ever to test the spirits of his teachings to see if they are of God.

Let me first say that it is absolutely critical to present the facts of Rick Warren's teachings by using his exact quotes and comparing them to Scripture, as the Lord considers it an abomination to bear false witness against a brother in Christ. I also have presented my articles to several fellow biblical discernment scholars, as iron sharpens iron, to help ensure the integrity of this document. There are a number of excellent documentaries, book reviews, and articles exposing Mr. Warren's teachings by other very capable discernment ministries throughout the world whom I list as resources for you throughout this book, as well as at the end. But finally, it is not my review of his teachings that you should ultimately test, though you should test mine as well, but more critically, that you be a good Berean and compare each quote and translation to Scripture, as the apostle Paul commended the Bereans and commands us to do.

And though I have spent years researching Rick Warren's teachings and the teachers he promotes and endorses, I have not included every error in his book. Some of the errors that I reveal have also been exposed by other scholars. I have not listed many problems and errors that have been documented by these scholars. Some of the selected resources, ministries, and web sites I have referenced in this book and in appendix E are mentioned because they are meant for the subject matter we will discuss throughout this book.

After reading *The Purpose Driven Life,* I could not help but wonder how it ever made it past the editors at Zondervan, his publisher, because there were so many colossal biblical blunders in the book. Then upon reviewing which translations he used, I discovered none other than Zondervan itself was the publisher of two such translations (*The Amplified Bible* and *The Revised Standard Version*). For further explanation on my use of the King James Version translation, I refer you to chapter three.

But no translation could be blamed for Rick Warren's error regarding the purposes of the forty days in each of the Old and New Testament characters he cites. These are purely factual errors, easily detectable! I have endeavored to document what I perceive to be the most glaring errors in his teaching and theology. In a manner similar to Martin Luther's *95 Theses,* I would simply like to list the problems with Warren's teaching. I address the errors in 113 pages of his 334-page book under each of the numbered "40 Days of Purpose" according to Rick Warren. In addition to the other resources I would like to equip you with, I invite you to read my chart comparing the Purpose Driven Church and Church Growth Movement to Scripture located at the end of this book (see appendix B). You can also access it at: *www.christianunplugged.com/cgm_chart.htm.*

Finally, for those who might believe that Rick Warren is above or exempt from criticism ("Don't criticize what God has blessed"), I exhort you to consider the following Scripture:

> Now the Spirit speaketh expressly, that in the latter times some
> shall depart from the faith, giving heed to seducing spirits, and
> doctrines of devils; . . . If thou put the brethren in remembrance of
> these things, **thou shalt be a good minister of Jesus Christ**, nour-
> ished up in the words of faith and of good doctrine, whereunto
> thou hast attained.
>
> —1 Timothy 4:1,6

I also would like to affirm that *every* Christian should expose a heretic
because "heretic" literally means schismatic or dividing or departing
from sound doctrine, i.e., a teacher of false doctrine. So to be a good
Berean as the apostle Paul commended the Berean church, we must
diligently search the Scriptures daily to see if any teaching is scriptural. We must all be vigilant to test every spirit to see if it is of God.
And those in eldership position are all the more required to guard the
flock against false teaching. Jesus Christ himself warned us to not be
deceived. And how would we even know deception without comparing a teaching to Scripture? The Lord has brought to the church another gift of the Holy Spirit, which is called "Discerner of Spirits." A
little leaven does not leaven just part of the lump, but if left unpurged,
will leaven the *entire* lump. One of the most precious doctrines and
resources of Christianity is *truth!* If we compromise truth, we will
have lost the savor in our salt and will eventually and rightfully be
trodden under foot.

Some Christians have used the term "heresy hunter" to describe
a person who exposes false teaching. But there remains a problem
with the negative connotation of "heresy hunter," at least in the case
of Rick Warren. The term implies that his teaching is obscure or hidden from obvious view like a hidden treasure or that we are going
on an unwarranted search-and-destroy mission. But the fact is that
there is *nothing* obscure or hidden about Warren's teaching. I did
not go out looking for it; it has come like a flood into a city, in which
no house is left untouched with water in its basement or worse. The
floodwaters of his teachings and books have permeated virtually every
city and denomination in the country. We did not ask for this! But it

is here nevertheless. I have tried to organize this book by separating in order the false translations from Warren's false teachings. But this was not always possible because his translations are often inextricably woven into his teachings. So my chapter headings are simply a general guide.

This is the list of abbreviations for all of the translations used by Rick Warren in his book:

AMP	*The Amplified Bible*, Grand Rapids: Zondervan (1965)
CEV	*Contemporary English Version*, New York: American Bible Society (1995)
GWT	*God's Word Translation*, Grand Rapids: World Publishing, Inc. (1995)
KJV	*King James Version*
LB	*Living Bible*, Wheaton, IL: Tyndale House Publishers (1979)
MSG	*The Message*, Colorado Springs: Navpress (1993)
NAB	*New American Bible*, Chicago: Catholic Press (1970)
NASB	*New American Standard Bible*, Anaheim, CA: Foundation Press (1973)
NCV	*New Century Version*, Dallas: Word Bibles (1991)
NIV	*New International Version*, Colorado Springs: International Bible Society (1978, 1984)
NJB	*New Jerusalem Bible*, Garden City, NY: Doubleday Publishers (1985)
NLT	*New Living Translation*, Wheaton, IL: Tyndale House Publishers (1996)
NRSV	*New Revised Standard Version*, Grand Rapids: Zondervan (1990)
Ph	*New Testament in Modern English* by J.B. Phillips, New York: Macmillan (1958)
TEV	*Today's English Version*, New York: American Bible Society (1992) (also called *Good News Translation*)

—Rick Warren, *The Purpose Driven Life*, appendix 3, page 325

False Premise of 40 Days of Purpose Comparing Warren's 40-Day Examples to Scripture

Rick Warren states: **"Don't you think it would be a wise use of time to set aside 40 of those days to figure out what God wants you to do with the rest of them? . . . Whenever God wanted to prepare someone for his purposes, he took 40 days."** [1]

Who decided, and by what authority, that forty days was required to determine your purpose in life? All who heard the message of repentance throughout both the Old and New Testaments and responded found out *immediately* God's purpose for their life. As many as five thousand who heard the message of the Gospel in the New Testament instantly became saved upon hearing it (see Acts 4:4). Paul received his calling and knew immediately what he was supposed to do the rest of his life. So Rick Warren's whole premise of purpose is fatally flawed. The events Warren describes in the Bible *transpired* in forty days, but that does not mean transformation took the entire forty days. I was most eager to determine what Rick Warren really meant by the term **"transformed."** It is safe to assume that he means what he quotes in Romans 12:2 (NLT) and attempts to then apply to various characters in the Old and New Testament: "Let God **transform** you into a new person by changing the way you think. Then you will know what God wants you to do."

---

1. Rick Warren, *Purpose Driven Life* (Zondervan Publishing, 2003), pp. 9–10.

Now let's see what that verse really says:

And be not conformed to this world: but be ye transformed by the renewing of your mind, that ye may prove what is that good, and acceptable, and perfect, will of God.

—Romans 12:2 (KJV)

In verse 1 of this chapter Paul states unequivocally who he is addressing when he says, "brethren." So the transforming can only apply to those who were already saved and at that point had already determined their purpose in life. The renewing of the mind Paul is talking about is the renewing of the minds of Christians or believers. Mr. Warren applies the term "transformed" to *both* believers and non–believers in the biblical examples he gives. Secondly, he assumes that at the beginning of forty days, each of his examples were still in a state of being conformed to this world, i.e., not yet transformed.

Here are the examples he cites:

1. Was Noah still conformed to this world at the beginning the forty days of rain? *No!* See Genesis 7 to determine for yourself!
2. Was Moses still conformed to this world at the beginning of forty days on Mount Sinai? *No!* See Exodus 24 to determine for yourself!
3. Was David still conformed to this world at the beginning of Goliath's forty-day challenge? *No!* See 1 Samuel 17 to determine for yourself!
4. Was Elijah still conformed to this world at the beginning of the forty days he received a single meal to strengthen him? *No!* See 1 Kings 19 to determine for yourself!
5. Were Jesus' disciples still conformed to this world at the beginning of the forty days commencing with Christ's resurrection? *No!* See Acts 1:3 to determine for yourself! Finally, if at any time the disciples were transformed it was at Pentecost, which even Christ told them to wait for! Pentecost is fifty days, not forty days. That is when they received power—not before—but they already had their purpose.

Now Rick Warren's example of Nineveh being conformed to this world at the beginning of the forty days would be true. But there is no evidence it took forty days for them to be transformed. In fact, the evidence in **Jonah** points to immediate repentance and the wearing of sackcloth. There is no text to support forty days of a process of transforming, assuming that this term can even apply to someone who was not a believer at the beginning or even during the forty days. The text in Jonah simply states that the city would be destroyed in forty days if the people therein did not repent. See the Book of Jonah to see if Warren is telling the truth!

In Romans 12:2, Paul addresses those who were already brethren, so his command to be transformed did not mean they became a new person. And certainly in none of Rick Warren's examples, except in Nineveh, did they become new persons.

Probably the most glaring error is Mr. Warren's statement: **"Jesus was empowered by forty days in the wilderness."**

Jesus was not empowered by forty days in the wilderness; He was tempted. He was all-powerful already. If anything, at least in the flesh, He was weakened, then strengthened only at the very end with food brought to Him by angels. There is no process of forty days required to get Jesus "empowered!" At any point during even Christ's earthly ministry He had the power to even call down a battalion of angels.

So I invite you to do a word search for "forty days" for each of the above biblical passages in a Blue Letter Bible or other great search engine. Type in "40 days." Read the entire text and context for Noah, Moses, Elijah, Nineveh, and Jesus Christ. You will see that nothing like the process of going from being conformed to this world to being transformed that Rick Warren describes even takes place at all, let alone is there a requirement of forty days.

You might ask, but doesn't God use forty-day periods repeatedly in the Bible? Yes, God used forty-day periods throughout the Bible; however, He never gave us liberty to invent what took place in those passages as Warren has done. The forty-day periods are descriptive, not necessarily prescriptive. Even if they were prescriptive, then by our invoking them we must follow the biblical pattern and schematic. We should not be following Rick Warren's ideas, which do not conform to those biblical models (together with his sprinkling in the doctrines or references to false teachers along the way of his journey), which collide with the true text of the forty-day examples in the Bible.

You might also ask, but isn't there a consistent recurring theme to God's use of forty-day periods in the Bible that we should apply to our lives to determine our purpose in life? Well, since all Scripture is profitable, as is recorded in 2 Timothy 3:16, then of course forty-day time frames have significance; however, I reiterate that the significance begins with first telling the truth about what occurred in those forty-day examples, which Mr. Warren does *not* do. Secondly, just because a number reoccurs does not mean we are to automatically plug that number into our lives. The Book of Numbers is full of myriads of numbers. And this book also is profitable as it says in 2 Timothy 3:16. But to go beyond what is written to suggest that this is God's blueprint with these numbers would constitute numerology, which is exactly what Warren's personality profile does by using a Carl Jung-based theory to score the information you acquire. One of the biggest problems of all is that none of the examples of forty days in the Bible is even used to determine your purpose. In fact, in most examples, God's purpose of the forty days is *judgment.* So, all of the forty-day examples are achieving very different purposes, not a homogenized schematic that all people follow according to what Rick Warren has dreamed up. I am sure God has a reason for the recurrence of forty days, and that it is not a coincidence, but that is known to the Lord. He does not tell us.

One example of forty days was the time frame used to mourn and embalm the body of Israel and Joseph in Egypt. Does this mean we should all take forty days to mourn and embalm every Christian or person when they die . . . just because we are certain that time frame must be there for a reason and that forty-day time frame is used often in the Bible? Just because forty days was used to mourn and embalm Israel and Joseph, does that mean it must be a template to use forty days to figure out our purpose in life? Do we string this together with all other occurrences of forty days in the Bible to say it must have something to do with figuring out our purpose in life? Do we include this forty-day example simply because the number reoccurs, so it must not be a coincidence, and therefore we will divine the meaning for our personal application to find our personal purpose in life?

Jesus spent forty days doing miracles and telling His disciples about the Kingdom of God between the time of His resurrection and ascension. But does this mean we are to now take that time frame as a template to figure out our purpose in life? To read these kinds of things into the text is poor hermeneutics at best, and divination at worst. **God sovereignly worked His purposes in these examples. There is no suggestion that therefore Christians should turn forty days over to Rick Warren to find "their" purposes. The use of forty days by Warren is intended to make people think that his material has God's imprimatur, when it does not. He is making the forty days a magic number.**

So Mr. Warren suggests that his book will transform our life? What if we are already a new person with a purpose and we just need our minds renewed (which is what Romans 12:2 is really saying)? The reason people aren't transformed is not because of impatience to read the next chapter, as Rick Warren alleges, but because they didn't read *the* book (the Bible), and because they weren't convicted. Warren's quote of Romans 12:2 implies that you will not know what God wants you to do until forty days have passed. But the fact is that in all of the Old and New Testament passages he cites, these men, with the exception of the people of Nineveh who found it during a forty-day period (but only part of a 40-day period), *already* knew what God wanted them to do *before* the forty days . . . not during, and not at the end! This is not a matter of opinion. The facts are not in dispute, as the Scriptures will easily verify, and you can verify yourself by simply examining the passages for yourselves.

❋   ❋   ❋

Rick Warren: "Real spiritual growth is never an isolated, individualistic pursuit." [2]

2. Ibid., p. 11.

I thought Mr. Warren just got through saying that Jesus was empowered in the wilderness where He was isolated. He was alone in the Garden of Gethsemane. Jesus himself commands us to go into our prayer closet when we pray. Do we now have company in our closet in order to achieve "real spiritual growth"? What about Paul being isolated for three years in order to prepare to begin his ministry? He was isolated for three years and experienced "real spiritual growth." (Remember, Paul did not need the three years to find out his purpose, that is, to preach the Gospel to the Gentiles; he was already given that upon being commissioned to be an apostle to the Gentiles by Christ himself.) The apostle John was exiled to Patmos whereby he would have been quite isolated. Are you going to say that John did not have real spiritual growth because he was isolated, during which time he wrote the Book of Revelation? And what an insult to all of the redeemed of the earth, *Foxe's Book of Martyrs,* and people like Richard Wurmbrandt who was put into solitary confinement for fourteen years, as well as all those saints who were persecuted and put in solitary confinement because of their faith. Are we to say they did not grow spiritually because they were in isolation? What about the countless persecuted and martyred saints that could not even assemble throughout the ages, in many cases because they were imprisoned *in isolation?* Rick Warren's generalization is not only biblically incorrect, it is an insult to all of those saints who suffered separation (isolation) for the cause of Christ, the very assurance Paul gives in Romans:

> Who shall separate us from the love of Christ? shall tribulation, or distress, or persecution, or famine, or nakedness, or peril, or sword? . . . Nor height, nor depth, nor any other creature, shall be able to separate us from the love of God, which is in Christ Jesus our Lord.
>
> —Romans 8:35, 39

So, in all of these examples, separation (isolation) often took place, yet Rick Warren tells his readers that no "real spiritual growth" can take place in isolation.

Chapter Two

Comparing Rick Warren's
Covenant to Scripture

Rick Warren: "With God's help, I commit the next 40 days of my life to discovering God's purpose for my life." [3]

Even if Christ had not warned us about taking pledges and oaths, and that indeed even if they were acceptable, why would anyone sign an oath *before* reading the book, without knowing anything about who Rick Warren is? What are his teachings? What teachers or false teachers does he endorse? What about testing the spirits to see if they are of God before going down this path or journey? Even if it were true that you need forty days to discover God's purpose for your life, how do you know that it is Mr. Warren's blueprint of forty days that will take you there? Maybe it is the wrong blueprint or map. What about the millions of Christians who discovered God's purpose for their life by simply reading the Bible, as opposed to Rick Warren's book? Since Mr. Warren is directing this in great part to non-believers, they have no correct concept of even who God is. God could simply be any higher power, or the god of this world (Satan), or Allah, or "God as we understand him" as in the Twelve-Step program. There is nothing in the covenant statement about the credentials of the partner's name that you are signing a covenant with. What if this person is a non-believer? If one person is a Christian (which Warren professes to be), then that person would be unequally yoked with an unbeliever who signs this covenant. Does Rick Warren have no concern about unholy

---

3. Ibid., p. 13.

alliances and treaties and their consequences, as Scripture reveals over and over again? And who is holding Mr. Warren accountable to hold up his part of the bargain, since he also signed this covenant? Finally, he quotes Ecclesiastes 4:9 (TEV). But this passage is about two working together or fighting together. There is nothing in the passage to back up Mr. Warren's statement of how this can help you discover God's purpose for your life.

So before you sign any pledge, vow, or covenant, whether it is Rick Warren's or anyone else's, I appeal to you to consider Jesus Christ's own words:

> Again, ye have heard that it hath been said by them of old time, Thou shalt not forswear thyself, but shalt perform unto the Lord thine oaths: But I say unto you, Swear not at all; neither by heaven; for it is God's throne: Nor by the earth; for it is his footstool: neither by Jerusalem; for it is the city of the great King. Neither shalt thou swear by thy head, because thou canst not make one hair white or black. But let your communication be, Yea, yea; Nay, nay: for whatsoever is more than these cometh of evil.
>
> —Matthew 5:33–37

And let us see if the apostle James confirms this very warning:

> But above all things, my brethren, swear not, neither by heaven, neither by the earth, neither by any other oath: but let your yea be yea; and your nay, nay; lest ye fall into condemnation.
>
> —James 5:12

Questions on Oaths and Covenants from Pastors Who Have Introduced *Purpose-Driven Life* Campaigns

Question or Comment
We are not going to make anyone in our church sign Rick Warren's covenant; we simply invite them to do so.

Response

Regarding signing a covenant, even if you were to believe this is biblically permissible, it would *never* be permissible to sign this covenant with a man that has already documented that he does not tell the truth in those forty-day examples contained in the pages prior to Mr. Warren's covenant. I challenge you to find agreement with his statements in *any* translation of the Bible (and you can even pick the translation). For pastors to offer your congregation the option to sign this document, knowing full well Warren has not told the truth, makes you his accomplice in falsehood. If Christians sign Warren's covenant in ignorance, God's Word holds true: " My people *still* perish for lack of knowledge." If they sign it after having been a good Berean and having investigated his statements to see if they are in the Scriptures, when they are not, then that is willful ignorance and a worse fate awaits them. And for pastors and leaders to lead them astray in inviting them to sign it—or even saying nothing but simply promoting the book which contains it—you are held to an even higher accountability for having stumbled the least one of His children (Mark 9:42). As this book reveals, his forty-day examples are not the only errors in his teachings which occur in these pages, even before you get to the covenant. If you have not read all of *The Purpose Driven Life,* you would only have to read up through the pages of Rick Warren's covenant to justify rejecting it.

> To the law and to the testimony: if they speak not according to this word, it is because there is no light in them.
>
> —Isaiah 8:20

The law says to tell the truth. *Prophets (and teachers) must tell the truth.* If Isaiah says there is no light in someone who does not tell the truth, then why are you promoting someone who does not tell the truth?

His covenant may not be mandatory for your church, but covenants are *mandatory* at Rick Warren's Saddleback Church in California in order to become a member. Once again, he is going beyond what is written, and he is laying a burden and requirement on the congregation, as well as compounding this erroneous requirement by compelling members to take an occult-based personality profile. This personality profile is the "P" in his SHAPE program. For complete proof and documentation, I refer you to chapters ten and eleven, as well as appendix C. I also refer you to the *Time* magazine article in the March 29, 2004, issue, page 56, which states that Rick Warren's own church requires its members to sign "strict covenants." One of the requirements is the personality profile. If all this is not bad enough and heretical enough, Warren then removes individuals from the congregation for failure to participate!

You may not be guilty of enforcing Warren's covenant, but I certainly hope you have a problem promoting a teacher who introduces these unbiblical and heretical demands. You may think that adding these kinds of burdens is perfectly harmless and not heretical. But Jesus Christ called the Pharisees who added unnecessary burdens to the people twice the sons of hell (Matt. 23:15). Paul, likewise, said to the church in Galatia that those who were trying to put people back under the law in Galatia were "accursed." You are not putting that requirement on the members of your church, but you are promoting a false teacher (and his book) who does advise congregants in churches to sign his covenant!

Finally, what if a Christian in Rick Warren's church were to actually believe the passage in Matthew and simply said: "Let my yea be yea!" This person also believes that going beyond letting his yea be yea, would be evil as the rest of the passage states. Would this be acceptable in Warren's church? Obviously not; otherwise they would not be prevented from becoming a member!

※　※　※

Question or Comment
I don't believe signing Rick Warren's covenant is a contradiction to Scripture for various reasons. *The Expositor's Commentary* seems to suggest that oaths are permissible and not abolished by Christ, so long as truth is not being threatened.

Response

So how is truth being threatened or evaded by simply following Jesus Christ's example and *not* signing an oath? What is the New Testament precedent for signing an oath, let alone requiring one of Christians, or worse, removing someone from the local church because they did not comply with such an oath, which they should not have had to take in the first place? And during the dispute in the Book of Acts as to what requirements should be laid on the Gentiles who were becoming Christians, is signing oaths on that list? Is any punishment or banishment advised for failing to comply with taking such an oath or failing to fulfill the oath? Who decides whether they complied? Rick Warren?

Here is that passage:

> That ye abstain from meats offered to idols, and from blood, and from things strangled, and from fornication: from which if ye keep yourselves, **ye shall do well.** Fare ye well.
>
> —Acts 15:29

What if a Christian decides that he shall "do well" by simply following this ruling of the council in Jerusalem? What if a Christian does not sign any covenant, but does as the passage suggests? Wouldn't he do well enough? Not according to Rick Warren! Christians *must* sign a covenant to become a member of his local church, and Warren is promoting this teaching to tens of millions of Christians and a host of denominations.

The Expositor's Commentary on this scriptural passage regarding oaths does not accurately reflect the meaning of the text. It is completely a fabrication of the expositor's opinion of the purpose that Christ clearly stated. I don't see any wriggle room when Christ said, ". . . for whatsoever is more than these cometh of evil." Isn't signing the oath doing more than saying "yea" or "nay"? Isn't compelling a person to sign the oath doing "more than these"? Isn't removing a Christian from the local congregation doing "more than these"?

This expositor has taken it upon himself to read into the text the "purpose" of Christ's words when there is not context or even compliance with the hermeneutic principle known as "unwarranted expansion of a grammatical field." Now I suppose that if Greek can be translated into English and is a constantly changing and developing process, as language constantly changes and develops, then we can't really be sure what Jesus means by the word "oath" or "evil." So in this case, there would be no caution or prohibition to signing covenants. But I pray you don't think that, and you do not hold this view.

※ ※ ※

Question or Comment
In the Scriptures God himself swears (Gen. 9:9–11; Luke 1:68, 73; Psalm 16:10; Acts 2:27–31), not because He sometimes lies, but in order to help men believe (Heb. 6:17). Therefore, oaths and covenants such as Warren's are perfectly warranted. Jesus himself testified under oath (Matt. 26:63–64).

Response
These are perhaps some of the most astonishing statements I have read on the subject of oaths! How can you compare what God can do regarding covenants or oaths to what man can do? God can swear to whatever He wants to, and He has the power to *guarantee* its fulfillment. Man cannot promise with any certainty to deliver anything in the future. This is one of the reasons Christ was telling His people not to take oaths. But God does not even need a reason. He simply tells us what to obey.

As to your statement of Jesus himself testifying under oath, Jesus Christ can testify under oath because He is God, and He can make any oath he wants; there is no power on earth or in the air that can prevent Him from completing it! But we can't make such an oath, because there are a host of unforeseen circumstances that can intervene to prevent us from fulfilling our oaths, such as financial pledges to the church to build a new building. Our fallen nature might prevent fulfillment. Satan could prevent us, as Paul was prevented by Satan to travel. We don't know with any certainty what tomorrow will bring; God does, and nothing is unforeseen to Him. So of course Jesus Christ can take an oath.

※   ※   ※

Question or Comment

The earliest Christians still took oaths, if we may judge from Paul's example (Rom. 1:9; 2 Cor. 1:23; 1 Thess. 2:5, 10; Phil. 1:8) for much the same reason.

Response

I looked up every one of these references you cited. Not one of them has Paul taking an oath, let alone signing one. All of these passages simply refer to witnessing various events, but nothing about an oath. In all of these passages but one, it is not about Paul's witness, but God's witness. It is Paul's testimony. The 1 Thessalonians 2:10 passage is also not about Paul's witness but about the witness of the church of Thessalonica. And even if Paul had taken an oath in Scripture, he was given direct apostolic authority, and he was penning Scripture itself. So such a binding oath would have been descriptive of Paul, but not prescriptive to us. But not to worry, for not even Paul took such an oath! So you have inserted and gone beyond what is actually written in your examples.

Here are the passages you supplied:

For **God is my witness,** whom I serve with my spirit in the gospel of his Son, that without ceasing I make mention of you always in my prayers.

—Romans 1:9

Moreover **I call God for a record upon my soul,** that to spare you I came not as yet unto Corinth.

—2 Corinthians 1:23

For neither at any time used we flattering words, as ye know, nor a cloke of covetousness; **God is witness:** . . . **Ye are witnesses, and God also,** how holily and justly and unblameably we behaved ourselves among you that believe.

—1 Thessalonians 2:5, 10

For God is my record, how greatly I long after you all in the bowels of Jesus Christ.

—Philippians 1:8

Where is the oath? Where is the covenant? These are simply statements of testimony made by Paul and witnesses. This is nothing more than testifying with and in compliance with "your yeas be yea and your nays be nay." And even if oaths are permitted, who determines that Rick Warren's composition of an oath should be written as it is? Who determines with absolute certainty that this is the oath God would have us take? We should not sign an oath penned by Rick Warren anymore than we should sign one penned by Pope John Paul II.

Chapter Three

Inaccurate vs. Accurate Translations

Time after time readers must think that they have the wrong biblical citation in this book, only to discover that Rick Warren really did mean that verse. Throughout the book there are statements indicating one position, only to find a contradiction somewhere else in the book. So alert readers are often left in complete confusion about what Mr. Warren meant or where he really stood on an issue.

Rick Warren states that he is against self-help books.[4] But the Twelve-Step program is a self-help book. The Twelve-Step program originated with Alcoholics Anonymous and is still the heart of AA. Christian twelve-step programs are simply spin-offs of the same model. Rick Warren has modified the steps and reduced them to eight principles of recovery and called it Celebrate Recovery. As you will see, chapter eight comments on Celebrate Recovery and supplies links to commentary on its close relative, the Twelve-Step program, as to whether or not it is biblical.

Mr. Warren then contrasts true self vs. false self. He quotes Matthew 16:25 (MSG): "Self-help is no help at all. Self-sacrifice is the way, my way, to finding yourself, your true self."

Even if the Bible taught this concept of "true self" vs. "false self," it is still self. Besides this, asceticism (which the apostle Paul opposed) teaches self-sacrifice. Paul goes on to even call the self-sacrifice of complying with the prohibitions of diet and marriage doctrines of demons. Islamic terrorists who destroyed the World Trade Center practiced self-sacrifice. In fact, some Buddhist monks literally sacri-

---

4. Ibid., p. 19.

fice themselves by immolating themselves. So, let's see what the text really says:

> For whosoever will save his life shall lose it: and whosoever will lose his life **for my sake** shall find it.
>
> —Matthew 16:25

"For my sake" (for Jesus Christ's sake) is obscured in *The Message* translation. And even if true, Christ is talking about losing your life (for Him), not simply self-sacrifice.

Rick Warren misquotes Isaiah 26:3 (TEV) by stating that the Lord keeps one in perfect peace whose purpose is firm.[5] But that is not what Isaiah said:

> Thou wilt keep him in perfect peace, **whose mind is stayed on thee:** because he trusteth in thee.

"DAY 7 – The Reason for Everything" begins on page 53

Rick Warren states: **"In heaven, God's glory provides all the light needed."** [6]

This is true, but he is quoting Revelation 21:23 (NIV). What is being described here is not heaven, but the New Jerusalem.

❈   ❈   ❈

Rick Warren: **"Jesus came to earth so we could fully understand God's glory."**

This is simply not true on two fronts. (1) Jesus came to save that which is lost and to give himself up as the perfect sacrificial Lamb for mankind. (2) We won't "fully" understand God's glory until we are glorified . . . not before. Even Paul said that we still see through glass dimly, not *fully,* until we see Him face to face. Other scriptures which disagree with Mr. Warren:

---

5. Ibid., p. 32.
6. Ibid., p. 54.

For since the beginning of the world men have not heard, nor perceived by the ear, neither hath the eye seen, O God, beside thee, what he hath prepared for him that waiteth for him.

—Isaiah 64:4

But as it is written, Eye hath not seen, nor ear heard, neither have entered into the heart of man, the things which God hath prepared for them that love him.

—1 Corinthians 2:9

Rick Warren quotes Psalm 147:11 (CEV): "The Lord is pleased only with those who worship him and trust his love." [7]

This mangled translation takes away the most important qualifier—the most important phrase—"for those who fear him." Proof:

The LORD **taketh pleasure in them that fear him**, in those that hope in his **mercy**.

—Psalm 147:11

Note that the CEV translation changes the word "mercy" to "love." Now, of course the Lord is full of both love and mercy. But they are not the same concepts. It is not surprising that Rick Warren leaves out the fear of the Lord, as later he states: "We give ourselves to him, not out of fear or duty, but in love." [8] But of course we give ourselves to Him out of the fear of the Lord. For more documentation on the fear of the Lord, I refer you to my article *Fear of the Lord* (Rock Salt Publishing).

On page 64 Warren quotes John 4:23 (does not indicate translation): "The Father seeks worshipers." But he leaves out the kind of worshippers He seeks:

But the hour cometh, and now is, when the **true** worshippers shall

---

7. Ibid., p. 64.
8. Ibid., p. 77.

worship the Father in spirit and in truth: for the Father seeketh such to worship him.

—John 4:23

Rick Warren's quotation of John 3:36 (MSG) takes away the second half of the verse.[9] This verse is not talking about life, but life everlasting.

Mr. Warren quotes Hebrews 11:7 (MSG), which says: ". . . Noah became intimate with God."

But once again, that is not what the original text says. It says Noah ". . . became heir of the righteousness which is by faith" (KJV).[10]

He also quotes Psalm 14:2 (LB): "The Lord looks down from heaven on all mankind to see if there are any who are wise, who want to please God." [11]

Is that what the text says? Let's read Psalm 14:2–3 for the complete context:

> The LORD looked down from heaven upon the children of men, to see if there were any that did understand, and seek God. They are all gone aside, they are **all together become filthy**: there is **none that doeth good, no, not one.**

Rick Warren leaves out the critical qualifier in verse 3 that says none seek after God. So the reader is left with the impression of deciding for himself if he is one of those who wants to please God. Mr. Warren doesn't tell you that the Bible says there are *none!* But this is not altogether surprising because the heart of the Purpose Driven theology is to stay positive, which is exactly the theme of his revered colleague, Dr. Robert Schuller. (See commentary on Robert Schuller in Questions and Comments and Resources at the end of this documentary).

---

9. Ibid., p. 58.
10. Ibid., p. 70.
11. Ibid., p. 76.

"DAY 11 – Becoming Best Friends with God" begins on page 85

Rick Warren quotes Romans 5:11 (NLT), 2 Corinthians 5:18a (TEV), 1 John 1:3, 1 Corinthians 1:9, and 2 Corinthians 13:14.[12] All of his translations use the term "friends" or "friendship" of God. (Mr. Warren does not even cite the source of the other translations.) Yet the word friend does not appear in *any* of the Authorized King James translations of these verses. Now if "friend" is the word God intended and meant, then it would appear in the text. Only once does Jesus call anyone "friends," and that was His disciples (John 15:15).

Warren quotes Exodus 34:14 (NLT): "He is a God who is passionate about his relationship with you."

This is nothing remotely reflective of the contents of the correct rendering of this passage:

> For thou shalt worship no other god: for the LORD, whose name is Jealous, is a jealous God.

Rick Warren mixes up passion with jealousy, and then completely misses the point of this commandment in Exodus that we are to worship no other gods. It is not just a declarative statement about one of God's attributes (which Warren could have at least gotten right), but the verse is a directive to *our* response and obedience to God.

Rick Warren once again misquotes "friendship" in Psalm 25:14 (LB).[13] But Psalm 25:14 (KJV) does not even contain this word:

> The secret of the LORD is with them that fear him; and he will shew them his covenant.

❈   ❈   ❈

Rick Warren: "Jesus is still the 'friend of sinners.'" [14]

But read Matthew 11:19 to see if that is what Jesus said. What

---

12. Ibid., p. 86.
13. Ibid., p. 91.
14. Ibid., p. 93.

He said was, "*They* say that I am a friend of sinners." But the text also relates that they said He was a glutton. Does that mean Jesus was a glutton? Read the text carefully:

> The Son of man came eating and drinking, and they say, Behold a man gluttonous, and a winebibber, a friend of publicans and sinners. . . .
>
> —Matthew 11:19; see also Luke 7:34

Rick Warren should not be so reckless as to confuse who is talking (Jesus) and to whom he is referring (the Pharisees).

Mr. Warren quotes Job 42:7b (MSG) in stating Job's friends have not been "honest" like his "friend" Job.[15] But if Warren says we should be honest, how about being honest with what the text really says. It does not say "honest," it says "right"; then it does not say "friend," it says "servant." Here's the proof: ". . . for ye have not spoken of me the thing that is right, as my servant Job hath" (Job 42:7b, KJV).

Warren quotes Philippians 3:10 (AMP):

> [For my determined purpose is] that I may know Him [that I may progressively become more deeply and intimately acquainted with Him, perceiving and recognizing and understanding the wonders of His Person more strongly and more clearly],[16] **and that I may in that same way come to know the power outflowing from His resurrection [which it exerts over believers], and that I may so share His sufferings as to be continually transformed [in spirit into His likeness even] to His death, [in the hope].**

(Note: Mr. Warren's quote of this passage had removed the brackets which indicate clarifying remarks not included in the original text; we have quoted the passage from the Amplified Bible as originally written.)

Note that even in the Amplified Version that Mr. Warren quotes,

---

15. Ibid., p. 93.
16. Ibid., p. 98.

he leaves out the entire second half of the verse, which I have high-lighted in bold. **Now let's read what the KJV says:**

> That I may know him, and the power of **his resurrection,** and the fellowship of his sufferings, being made conformable unto his death.

—Philippians 3:10

There is nothing in Rick Warren's quote, or even context about His resurrection, the fellowship of His suffering, and conformity to His death.

❈   ❈   ❈

Rick Warren: **"Jesus called thoughtless worship 'vain repetitions.'"** [17]

Well let's examine Matthew 6:7 to see if this is precisely what Jesus said:

> But when ye pray, use not vain repetitions, as the heathen do: **for they think** that they shall be heard for their much speaking.

It is true that Jesus is making it perfectly clear that methods and techniques *do* matter in how we pray . . . technique is *not* neutral. The word in Greek for vain repetitions means "babbling." But it is very confusing to me that Rick Warren would quote this verse in Matthew prohibiting vain repetitions as well as state that meditation is not the emptying of the mind but engaging it, while he simultaneously promotes the teachers who promote mantras, chants, and other New Age techniques, meditation, and Roman Catholic repetitions in their form of meditation, as well as in the rosary. It is difficult to see where Rick Warren ultimately stands regarding contemplative prayer, prayer centering, meditation, guided visualization, breath prayers, etc. Also refer to appendix E.

Jesus is not condemning all repetition in prayer, for He himself

---

17. Ibid., p. 103.

repeated His prayer in Gethsemane: "And he left them, and went away again, and prayed the third time, saying the same words" (Matt. 26:44; also Mark 14:39). Jesus then tells the parable of a persistent widow who continually pleaded with an unjust judge, "Avenge me of mine adversary" (Luke 18:2–8). The widow's **repetitious pleading,** according to Christ, should be our model for prayer to God! This kind of prayer is travailing in the spirit. Jesus' prayer in the Garden of Gethsemane (which he repeated) was resisting temptation to the point of sweating drops of blood. We see a similar sobriety and need for being circumspect in how we are to meditate in Psalm 119 (while on guard duty), which bears no resemblance to the techniques for meditating prescribed by Richard Foster and many other mystics that Rick Warren promotes. Psalm 136 repeats the phrase "for his mercy endureth forever." There is not an absolute prohibition to repetition. For more discussion on when repetition is permissible, see chapter seven on "How to Worship." It is the pagan techniques we are to not to use as a model. So why are Christians who promote comtemplative prayer using them as a model? Finally, when the Lord actually gives us the Lord's Prayer, it is filled with petitions in which the mind must be fully engaged, not emptied.

✵   ✵   ✵

Warren quotes Job 29:4 (NIV): "God's intimate friendship." [18]

Once again the KJV makes no mention of "friendship," but says "secret of God." Using terms not even in the original text is a persistent pattern of Rick Warren adding to, subtracting from, omitting critical qualifiers, and changing words and concepts in the Bible.

Rick Warren quotes 2 Corinthians 5:21 (TEV), which states: ". . . God made him [Jesus Christ] share our sin. . . ." [19]

No, Jesus Christ did not share in our sin; He took all of our sin on the cross!

"DAY 19 – Cultivating Community" begins on page 145

18. Ibid., p. 110.
19. Ibid., p. 113.
20. Ibid., p. 145.

Rick Warren quotes Ephesians 4:3 (NCV), which says: "You are joined together with peace through the Spirit, so make every effort to continue together in this way." [20]

But if you read the KJV you will see the glaring omissions where he leaves out "one body, one spirit, and one hope." The word "one" is so important that it is repeated four more times in verses 5 and 6. Without these qualifying verses we have no context for even understanding what is meant by unity.

> Endeavouring to keep the **unity** of the Spirit in the bond of peace. There is **one body**, and **one Spirit**, even as ye are called in **one hope** of your calling; **One Lord, one faith, one baptism, One God** and Father of all, who is above all, and through all, and in you all.
>
> —Ephesians 4:3–6

"DAY 20 – Restoring Broken Fellowship" begins on page 152

Rick Warren quotes Matt 5:23–24 (MSG).[21]

> If you enter your place of worship and, about to make an offering, you suddenly remember a grudge a friend has against you, abandon your offering, leave immediately, go to this friend and make things right. Then and only then, come back and work things out with God.

This is another corrupt translation because the text in the Greek does not say the offended brother has a grudge. That makes it appear that the victim is the one with the problem. The offended brother might have a legitimate grievance!

Here is the correct rendering of Matthew 5:23–24 (KJV):

> Therefore if thou bring thy gift to the altar, and there rememberest that thy brother hath ought against thee; Leave there thy gift

---

21. Ibid., p. 154.

before the altar, and go thy way; first be reconciled to thy brother, and then come and offer thy gift.

Mr. Warren then quotes Job 5:2, 18:4 (TEV), where he recommends following Job's friends' advice.[22]

To worry yourself to death with resentment would be a foolish, senseless thing to do. . . . You are only hurting yourself with your anger. . . .

Now let's see what those passages really say:

For wrath killeth the foolish man, and envy slayeth the silly one. . . . He teareth himself in his anger: shall the earth be forsaken for thee? and shall the rock be removed out of his place?

But the Lord stated to Job that his friends needed to repent of their advice. Rick Warren knows that, as he later even quotes the verse in Job where the Lord tells Job that it is his friends that need to repent.

Warren quotes Matthew 5:9 (MSG): "You're blessed when you can show people how to cooperate instead of compete or fight. That's when you discover who you really are, and your place in God's family." [23]

Compare this translation to the KJV:

Blessed are the peacemakers: for they shall be called the children of God.

The Message translation is so far off the mark, you have to wonder if you have the same verse. There is nothing in the correct rendering about competing and fighting. Paul **competed** to run a good race to win the prize, and he fought the good **fight**. When is it right (for Christians) to fight is a very legitimate question one might ask. Of

22. Ibid., p. 155.
23. Ibid., pp. 157–158.

course, Christians should not fight with each other by quarreling and causing strife and wrongful division. But all Christians fight on the same team in the good fight of faith in the great spiritual war we are in. Omitted or taken away from the Scripture is "children of God," and added to Scripture is a completely foreign idea of the New Age concept of "self-discovery." Competitive vs. cooperative is an idea we can trace back to Aristotle, who wrote that it is those who cooperate who are happy. All of the pastors who read this book and implemented Rick Warren's programs should have recognized this corrupt rendering. Any Christian reasonably grounded in His Word should equally recognize it. (See chapter eleven in this book which further describes Rick Warren's implementation of balancing personality traits.)

"DAY 34 – Thinking Like a Servant" begins on page 265

Rick Warren quotes Philippians 2:4 (MSG) which states: "Forget yourselves. . . ." [24] But that is once more an altered rendering, as there is nothing in the text to suggest forgetting yourselves.

Here is the proof:

> Look not every man on his own things, but every man **also** on the things of others.

As you can see, Rick Warren's translation is so far off track, you wonder if he meant a different verse. His removing the word "also" from God's Word completely changes the meaning. Is this another example of Rick Warren rightly dividing the truth, which he professes that we should do?

Purpose Five Section: "You Were Made for a Mission"

"DAY 36 – Made for a Mission" begins on page 281

Rick Warren quotes 2 Corinthians 5:18 (TEV): "Christ changed us

---

24. Ibid., p. 265.

from enemies into his **friends** and gave us the task of making others his **friends** also." [25]

Once again, Mr. Warren finds a translation that adds words to God's Word. Inserting "friends" is one of his favorites. But let's see if it is in the original:

> And all things are of God, who hath **reconciled** us to himself by Jesus Christ, and hath given to us the ministry of **reconciliation.**

So, do you see the word "friends" in there? I don't! Furthermore, the issue in this verse is reconciliation. So, do you see that word or even that concept in Rick Warren's chosen translation? And reconciliation to Christ can only come through the blood of Jesus. Some argue that the TEV, *The Message,* the NCV, and other translations that Rick Warren uses are not translations, but paraphrases. But if a paraphrase completely changes the meaning of the text, it is useless!

❊   ❊   ❊

Rick Warren: "Your mission is a continuation of Jesus' mission on earth" (p. 282).

It is true that just as Jesus was sent, we are sent. Jesus and Christians do have "sent" in common. But this is very misleading. Christ's mission was not our mission. His mission was to be crucified for our sins. Only He could do that! We can't continue that mission. Besides, that mission was finished (not continued) when Jesus said on the cross, "It is finished!" Our mission is to declare His mission. That is the Great Commission.

Rick Warren continues his pattern with inserting "friends" into God's Word when it is not there by quoting still another verse from still another translation containing the word "friends." [26]

He quotes 2 Corinthians 5:20 (MSG), which states: "God uses us to persuade men and women to drop their differences. . . . Become **friends** with God. . . ."

---

25. Ibid., p. 282.
26. Ibid., p. 282.

But there is nothing like this word or even concept in the proper rendering of this passage. There is nothing about the differences between each other and nothing about being friends with God. Here is the proof:

> Now then we are ambassadors for Christ, as though God did beseech you by us: we pray you in Christ's stead, be ye reconciled to God.
>
> —2 Corinthians 5:20 (KJV)

Once again, Rick Warren misses the most important concept, which is reconciliation to God. Becoming friends with God is a completely different meaning from becoming reconciled to God. Mr. Warren makes the same mistake here as he did in 2 Corinthians 5:18 (TEV) discussed above.

"DAY 37 – Sharing Your Life Message" begins on page 289

Rick Warren: "There is almost nothing God won't do for the man or woman who is committed to serving the kingdom of God." [27]

Mr. Warren quotes Matthew 6:30 (NLT). But this is a bad rendering because it screams of Word of Faith Movement and Kingdom Now Theology. A Christian could be 100 percent committed to serving the Kingdom of God but receive none of the promises in this life. The last section of Hebrews 11 is devoted to all of the persecuted and mistreated saints who waited for a better country . . . this world is not worthy of. And a totally committed Christian is still one who the Scripture would describe as:

> But as it is written, **Eye hath not seen, nor ear heard, neither have entered into the heart of man, the things which God hath prepared for them that love him.**
>
> —1 Corinthians 2:9

---

27. Ibid., p. 287.

Rick Warren quotes 1 John 5:10a (GWT): "Those who believe in the Son of God have the testimony of God in them." [28]

But he leaves out 1 John 5:10b . . . the rest of the sentence (in bold) which is absolutely crucial to the content and context, which states in the KJV:

> He that believeth on the Son of God hath the witness in himself: **he that believeth not God hath made him a liar; because he believeth not the record that God gave of his Son.**

※ ※ ※

Rick Warren states: "We were chosen by God," then he quotes 1 Peter 2:9 (MSG): "to do his work and speak out for him, to tell others of the night-and-day difference he made for you." [29]

But is that what the verse says?

> But ye are a chosen generation, a royal priesthood, an holy nation, a peculiar people; that ye should shew forth the praises of him who hath called you out of darkness into his marvellous light.

Rick Warren quotes 2 Peter 3:9 (NCV): "He [God] does not want anyone to be lost, but he wants all people to change their hearts and lives." [30]

But a change of heart without true biblical repentance can result in following other religions or cults. The text really says "repent," not simply changing their hearts.

Mr. Warren quotes 2 Chronicles 14:4 (MSG), which says: "**Center** their lives in GOD"; and Philippians 4:7 (MSG): "Christ displaces worry at the **center** of your life." [31] But the KJV, in these two passages, saying nothing about centering . . . not in the Hebrew and not in the Greek.

---

28. Ibid., p. 289.
29. Ibid., p. 290.
30. Ibid., p. 294.
31. Ibid., p. 314.

And commanded Judah to seek the Lord God of their fathers, and to do the law and the commandment.

—2 Chronicles 14:4

And the peace of God, which passeth all understanding, shall keep your hearts and minds through Christ Jesus.

—Philippians 4:7

So, where is the word or even concept of centering in these passages? Answer: *Nowhere!* Centering is a New Age concept. See my article entitled "Christian Meditation—Centering Prayer: Is It Christian?" at *www.abrahamic-faith.com/James/Part%20XI%20Christian%20Me ditation-Centering%20Prayer.html*

On page 318 Rick Warren quotes 2 Corinthians 10:13 (LB): "Our goal is to measure up to God's plan for us." I thought he said on page 313 that "goals are temporary." [32] Wouldn't measuring up to God's plan for us be a permanent pursuit?

❈ ❈ ❈

Rick Warren: "Neither past nor future generations can serve God's purpose in this generation." [33]

Really? All Scripture was written in past generations and God's purpose in them is for this and future generations. This is another unbelievable statement by Rick Warren.

Bible Translation Questions

Question or Comment
Isn't there a place within God's Kingdom for paraphrases and all of the various translations that Rick Warren uses, recognizing that I would not build my doctrine upon these translations? Certainly you are not suggesting that God endorses only one translation, the King James Version?

---

32. Ibid., p. 318.
33. Ibid., p. 318.

Response

A teacher should not introduce material to your congregation that you don't want to develop your doctrine from! A teacher should not be teaching anything not based on sound doctrine. The KJV conforms to the Majority Texts. One thing God does not endorse is translations that add and subtract the content and intent of the authors, as Warren has clearly done.

Of course, the KJV is not the original text in its most literal sense. But the issue is, does it conform to what the Greek and Hebrew actually say? Does the translation conform to the Majority Texts? Another reason I use the King James Bible is that it is also accessible as the BlueLetter Bible, which you can access online and is a gateway to both the Hebrew and Greek renderings so that you can directly compare all of the Scripture translations that Rick Warren uses. I checked these translations against the Hebrew and Greek. In the verses I quoted, the KJV conformed. In the translations I cited that Mr. Warren uses, they did *not* conform. If this is not bad enough, he introduces many more ideas that also do not conform to the Scriptures.

❧   ❧   ❧

Question or Comment

Isn't how Hebrew and Greek can be translated into English a constantly changing and developing process as language constantly changes and develops?

Response

Given your question, you are suggesting that we can never really know what the English really says or means? We can never really know for sure what is true teaching vs. false teaching in order to identify false teachers? And we then can never really know for sure what is meant by the "faith once and for all delivered to the saints?"

Paul taught that in the last days the very same doctrines of demons and seducing spirits that Paul opposed in his day, would be given heed to . . . but because language has been changing and developing so much for two thousand years, then certainly you are not suggesting that we really can't be sure what the words mean and what to believe, how to behave, when to rebuke, when to mark someone for teaching doctrines contrary to the doctrines of the apostles, when to judge a teaching, and when to separate from such a teacher! And who is the authority to determine the meaning today of any word in the Bible? So much for God's counsel being immutable (unchanging), as it says in Hebrews! This kind of thinking is *exactly* why we have different gospels and different Jesus Christs being taught . . . the very thing Paul so passionately opposed and warned us about. You have projected a very alarming statement: that we cannot ultimately determine truth even from the Hebrew and Greek. I have prepared a file of two pages of just some of Warren's false translations and was going to insert the actual Greek or Hebrew. But it will be much less cumbersome to simply invite you to take any of *The Message* translation citations and any other translations he uses, then go to *www.blueletterbible.org,* go to that citation, then click the "C" on the left and it will supply you with the Hebrew or Greek rendering. If the Hebrew or Greek renderings are indeed even a problem, what is your solution? Are we to correct the Greek by using translations such as *The Message,* which Warren often quotes? You are suggesting a solution to a nonexistent problem. The apostle Peter says that no scripture is open to private interpretation, yet that is precisely what Eugene Peterson (editor of *The Message*) stated:

> Peterson says that *The Message* is "not . . . a word-for-word conversion" of God's Holy Word into modern language but *what he thinks God's Word means*—not a translation but an *interpretation* (introduction). What audacity to rewrite the Bible!
> —Dave Hunt, *The Vanishing Gospel*, February 1, 2004

Warren says "the Bible says" in referring to quotes from *The Message.* Well, no, the Bible does not say! And Mr. Warren follows suit by giving his own spin to the purpose of prophecy, as I point out in my document. Eugene Peterson's *The Message* translation is so often quoted in Rick Warren's *PDL* book. **For more information about "What kind of message is The Message?" go to Berit Kjos' web site:**

http://crossroad.to/Bible_studies/Message.html, which gives a more extensive list of the corruptions in *The Message* translation often quoted by Warren in his book.

Chapter Four

False Teachings

Pastors and other Christians who use or are promoting Rick Warren's books and campaigns argue that even if Rick Warren says a lot of things that are not true, he still believes and teaches the essential doctrines of Christianity (such as the virgin birth, the resurrection of Christ, etc.), so therefore he is not a false teacher and we should support him.

The apostle Paul delineates teachings in which we have liberty, such as days and diets. But he never suggests there is liberty regarding doctrine. There are *no* nonessential doctrines. And if there were, who would decide which ones are dispensable and which ones can be changed? But Rick Warren does not even qualify that when he makes a general statement about how doctrine is not important (please refer to chapter five). The apostle Paul does not make any distinctions or excuses for any false teaching. He articulates the false teaching and then in many cases even names names.

We must do the same with Rick Warren's teaching. How do those who justify error in Warren's "nonessentials" possibly think that telling the truth is not a central doctrine to orthodox Christianity? So we are compelled to reveal every single instance in which Rick Warren's own documented teaching strays from the plumb line of Scripture. We must list his quotes, then compare them with Scripture, exactly what Paul commended the Bereans for doing. But we are even more compelled to do so if his teachings are permeating virtually every Christian denomination. The greater the tidal wave, the greater the need for emergency action. Many are also taken aback that we dare call Rick Warren a false teacher. Well, I don't know why that is difficult. A false teacher is simply someone who systematically does not tell or teach the truth about what Scripture teaches. No rocket science here. Again, this is not a matter of an occasional blunder, but rather a systematic and extensive paradigm shift in the authority of Scripture in which the errors are extensive and far-reaching and in many cases have reached the point of no return.

Related to this issue, a retirement home resident recently asked in a Bible study that I teach whether Scripture can be interpreted differently by every reader. My response was the same as the apostle Peter's:

> Knowing this first, that no prophecy of the scripture is of any private interpretation.
>
> —2 Peter 1:20

I then told her very kindly that if Scripture were that flexible, there would be no such thing as a false teacher, because there would be no absolute truth. Every scripture could be subjectively interpreted by every person . . . there would be no false teaching, no false teachers to even mark. We could even add Scripture, or take it away. Everyone would be a legitimate teacher. But since Scripture itself goes into great depth describing false teaching and what we are to do about it, we must therefore be vigilant and sober and hold Rick Warren's private interpretations and pure inventions to the same holy standard of accountability.

In a sense, Rick Warren's false translations and the false teachers he promotes would also constitute his being rightly marked as a false teacher. These are already addressed in other chapters in this book. Also refer to appendix E for more resources on his teachings. This chapter lists the rest of Rick Warren's teachings and compares them to Scripture. I document each one of his quotes from his book, then cite scripture or scriptures which refute each teaching.

Rick Warren states that after killing Abel, Cain wandered without a purpose the rest of his life.[34]

---

34. Ibid., p. 28.

This is simply not true, as God marked him for protection. He then built a city . . . does that sound like someone without a purpose?

Rick Warren states that Job said he had no purpose and then he states: "Hope comes from having a purpose." [35]

Does this mean Job had no hope?

Rick Warren quotes Proverbs 13:7 (MSG): "A pretentious, showy life is an empty life; a plain and simple life is a full life." Warren comments: "People who don't know their purpose try to do too much." And, "Knowing your purpose simplifies your life."

Do these statements by Rick Warren describe Paul when he pressed on, was constrained, ran a good race? Paul had a purpose yet his life became even busier, at least compared to the other apostles. In fact, Paul even describes himself as having done *more* than all of the other disciples. Even Rick Warren states that this is how "Paul almost single-handedly spread Christianity throughout the Roman Empire." As to whether Paul's life was any busier or more simplified than before his conversion, that is pure speculation, as he was zealous in both cases. David's life was much simpler as a shepherd boy than it was as king of Israel. But an imprisoned saint might have had an unsimplified life prior to being imprisoned for his or her faith, then lead a simple life in prison. Or he might have been a busy business executive before conversion, found their purpose, then decided they wanted to be more of a servant and lead a life as a janitor for a church. A Christian who knows his or her purpose might have a simpler life or a more complex life. There is no foundation for Mr. Warren's statement and conclusion, let alone trying to extract this teaching from a faulty Bible translation verse.

"DAY 4 – Made to Last Forever" begins on page 36
"DAY 5 – Seeing Life from God's View" begins on page 41

Rick Warren: "How you define life determines your destiny." [36]

---

35. Ibid., pp. 30–31.
36. Ibid., p. 41.

No! How *God* defines your life determines your destiny!

❋ ❋ ❋

Rick Warren: "It's the view of life that you hold, consciously or unconsciously, in your mind." [37]

Sorry, we don't view anything in our unconscious unless we believe in the psychology teachings of Freud and/or Carl Jung. If we are able to obtain our views and refine our views by renewing our conscious mind through the study and application of Scripture, then why do we need be "conformed to this world" through psychological profiles based on Carl Jung to help us determine our SHAPE? (See chapters ten and eleven in this book, which defines and further describes Rick Warren's SHAPE and his implementation of his personality theory.)

I agree that character is developed and revealed by tests,[38] but these are God's tests, not psychological world-based personality profiles.

"DAY 6 – Life Is a Temporary Assignment" begins on page 47

Rick Warren calls flirting with the world spiritual adultery.[39] I agree, so why then does he require his members at Saddleback Church to take personality profiles, which were conceived by the world? For complete documentation of Warren's personality profiling of his members, I refer you to chapters ten and eleven, as well as appendix C. I also refer you to the *Time* magazine article in the March 29, 2004, issue, page 56, which states that Rick Warren's own church requires its members to sign "strict covenants." One of the strict covenant requirements is the personality profiling. He quotes James 4:4 (MSG), which uses the phrase, "flirting with the world." But the true rendering is "friendship of the world." Secondly, it is in error when it says, "you end up

37. Ibid., p. 42.
38. Ibid., p. 43.
39. Ibid., p. 48.

enemies of God." The correct rendering is not "end up," but rather it is present tense, i.e., you "are" enemies with God. *The Message* translation then adds unto God's Word by adding a phrase that is not even in the original: "If all you want is your own way."

Rick Warren quotes 1 Peter 2:11 (MSG) which contains the word *ego.*[40]

Ego in the context Rick Warren presents it is another Freudian and Jungian psychology term. Although *ego* is used in the Greek in the Bible, it has an entirely different meaning in the personality theory of Jung and Freud from which Rick Warren derives his personality profile. *Ego,* in terms of personality theory is used in conjunction with *id* and *super ego.* There is not even any such thing as *id* and *super ego.* Freud's definition of *ego* is certainly not what is meant by the word *ego* in the Bible.

> EGO: For Freud, the ego is "the representative of the outer world to the id" ("Ego and the Id," 708). In other words, the ego represents and enforces the reality-principle whereas the id is concerned only with the pleasure-principle. Whereas the ego is oriented towards perceptions in the real world, the id is oriented towards internal instincts; whereas the ego is associated with reason and sanity, the id belongs to the passions. The ego, however, is never able fully to distinguish itself from the id, of which the ego is, in fact, a part, which is why in his pictorial representation of the mind Freud does not provide a hard separation between the ego and the id. The ego could also be said to be a defense against the superego and its ability to drive the individual subject towards inaction or suicide as a result of crippling guilt. Freud sometimes represents the ego as continually struggling to defend itself from three dangers or masters: "from the external world, from the libido of the id, and from the severity of the super-ego" ("Ego and the Id," 716).
>
> SUPER-EGO: The super-ego is the faculty that seeks to police what it deems unacceptable desires; it represents all moral restric-

---

40. Ibid., p. 49.

tions and is the "advocate of a striving towards perfection" ("New Introductory Lectures," 22.67). Originally, the super-ego had the task of repressing the Oedipus complex and, so, is closely caught up in the psychodramas of the id; it is, in fact, a reaction-formation against the primitive object-choices of the id, specifically those connected with the Oedipus complex. The young heterosexual male deals with the Oedipus complex by identifying with and internalizing the father and his prohibitions: "The super-ego retains the character of the father, while the more intense the Oedipus complex was and the more rapidly it succumbed to repression (under the influence of discipline, religious teaching, schooling and reading), the more exacting later on is the domination of the super-ego over the ego—in the form of conscience or perhaps of an unconscious sense of guilt" ("Ego and the Id," 706). Given its intimate connection with the Oedipus complex, the super-ego is associated with the dread of castration. As we grow into adulthood, various other individuals or organizations will take over the place of the father and his prohibitions (the church, the law, the police, the government). Because of its connection to the id, the superego has the ability to become *excessively* moral and thus lead to destructive effects. The super-ego is closely connected to the "ego ideal."

Id. The id is the great reservoir of the libido, from which the ego seeks to distinguish itself through various mechanisms of repression. Because of that repression, the id seeks alternative expression for those impulses that we consider evil or excessively sexual, impulses that we often felt as perfectly natural at an earlier or archaic stage and have since repressed. The id is governed by the pleasure-principle and is oriented towards one's internal instincts and passions. Freud also argues on occasion that the id represents the inheritance of the species, which is passed on to us at birth; and yet for Freud the id is, at the same time, "the dark, inaccessible part of our personality" ("New Introductory Lectures," 22.328). See also Freud Module I on psychosexual development.

—www.sla.purdue.edu/academic/engl/theory/
psychoanalysis/definitions/ego.html

But these definitions are pure myth, exactly what the apostle Paul opposed.

Here is the incorrect translation Rick Warren invokes: "Friends, this world is not your home, so don't make yourselves cozy in it. Don't indulge your ego at the expense of your soul" (1 Pet. 2:11 [MSG]).

So which *ego* does Rick Warren mean? The biblical definition from the Greek, or Freud's which collides with Scripture? I submit that Warren's use of the word is more in compliance with Freud's definition and ultimately Jung's application to personality theory.

Following is a definition of *ego* from still another psychology source:

> Ego: Freud's term for the aspect of the "psyche" that processes a person's "conscious" perception of reality. In a healthy person, it also controls the "id", so that satisfaction occurs only in socially acceptable and/or personally meaningful forms, and decides when to obey or disobey the "superego."
>
> —*www.hkbu.edu.kh/~ppp/dow/dowglos.html*

Now let's see what the 1 Peter 2:11 really says:

> Dearly beloved, I beseech you as strangers and pilgrims, abstain from fleshly lusts, which war against the soul.

So, where is *ego* in this passage? Where is the war in *The Message* translation?

❋   ❋   ❋

Rick Warren states: "The greatest heroes of faith are not those who achieve prosperity, success, and power in this life." [41]

Well this is certainly true of many heroes of faith. But it applies equally to those who achieved prosperity, success, and power in this life. Rick Warren's statement would then have to exclude Abraham, Joseph, Solomon, Esther, Job, and many others who had all three

---

41. Ibid., p. 51.

characteristics. And now Mr. Warren is considered a great hero of the faith by some, and even the modern-day Luther in launching a New Reformation. But Warren has been prosperous, well-known, and wields enormous power and influence in this life! So from Rick Warren's own testimony, wouldn't he then be excluded as a great hero of the faith?

❋ ❋ ❋

Rick Warren quotes **Irenaeus**: "The glory of God is a human being fully alive!" [42]

I hardly know where to begin refuting this troubling idea except to say that there are a host of scriptures to refute it, such as Isaiah's own words speaking of God:

> I am the Lord: that is my name: **and my glory will I not give to another,** neither my praise to graven images.
>
> —Isaiah 42:8

It is most unfortunate that Irenaeus made such a statement because he was devout early church father who was a passionate opponent of gnosticism and would certainly have opposed a number of the Catholic mystics that Rick Warren quotes and endorses. I refer you to Irenaeus' several volumes entitled ***Against Heresies.***

❋ ❋ ❋

Rick Warren quotes **John Piper:** "God is most glorified in us when we are most satisfied in him." [43]

Jonah, Job, and Ezekiel were not most satisfied in him and yet God was still glorified. Lazarus wasn't even alive and hardly knew what hit him when he was resurrected, yet God was glorified.

❋ ❋ ❋

Rick Warren: "Worship is . . . enjoying God." [44]

Worship could be a time of enjoying God, but not always. Worship is honoring the "worthship" of God, prostrate and travailing be-

42. Ibid., p. 55.
43. Ibid., p. 56.
44. Ibid., p. 56.

fore the Lord in total humility, in recognition of our own unworthiness. (See chapter seven on worship.)

Purpose One Section:
"You Were Planned for God's Pleasure"

"DAY 8 – Planned for God's Pleasure" begins on page 63

Rick Warren: "When you fully understand this truth" [that your first purpose is "living for God's pleasure"], you will never again have a problem with feeling insignificant." [45]

If this is true, then why did David, who was *already* a man after God's own heart, ask the question, "What is man that thou art mindful of him?" (Ps. 8:4). Why did Jeremiah despise the day he was born if he thought he was so significant? There are many examples throughout the Bible of men and women of faith who already understood their purpose, yet still had times of feeling insignificant, let alone *never again* feeling insignificant. Besides this, our feelings are mercurial; we can't always depend on our feelings, but on faith. Furthermore, there is nothing in the Bible to suggest that recognizing "living for God's pleasure" is God's "first" purpose in your life!

❀ ❀ ❀

Rick Warren: "The moment you were born into the world . . . you are a child of God, and you bring pleasure to God like nothing else he has ever created." [46]

He quotes Ephesians 1:4–5 (TEV) to prove this which states: ". . . Because of his love God had already decided that through Jesus Christ he would make us his children—this was his pleasure and purpose."

So even in this translation, Mr. Warren contradicts his own premise . . . that simply being born does not give God His greatest pleasure and there is not one single scripture to support that idea. If anything,

---

45. Ibid., p. 63.
46. Ibid., p. 63.

it is us being ***born again*** (literally, "born from above") that gives God His greatest pleasure. This is confirmed by the angels praising the Lord when one person comes to repentance, not when one person is simply born. Rick Warren's use of translations, or even paraphrasing a scripture, completely changes and/or adds words to the meaning intended by the author. The correct rendering of this text is even clear in that we are adopted by Jesus Christ. But you can't be adopted until you are first born physically. So, let's see what Ephesians 1:5 has to say:

> Having predestinated us unto the **adoption** of children by Jesus Christ to himself, according to the good pleasure of his will.

❋ ❋ ❋

Rick Warren: "God loves all kinds of music." [47]

This is a most astonishing statement considering that Rick Warren's whole thrust in his ***Purpose Driven Church*** book is "out with the old" (music) and in with the new! It is all the more a contradiction of Mr. Warren's statement in that book, "To insist that all 'good' music came from Europe two hundred years ago is cultural elitism" (**Rick Warren**, ***The Purpose Driven Church***, p. 281). Furthermore, music is not neutral, it too must be judged by its fruit. For more scriptural proof of what the Lord thinks of music, I refer you to ***What Is Worship, Parts I & II,*** available from Rock Salt Publishing.

❋ ❋ ❋

Rick Warren: ". . . falling in love with Jesus." [48]

This is a very troubling term and very misleading to non-believers who will mistake it for romantic *eros* love. Besides this, the term implies a helpless free fall vs. purposeful obedience, picking up the cross and denying yourself, and resisting temptation. Having an *eros* love for Jesus is a concept found nowhere in Scripture. Yes, we are to love Jesus with all of our hearts. But we are also to fear God.

47. Ibid., p. 65.
48. Ibid., p. 67.

"DAY 9 – What Makes God Smile?" begins on page 69

Rick Warren: "Noah . . . trusted God, even when it didn't make sense." [49]

But if you read the account of Noah in Genesis, you will see that the passage does *not* say building the Ark for the coming global flood did not make sense; it was simply unseen by Noah. In fact, being "unseen" is a major component of faith. Just because something is unseen, doesn't mean it doesn't make any sense. Read the entire chapter eleven in Hebrews, which describes many examples of faith being exercised for things unseen. Only one of these examples implies that trusting God did not make sense, and that was Sarah being too old to conceive.

❋ ❋ ❋

Rick Warren: "There are no unspiritual abilities." [50]

If this statement is true, then you would have to say that all abilities are spiritual. But there are a host of human abilities that have nothing to do with the spirit. One has to also ask what one could easily and reasonably infer from his statement, and that is to ask what spiritual abilities are *forbidden* by Christians. Divination and necromancy are spiritual abilities too! But they are an abomination to the Lord.

"DAY 10 – The Heart of Worship" begins on page 77

Rick Warren: "Love casts out all fear." [51]

Yes it is true that perfect love does cast out all fear of punishment and fear of man, but it *never* casts out the fear of the Lord.

"DAY 12 – Developing Your Friendship with God" begins on page 92

49. Ibid., p. 69.
50. Ibid., p. 75.
51. Ibid., p. 78.

Rick Warren: "God doesn't expect you to be perfect, but he does insist on complete honesty." [52]

Please show me chapter and verse that supports this idea. Saul was honest, too, in bringing a sacrifice to the Lord. But the Lord demanded obedience, not sacrifice. In several examples in the Old Testament, God's people murmured and complained . . . but at least they were completely honest. And what did God do? Was He pleased simply because they were honest? Of course not. He opened up the earth and swallowed these "honest" people and killed the rest of them with plagues . . . 14,700 of them (see Numbers 16, 26; and Deuteronomy 11)! If you think Rick Warren's theology is correct about God insisting on complete honesty, do a word search with the word "murmur" in the Bible and see if it ever made any difference to God simply because they were completely honest.

> Neither murmur ye, as some of them also murmured, and were destroyed of the destroyer.
>
> —1 Corinthians 10:10

> Do all things without murmurings and disputings: That ye may be blameless and harmless, the sons of God, without rebuke, in the midst of a crooked and perverse nation, among whom ye shine as lights in the world.
>
> —Philippians 2:14–15

Finally, Mr. Warren's above statement that God does not want perfection collides with the Scriptures of what God really expects as the process of sanctification as Christians until we are glorified, and that is:

> Be ye therefore **perfect**, even as your Father which is in heaven is **perfect**.
>
> —Matthew 5:48

---

52. Ibid., p. 92.

> But let patience have her **perfect** work, that **ye may be perfect** and entire, wanting nothing.
>
> —James 1:4

✻ ✻ ✻

Rick Warren states: "**There is nothing—absolutely nothing—more important than developing a friendship with God.**" [53] Then he quotes 1 Timothy 6:21 (LB) to try to back this up: "Some of these people have missed **the most important thing in life**—they don't know God."

Well, let us once again see if that is what the text really says:

> O Timothy, keep that which is committed to thy trust, avoiding profane and vain babblings, and oppositions of science falsely so called: Which some professing have erred concerning the faith. Grace be with thee. Amen.
>
> —1 Timothy 6:20–21

It is unthinkable that Rick Warren would once again leave out the critical qualifier and context of this quote, and that is verse 20 . . . really the rest of the sentence! There is nothing in the text which says "the most important thing," let alone "the most important thing in life." Besides, Paul is not saying these people in the church don't know God, but rather were erring in dabbling in vain babblings and science falsely so-called. Mr. Warren's quote is one more example of leaving me in complete disbelief that I had even had the right citation because his statements are so far off track from what the text actually says. Later in this book you will see that it is this very "science falsely so-called" (i.e., psychology) that Rick Warren himself integrates into the church with his SHAPE personality profile (see chapters ten and eleven), whose roots go back to the very Greek and pagan ideas that Paul himself opposed. Timothy took the warning to heart. It is too bad that Rick Warren did not!

---

53. Ibid., p. 99.

"DAY 13 – Worship That Pleases God" begins on page 100

Rick Warren: "God is pleased when our worship is **accurate**." [54]

This is one of the most brazen statements in the book, that Rick Warren would champion accuracy, yet use one corrupt, inaccurate, incomplete translation and paraphrase of the Bible after another, and promote and endorse false teachers throughout the book who are anything but accurate in conveying the authority of Scripture. I have already identified some of these false teachers and will document more later in this commentary.

In Day 14 Rick Warren quotes **A. W. Tozer.**[55] Tozer is a highly revered scholar. But if anyone has ever read any of his work, you would easily see that Tozer would oppose the Purpose Driven theology of Rick Warren. Here are some quotes from A. W. Tozer:

> If the Holy Spirit was withdrawn from the church today, 95 percent of what we do would go on and no one would know the difference. If the Holy Spirit had been withdrawn from the New Testament church, 95 percent of what they did would stop, and everybody would know the difference.

> That religion and amusement are forever opposed to each other by their very essential natures is apparently not known to this new school of religious entertainers.

> The emotions have had a beautiful time, but the will is left untouched.

> The best they can do is to appeal to the world's psychology or repeat brightly that "modern times call for modern methods."
> —*The Menace of the Religious Movie* by A. W. Tozer

These quotes of A. W. Tozer do not resemble the philosophy and the-

---

54. Ibid., p. 101.
55. Ibid., p. 108.

ology of Rick Warren's *Purpose Driven Life*. I am confident that Tozer would kindly thank Rick Warren to not quote him and create any false impression that he would have supported his theology.

Purpose Two Section:
"You Were Formed For God's Family"

"DAY 15 – Formed for God's Family" begins on page 117
"DAY 16 – What Matters Most" begins on page 123

Rick Warren: "Why is **baptism** so important? . . . It symbolizes God's second purpose for your life: participating in the fellowship of God's eternal family." [56]

Where does it say that in the Bible? No, if anything, it symbolizes the first purpose in your life, which is to be born again. So what it really symbolizes is our death, burial, and resurrection, passing from death unto life . . . not participating in fellowship.

❀   ❀   ❀

Rick Warren: "You become a church member by committing your-self to a specific group of believers." [57]

Simply not true. You become a church member the day you become a member of the Body of Christ, which is the day you become a believer. Of what specific local church was Paul a member? Titus? Timothy? They were committed to a number of churches!

"DAY 18 – Experiencing Life Together" begins on page 138

Rick Warren: "It is only when we become open about our lives that we experience real fellowship." [58] He quotes 1 John 1:7–8 (NCV): "If we live in the light, as God is in the light, we can share fellowship with each other. . . ."

But being open with each other about our lives does not define

---

56. Ibid., p. 120.
57. Ibid., p. 137.
58. Ibid., p. 140.

walking in the light. You could be open with each other and walking in total darkness. Rick Warren's statement does not even agree with the very scripture he quotes. Furthermore, we don't automatically walk in the light just because we have fellowship. By walking in the light, God supplies the fellowship, or adds unto the church as should be added. The critical flaw and fatal attraction to the Church Growth Movement that Mr. Warren espouses is his own thinking.

"DAY 21 – Protecting Your Church" begins on page 160

Rick Warren: "Unity is the soul of fellowship. . . . But for **unity's sake** we must never let differences divide us." [59]

This is the great argument for ecumenism in which Rick Warren reveals his true colors throughout this book, as I have documented. But unity can never be at the expense of truth! The fact is that doctrine *does* divide and it is intended to:

> For **there must be also** heresies [**divisions**] **among you,** that they which are approved may be made manifest among you.
> —1 Corinthians 11:19

> Holding fast the faithful word as he hath been taught, that he may be able **by sound doctrine** both to exhort and to convince the gainsayers.
> —Titus 1:9

> For the time will come when they will not endure sound doctrine; but after their own lusts shall they heap to themselves teachers, having itching ears.
> —2 Timothy 4:3

No, unity is not the soul of fellowship; truth is the soul of true fellowship. Light cannot have fellowship (unity) with darkness. What

---

59. Ibid., pp. 160–161.

do the cup of Belial and the cup of the Lord have in common? If we don't let our differences divide us (other than nonessentials such as days and diet) we are on a sure path to heresy!

※   ※   ※

Rick Warren: "Conflict is usually a sign that the focus has shifted to less important things." [60]

Tell this to Martin Luther who penned the *95 Theses* in which conflict was the focus of the *most* important things! Rick Warren then calls interpretations "disputable matters." Interpretation of Scripture is not a less important thing, nor is it a disputable matter. Peter says that no scripture is open to private interpretation (2 Pet. 1:20). So private interpretations *should* produce conflict and correction! Mr. Warren then calls styles and methods disputable matters that we should not engage in, yet disparages a host of other church styles and methods in his *Purpose Driven Church* book.

It is ironic that Rick Warren quotes Dietrich Bonnhoffer regarding disillusionment with the church during Hitler's reign so that we should not divorce the church.[61] But thank God Bonnhoffer *did* divorce the church as an institution for its allegiance to Hitler and then helped build the underground church. Finally, we are not really married to the church in the first place, we as the Bride of Christ (both individually and corporate) are betrothed to Christ the Groom. For a Christian to be married to the church would mean they are married to themselves.

※   ※   ※

Rick Warren: "At Saddleback Church, every member signs a covenant that includes a promise to protect the unity of our church." [62]

Two problems with this statement. One is signing a covenant, which is addressed in the commentary on Rick Warren's *Purpose Driven Life* book (chapter two of this book), and the other pertains to unity at what price (addressed in the commentary on Mr. Warren's *Purpose Driven Life* book, pp. 160–161 above).

---

60. Ibid., p. 162.
61. Ibid., p. 163.
62. Ibid., p. 167.

Purpose Three Section:
"You Were Created to Become Like Christ"

"DAY 22 – Created to Become Like Christ" begins on page 171
"DAY 23 – How We Grow" begins on page 179

Rick Warren: "Every behavior is motivated by a belief, and every action is prompted by an attitude. God revealed this thousands of years before psychologists understood it." [63]

The truth is that psychologists *never* understood it and still don't because their worldview is the opposite of Christianity's. But it is not surprising that Rick Warren thinks that psychologists understand it now because he promotes and endorses so many of them and has integrated psychological profiling into his SHAPE program. He quotes Proverbs 4:23 (TEV) to prove this. But this verse states in the King James Version:

Keep thy heart with all diligence; for out of it are the issues of life.

Jesus reaffirms this:

But those things which proceed out of the mouth come forth from the heart; and they defile the man.

—Matthew 15:18

Psychologists don't believe the above proverb any more than they believe the proverb that says, "The fear of the Lord is the beginning of wisdom" (Prov. 9:10).

Psychologists such as Jung, whom Warren uses in his personality profiling, believe that it is out of our unconscious and collective unconscious that pour the issues of life. Psychologists don't agree on much, but they do agree that the nature of man is not what is de-

---

63. Ibid., p. 181.

scribed in the Bible. For those who are still not sure whether or not psychologists even presently understand why we behave the way we do and what is the solution, I invite you to read my book review of *Psychology Debunked*, then read the book, available at: *www.psychologydebunked.com/sundquistreview.htm.*

For a comprehensive comparison of psychology's worldviews vs. Scripture, please see appendix A.

❋   ❋   ❋

Rick Warren quotes Romans 12:2b (TEV): "Let God transform you inwardly by a complete change of your mind. Then you will be able to know the will of God—what is good and is pleasing to him and is perfect." [64]

It is surprising to me that Rick Warren would quote this verse (which tells us that the perfect will of God in a believer can be achieved by the renewing of our mind which we are able to fully do with Scripture and prayer alone) and suggest we need his SHAPE program in order to find God's will and purpose for our life. This is one of many verses Rick Warren cites that I would quote to refute his theology.

"DAY 24 – Transformed by Truth" begins on page 185

Rick Warren: "Spiritual growth is the process of replacing lies with truth." He even quotes Jesus' prayer, "Sanctify them by the truth; your word is truth" (John 17:17 [NIV]). [65]

But if Mr. Warren believes this, then why does he replace Jesus' command to *not* make covenants, such as Warren's covenant at the beginning of this book and the one you have to sign to become a member of his church? Why does he use corrupt and inaccurate translations that are not truth? Why does he does not even have the facts right regarding his examples of forty-day scenarios in the Bible he describes? Why does he allow the influence of the teaching of Carl Jung? Why does he promote and work with a host of false teachers

---

64. Ibid., p. 184.
65. Ibid., p. 185.

who have replaced the truth with lies, as documented in this commentary and by many discernment ministries around the world?

⁑   ⁑   ⁑

Rick Warren: "Meditation is focused thinking." [66]

If this is true, then why does Rick Warren endorse Richard Foster and so many Catholic mystics such as Henri Nouwen and Thomas Merton? (See commentary on pages 90–91 and visit *www.lighthousetrails.com* for commentary on Thomas Merton.)

⁑   ⁑   ⁑

Rick Warren: "He [God] depends more on circumstances to make us like Jesus than he depends on our reading the Bible." [67]

This statement is so far off track from the canon of Scripture that I think I will mostly just let it speak for itself. Rick Warren would not even know the purpose of circumstances or trials if he had not been "reading the Bible" when he quotes Peter. How would we know what to obey and how to respond to circumstances without first having read the Bible? His statement hardly harmonizes with Jesus Christ's own words that state:

> But he answered and said, It is written, Man shall not live by bread alone, but by every word that proceedeth out of the mouth of God.
>
> —Matthew 4:4

> But **seek ye first** the kingdom of God, and his righteousness; and all these things shall be added unto you.
>
> —Matthew 6:33

⁑   ⁑   ⁑

Rick Warren quotes 2 Timothy 2:15 (NIV): "Do your best to present yourself to God as one approved, a workman **who does not need to be ashamed** and **who correctly handles the word of truth.**" [68]

---

66. Ibid., p. 190.
67. Ibid., p. 193.
68. Ibid., p. 256.

Of course I agree with this Scripture. But you have to ask yourself, then why didn't Rick Warren correctly handle the truth when he used a host of corrupt translations and quote and endorse so many false teachers in his book?

"DAY 32 – Using What God Gave You" begins on page 249
"DAY 33 – How Real Servants Act" begins on page 257

Rick Warren: "God determines your greatness by how many people you serve." [69]

Christ did say that we must be servants of all. But He didn't mean quantity, he meant quality in the individual's heart so that whomever a person encounters, they should have a servant's heart. Mr. Warren's fatally flawed spin on the word "all" is another trap for unsuspecting people to become prey to his Church Growth philosophy.

※　※　※

Rick Warren: "God often tests our hearts by asking us to serve in ways we're not shaped." [70]

Warren's SHAPE personality profile asks us to make the quantum leap from a premise that is not even sound. It assumes that how we are shaped is how Warren says we are shaped. And if we don't know how we are shaped, then we are to take Warren's SHAPE profile to figure it out. This all assumes that the integrity of Rick Warren's model is even an accurate profile or schematic for determining a person's personality or that if the results of such a profile should even have any appreciable impact on determining how one is to serve the Lord in the church. The problem is that Warren's profile is fundamentally and fatally flawed because it is modeled after (in great part) Carl Jung's personality theory, which Jung obtained by divination (divination is forbidden in Scripture). For complete proof and documentation I refer you to chapters ten and eleven, as well as appendix C.

※　※　※

---

69. Ibid., p. 257.
70. Ibid., p. 258.

Rick Warren: "Faithfulness has always been a rare quality." [71]

He cites Psalm 12:1, Proverbs 20:6, and Philippians 2:19–22 to prove this.

But these passages emphasize faithfulness to God and Jesus Christ, not faithfulness to the church as Mr. Warren defines it, or faithfulness to your shape. His argument is very clever, but very dangerous because it is the argument I have observed in how cults and the shepherding movements manipulate people into serving. He implies that faithfulness to the local church is automatically faithfulness to God. But if the local church strays from the truth, a loyal congregation would also stray from the truth. This, in part, is why so much error has seeped into the Church Growth Movement. It is misplaced loyalty. Our allegiance and faithfulness must always first and foremost be to the truth! If believers simply prayed and studied the roots of Rick Warren's SHAPE personality profile and compared it to Scripture, they should see that it is *not* faithful to the truth.

✻ ✻ ✻

Rick Warren: "Self-denial is the core of servanthood." [72]

It is surprising to me that Rick Warren would make this statement in light of Paul's own teaching to the Colossian church. This was the religion of the ascetics that Paul so opposed. This heresy is well described in an article by David Treybig entitled "Does the New Testament Abolish Meat Distinctions?"

> The false teaching Paul condemned contained many elements of asceticism—avoidance of anything enjoyable—which was intended to make its followers more spiritual. This deluded attempt to attain greater spirituality included "neglect of the body" (Colossians 2:23). Paul characterized the ascetics' misguided rules as "Do not touch, do not taste, do not handle" (verse 21). These efforts only created a "false humility" (verse 23) and were destined to fail

71. Ibid., p. 261.
72. Ibid., p. 266.

> because they were based on "the commandments and doctrines of men" (verse 22) rather than God's instruction.
>
> —*www.gnmagazine.org/issues/gn11/ntmeats.html*

Paul went on to say that all these things were meant to be eaten, so long as they were eaten with thanksgiving to the Lord. Paul even went so far as to call this self-denial theology a doctrine of demons in reference to the prohibition to marry and the eating of certain foods.

> Now the Spirit speaketh expressly, that in the latter times some shall depart from the faith, giving heed to seducing spirits, and doctrines of devils; Speaking lies in hypocrisy; having their conscience seared with a hot iron; Forbidding to marry, and commanding to abstain from meats, which God hath created to be received with thanksgiving of them which believe and know the truth. For every creature of God is good, and nothing to be refused, if it be received with thanksgiving. For it is sanctified by the word of God and prayer.
>
> —1 Timothy 4:1–5

❋ ❋ ❋

Rick Warren: "The closer you get to Jesus, the less you need to promote yourself." [73]

Does this mean you need to promote yourself more when you are farther from Jesus? If Mr. Warren is now closer to Jesus than ever before, why does he promote himself and his own resources, listed in appendix 2 of his book (which are mostly him)? Why is he promoted globally now more than ever? It is true that one of the central themes of the Bible is selflessness as a godly attribute. But the fact is that most ministries promote themselves. Those mature in the faith will be in discernment ministry and will often be working for missionary organizations that do promote themselves. So if anything, rather than promoting yourself less, you would be promoting yourself more, not for selfish reasons, but for the sake of the Gospel. Scripture

73. Ibid., p. 270.

speaks with commendation to those who publish the "good news." So wouldn't it be appropriate for publishing houses that publish the Bible to advertise? Wouldn't advertising be construed as promotion for a good cause? Paul even speaks of bringing a letter of recommendation into a city to ensure that a teacher of Christianity is sound in doctrine. One should let another speak well of them, but it is still promoting yourself. Don't thousands of Christian businessmen promote themselves? Haven't you ever bought a Christian book or product from a Christian that you would never have found or known about if that person had not promoted himself?

Mr. Warren quotes Albert Schweitzer: "The only really happy people are those who have learned how to serve." But serve whom? The pope? The Dalai Lama? The Rajneesh?

"DAY 35 – God's Power in Your Weakness" begins on page 272

Rick Warren: "Gideon's weakness was low self-esteem." [74]

There we go again with this teaching of self-esteem, promoted by Robert Schuller and James Dobson, as well as a host of psychologists. So the answer to Gideon's problem was a dose of high self-esteem? High self-esteem is exactly what Lucifer had and fell from heaven. High self-esteem is what built the Tower of Babel. I invite you to re-read the account of Gideon to see if Gideon even had this nonexistent weakness! If low self-esteem was Gideon's problem, he simply needed a dose of *high* self-esteem in order to conquer the Midianites. But he did not even know he was supposed to go into battle against them until the Lord commanded him to do so. In fact, the whole purpose of God reducing the size of Gideon's army from thirty thousand to three hundred was so they would *not* take the credit and thereby increase their self-esteem. They were to give God the glory and exalt Him, not themselves! If low self-esteem was Gideon's problem, then high self-esteem would have been provided him when all of the people asked Gideon to rule over them. But what was Gideon's response, when he

---

74. Ibid., p. 275.

could easily have satisfied his self-esteem by becoming king over the Israelites? He said neither he nor his son would rule over them, that the Lord would rule over them! He could have also strengthened his "weakness" of "low self-esteem" by taking plunder. After all, didn't he deserve it for his victory over the Midianites? But what was his response? He only asked for earrings from the plunder (the rest of the plunder went to his soldiers), though sadly these earrings were used to build idols. (See Judges 6–8 to see if Rick Warren is telling you the truth!) It is amazing to me how many times I see Mr. Warren using revisionist history to force his theological and psychological ideas into the biblical text that are simply not there! Finally, one of the best examples of what Jesus Christ himself thinks of more self-esteem is His account of the Pharisee who had high self-esteem vs. the tax collector who had very low self-esteem. Which one of the two went home justified? The tax collector. But this should not be difficult to see because the Old Testament had already told us that it is a broken and contrite spirit that the Lord esteems . . . not high self-esteem!

> The Lord is nigh unto them that are of a broken heart; and saveth such as be of a contrite spirit.
>
> —Psalm 34:18

> The sacrifices of God are a broken spirit: a broken and a contrite heart, O God, thou wilt not despise.
>
> —Psalm 51:17

For more information on self-esteem vs. Christianity see: *www.rapidnet.com/~jbeard/bdm/Psychology/self-est/self.htm.*

※   ※   ※

Rick Warren: "The more honest you are, the more of God's grace you get." [75]

As I discussed earlier, the murmurers in the Old Testament were honest too, and they did not get more of God's grace; their hones-

---

75. Ibid., p. 276.

ty angered God and so He had the earth swallow them up! Besides which, honesty, at least as opposed to dishonesty, is its own reward. God does necessarily give you more grace because you are simply being obedient to what He commanded you to do in the first place. God dispenses His grace for His own purposes, not ours!

❈ ❈ ❈

Rick Warren: "Your personal testimony is more effective than a sermon." [76]

This sounds like the theme of his Celebrate Recovery, when he says, "When a sermon is not enough." (For a complete analysis of Rick Warren's Celebrate Recovery, see chapter eight.) It is not our personal testimony that is ultimately effective, but by the hearer hearing the Word being preached. Faith comes by hearing the Word of God, not our testimony whether in person or from the pulpit.

❈ ❈ ❈

Rick Warren: "Personal stories are also easier to relate to than principles, and people love to hear them." [77]

Then why are there eight "principles" to recovery at the heart of his Celebrate Recovery program?

❈ ❈ ❈

Rick Warren: "Unbelievers would probably lose interest if you started quoting theologians." [78]

What an insult to Jan Hus who was martyred, to Martin Luther and A. W. Tozer (whom Warren quotes). I am all for personal testimonies, but they should never supersede preaching the Word. The entire Bible is full of examples of simply preaching repentance and quoting Scripture to bring about repentance! But even if no one comes, as in the case of Noah, you still preach repentance. Of course people love to hear personal stories. But personal stories don't bring repentance, the Word does!

❈ ❈ ❈

76. Ibid., p. 290.
77. Ibid., p. 290.
78. Ibid., p. 290.

Rick Warren: "Shared stories build a relational bridge that Jesus can walk across."

No, that is not the bridge Jesus walks across. Once again, it is by His Word being preached!

❋ ❋ ❋

Rick Warren: "Many people who won't accept the authority of the Bible will listen to a humble, personal story. That is why on six different occasions Paul used his testimony to share the gospel instead of quoting Scripture (Acts 22–26)." [79]

We certainly can share our testimony. But Paul's testimony ***is*** Scripture. So when we share his testimony, we are preaching Scripture. But it is recorded that Paul ***always*** also reasoned from Scripture to bring about conversions. More critically, it is not Paul's personal testimony *per se* that is what is at stake here, but his testimony of Jesus. That is what we testify! That is how the saints overcame in Revelation by the testimony of Jesus:

> And they **overcame** him by the blood of the Lamb, and by the word of their testimony; and they loved not their lives unto the death.
>
> —Revelation 12:11

❋ ❋ ❋

Rick Warren: "The church that doesn't want to grow is saying to the world: 'You can go to hell.'" [80]

That is not necessarily true. God wanted Gideon's army to shrink, not grow. He was looking for a few good men. Only a remnant will be saved. Because of the great falling away in the last days, a church may not grow which is faithful, but will shrink. It might only grow if it chooses to compromise. In no way would these people be saying, "You can go to hell." If anything, it is because they don't want them to go to hell that they are risking not growing so that truth will not suffer! In fact, the true Gospel may cause everyone to walk away or

---

79. Ibid., p. 291.
80. Ibid., p. 294.

refuse, as in the case of Noah and as occurred to Jesus Christ himself, when He asked, "Will you also walk away?"

"DAY 38 – Becoming a World-Class Christian" begins on page 297

Rick Warren: "You will be either a world-class Christians or a worldly Christian. . . . The only barrier is the way we think. To be a world-class Christian you must make some mental shifts. Your perspective and attitudes must change." [81]

According to whom? I don't see any scriptural basis for this justification or mandate for this Kingdom Now and Word of Faith theology. This "power of positive thinking" teaching reminds me of Norman Vincent Peale, Tony Robbins, Robert Schuller, Dale Carnegie (remember his book *How to Win Friends and Influence People?*) and a host of other self-realization and self-actualization gurus. And where is faith in this axiom? ". . . Without faith it is impossible to please him [God]" (Heb. 11:6).

By Rick Warren's using the phrase "world-class," it seems to imply measuring Christianity by the world's standards. This term is wrong. Even though Rick Warren contrasts world-class with worldly, it still projects self-exaltation if even for a good cause. Nevertheless, it is still a confusing and misleading statement. It should read, "You will either be a 'not-of-this-world' Christian or a worldly Christian," since Jesus said that His Kingdom is *not* of this world . . . whether world-class or worldly. Mr. Warren's terminology also defies the humility talked about in the Book of James and the desire to *not* be world-class Christians in this life in the last verses of Hebrews 11. Many martyred saints chose not to have any earthly reward or earthly calling, but loved their lives not unto death that they might have a more excellent city whose builder and foundation is God himself. In fact, Warren's statement gives the appearance of even contradicting his own statements about being a servant to be great in God's Kingdom. Someone with a servant's heart is not thinking about being a world-class Chris-

---

81. Ibid., pp. 297–298.

tian in any sense of the word. I keep hearing from people who attend Rick Warren's Purpose-Driven churches that they are going to do great things for God . . . they are going to think globally. But maybe God does not want them to do great "world-class" things, but simply and humbly perform faithfully the most miniscule of tasks, virtually unnoticed by anyone. And how might it make someone feel who is not as talented or driven who has not succeeded in being a "world-class" Christian? This could only contribute to producing envy and strife. This is simply the wrong word to be using.

> For we are unto God a sweet savour of Christ, in them that are saved, and in them that perish: To the one we are the savour of death unto death; and to the other savour of life unto life. And who is sufficient for these things?
>
> —2 Corinthians 2:15–16

Also, Jesus said we would be hated by the world. Are world-class Christians loved by the world? Paul said:

> Not that I speak in respect of want: for I have learned, in whatsoever state I am, therewith to be content. I know both how to be abased, and I know how to abound: every where and in all things I am instructed both to be full and to be hungry, both to abound and to suffer need.
>
> —Philippians 4:11–12

Elsewhere Paul says: "But godliness with contentment is great gain" (1 Tim. 6:6).

So how does Rick Warren's teaching square with being content if you are simply a faithful Christian, *not* a world-class Christian. Will those who will refuse the mark of the beast be considered world-class Christians? Or will they be as Scripture says of those Christians who were martyred and persecuted: This world is not worthy of them . . . if they are "world-class" Christians?

(Of whom the **world** was **not worthy:**) they wandered in deserts, and in mountains, and in dens and caves of the earth.

—Hebrews 11:38

※ ※ ※

Rick Warren: "It has never been easier in history to fulfill your commission to go to the whole world." [82]

Once again that is a misinterpretation of the Great Commission. This commandment by Jesus Christ is for the whole church collectively, not lone crusaders.

※ ※ ※

Rick Warren once again mentions "breath prayers." This teaching comes from John Mains. This web site describes his teaching: *www.basilica.org/meditationgrp.html.*

The following web site describes the **Benedictine Order's** teaching: *www.osb.org/acad/benval1.html#I.D*

(Disclaimer: I do not endorse the teachings on these two sites. They are here for reference and confirmation from their own advocates.) (Source: *www.lighthousetrailsresearch.com/Rick Warren.htm*)

"DAY 39 – Balancing Your Life" begins on Page 305

Rick Warren: "Blessed are the balanced, they shall outlast everyone." [83]

Does this mean that the unbalanced (assuming there is such a thing as balanced) are not blessed? Mr. Warren comments upon the above statement with 2 Peter 3:17 (CEV), which says: "Don't let the errors of evil people lead you down the wrong path and make you lose your balance."

Now let's compare this to the KJV:

Ye therefore, beloved, seeing ye know [these things] before, beware lest ye also, being led away with the error of the wicked, fall from your own stedfastness.

---

82. Ibid., p. 297.
83. Ibid., p. 305.

So where is there anything in this verse about outlasting everyone? This certainly describes falling, but that is due to choosing a different path; it has nothing to do with balance. This is the exact same thinking that Rick Warren integrates into his Jung-based personality theory. (See chapter eleven.)

※ ※ ※

Rick Warren: "Our minds are sharpened and our convictions are deepened through conversation." [84]

Rick Warren quotes Proverbs 27:17 (NCV) which states that "iron sharpens iron." But this assumes that in a conversation, both parties are believers in God. It is not conversation as such that sharpens us, but by two brothers holding each other accountable to Scripture and right teaching. Conversation in and of itself does not necessarily have any value. If Mr. Warren believes this, why isn't he subject to the iron of other discernment ministries that have rightfully opposed him for his errors and false teaching and the obvious errors in his book(s)?

※ ※ ※

Rick Warren quotes 1 Timothy 4:6 (CEV): "If you teach these things to other followers, you will be a good servant of Christ. . . ." [85]

Actually, if I pass on Rick Warren's teaching that I have exposed in this commentary (without the commentary), then I will have been a poor servant, and I will not have served either Mr. Warren or the thousands of pastors and churches reading this book and drinking in his teaching. I will have been a poor steward of God's Word to refrain from opposing his use of pagan and occult-based personality profiles.

"DAY 40 – Living with Purpose" begins on page 312

Rick Warren quotes John 13:17 (NIV): "Now that you know these things, you will be blessed if you do them." [86]

---

84. Ibid., p. 307.
85. Ibid., p. 310.
86. Ibid., p. 312.

He presumes that "these things" are what Rick Warren says. This is a classic bait-and-switch tactic! "These things" refer directly to Christ's own commandments, not Rick Warren's program!

※   ※   ※

Rick Warren: "As we come to the end of our forty-day journey together, now that you know God's purposes for your life, you will be blessed if you do them!" [87]

I have several problems with this statement. First of all, I already knew my purpose the minute I heard the Gospel and believed it, as would anyone who heard or read the Gospel and obeyed it for the last two thousand years prior to Warren's *40 Days of Purpose!* For those who haven't, we still preach the Gospel . . . and, yes, quote Scripture to do so! That still remains the way we secure our purpose. Following Rick Warren's plan will lead to more confusion and a worse state. Even Mr. Warren does not believe you will know your purpose or SHAPE even at the end of the forty days because you can't determine your SHAPE until you have taken his SHAPE profile and obtained your score which is his Discovery 301 class available as one of the resources in his appendix 2!

※   ※   ※

Rick Warren: "Goals are temporary, purposes are eternal." [88]

Now even assuming you buy into this, Rick Warren does another bait-and-switch by presuming his SHAPE model is how you can find your purpose . . . remember what he said at the beginning of the book, that it is his book that will lead you to God's purpose for your life. Later on Mr. Warren contradicts this statement when he gives examples where goals are eternal. His statement also contradicts the Scripture itself when Paul states in 1 Timothy 1:5: " Now the end of the commandment is charity [love] out of a pure heart, and of a good conscience, and of faith unfeigned." Isn't love eternal?

Or what about Paul running straight to the prize? The prize of the upward call of God in Christ Jesus is the goal (Phil. 3:13). Are we

---

87. Ibid., p. 312.
88. Ibid., p. 313.

to suggest that the prize is temporary? If anything, it was each step in the race that was temporary. Warren also quotes John 14:28 in another place which states the "Father is the goal" (MSG). Does this mean the Father is temporary or eternal?

※　　※　　※

Rick Warren: "Before most unbelievers accept the Bible as credible they want to know that we are credible." [89]

As Isaiah says in Isaiah 53, "Who hath believed our report?" Our report *is* the Bible. We are credible because we have believed His report and preach His report. When the Lord spoke to Ezekiel, Ezekiel didn't think he would be credible. So was Ezekiel going to be credible because he was a sincere person or because he told his listeners a wonderful story? Of course not. God told him to preach the Word of the Lord whether they listened or failed to listen! Jonah had no relationship whatsoever with Nineveh; in fact, Assyria was Israel's sworn enemy to have established or developed any credibility with them. He simply preached repentance . . . the Word of the Lord that God told him to preach! In this example, *all* unbelievers in Nineveh repented. But earlier, Noah had no credibility either, and in fact was mocked, yet he preached the same message and no one repented. Paul could have boasted about all of his credentials (being a Pharisee of Pharisees, etc.), but his view was to count it all loss and his desire was to simply preach Christ crucified.

※　　※　　※

Rick Warren: "If you would like to see some examples from other people, just email me (see appendix 2)." [90]

I have e-mailed Rick Warren with two appeals and he has never responded. Here are the two letters:

February 22, 2003

Dear Rick Warren,

I invite you to consider the following documents which prove

---

89. Ibid., p. 316.
90. Ibid., p. 316.

the Clear and Present Danger of Carl Jung and Psychology which has already become the Trojan Horse and Strange Fire in the Body of Christ. This movement has affected even our closest friends and relatives!

I fervently pray that you take it to heart.

Sincerely in Christ,

James Sundquist

In the above letter I sent him the documentary by Reverend Ed Hird (appendix C in this book) as well as Gary Gilley's article (see resources at the end of this book).

❈ ❈ ❈

February 26, 2003

Dear Rick Warren,

I wish to confirm that you have received my last letter and exhortation re Carl Jung and your S.H.A.P.E. program.

If you still remain unconvinced, I appeal to you to read the following articles:

> *http//www.crmspokane.org/myths2.htm*
>
> and
>
> *http//www.crmspokane.org/Philemon.htm*

Your biblical response to the content of these e-mails is of the utmost urgency!

Sincerely in Christ,

James Sundquist

To date, Rick Warren has still not replied. If Rick Warren champions keeping pledges and promises, wouldn't he be required to respond to a legitimate inquiry?

❈ ❈ ❈

Rick Warren: "It isn't going to matter at all what other people say about you." [91]

If that is true, then why did Rick Warren just get done telling us

---

91. Ibid., p. 317.

on page 316 that we must be credible before we can get most unbelievers to accept the Bible? In other words, to get through to them and be credible, we would need to care what others say about you. Don't you see the contradiction here? And there are many contradictions in his book.

Chapter Five

Does Doctrine Really Matter?

Rick Warren: "God won't ask about your religious background or doctrinal views." [92]

Say what? Doctrine doesn't matter? So why did the apostle Paul spend so much time and effort warning us about doctrines of demons? Why bother to even warn the Galatians who had been bewitched? More of what Paul thought about doctrinal views:

All scripture is given by inspiration of God, and is profitable for doctrine, for reproof, for correction, for instruction in righteousness.

—2 Timothy 3:16

For the time will come when they will not endure sound doctrine; but after their own lusts shall they heap to themselves teachers, having itching ears.

—2 Timothy 4:3

Holding fast the faithful word as he hath been taught, that he may be able by sound doctrine both to exhort and to convince the gainsayers.

—Titus 1:9

What the apostle John thought of doctrinal views:

---

92. Ibid., p. 34.

> If there come any unto you, and *bring not this doctrine,* receive him
> not into your house, neither bid him God speed.
>
> —2 John 1:10

And God won't ask about doctrinal views? Well, Jesus Christ (who is
God) also did not agree with Rick Warren regarding the importance
of doctrine, as we read His words directly to the church in Pergamum
in the Book of Revelation:

> But I have a few things against thee, because thou hast there them
> that hold the **doctrine of Balaam,** who taught Balac to cast a stum-
> blingblock before the children of Israel, to eat things sacrificed
> unto idols, and to commit fornication. So hast thou also them that
> hold the **doctrine of the Nicolaitanes, which thing I hate.**
>
> —Revelation 2:14–15

Doctrinal views do matter! Warren's belittling the importance of
sound doctrine might explain why so few in his congregation and
those who have become Rick Warren churches, have opposed him . . .
they took his advice of less Bible and more stories and personal testimonies, so no one would recognize even the most blatant heresy. And
even where the Bible is taught, where they might get grounded to recognize error, they are given diluted and obscured translations which
have added to, deleted, subtracted from, and completely changed the
meaning of God's Word. So, from Rick Warren's own testimony and
advice, we see prophecy of 2 Timothy 4:3 being fulfilled in these last
days in his own church and in the thousands of churches who believe
his statement(s).

Chapter Six

Promoting False Teachers

What follows in this chapter are concerns over the teachers quoted by Rick Warren in *The Purpose Driven Life* and recommended on his *pastors.com* website. Rick Warren is utilizing these teachings to form the mortar of his Purpose Driven theology, not just as anecdotal quotes. In spite of the well-known concerns regarding many of these teachers, Rick Warren gives no warning label or disclaimer.

Rick Warren quotes **Brother Lawrence** and advises us to **"practice his presence."** [93]

What Rick Warren does not tell you is that Brother Lawrence was a lay Carmelite Order Roman Catholic, which was one of the first orders to elevate Mary to a status beyond what is written in the Bible. And there is nothing in Scripture to support the idea of "practicing His presence" as Brother Lawrence describes it. Brother Lawrence is not the only Catholic mystic that Rick Warren endorses, or author he endorses who also promote mysticism and the desert fathers, as you will see later.

Facts on Brother Lawrence:
- His real name was Nicholas Herman.
- He was a lay Carmelite monk. The Carmelites go back to 1562 when Teresa of Avila took it upon herself to reform the Carmelite Order instituted in 1154 on Mount Carmel, Israel. When the order fell victim to a lack of discipline

---

93. Ibid., p. 162.

among its monks and nuns, Teresa resolved to revive it by restoring the primitive rule and emphasizing a contemplative life. John of the Cross joined forces with Teresa to reform the monk's houses of the order. Now besides the fact the Carmelites are a Roman Catholic order, here are some quotes from these Carmelites which are quite alarming and why New Agers just love them.

Here is a quote from **Basil Pennington**, who wrote the preface for Brother Lawrence's *Practicing the Presence of God:* "The soul of the human family is the Holy Spirit."

Here is what **John of the Cross** says about God: "My beloved [God] is the high mountains, and the lovely valley forests, unexplored islands, rushing rivers."

No, God is not the high mountains. He is the Creator of the high mountains. Anyone worshipping the mountains, thinking they are God, is a pantheist.

Rick Warren endorses "breath prayers" and invites us to pray as the Benedictine monks do.[94]

Where did he get that concept? Not from the Bible. But I can tell you where he did get it. From none other than Benedictine monk John Main, who promotes **universalism** through his identification with the Benedictine Order. Here's a quote from **John Main:**

> Benedict's utter faith in the divine Son of God casts into even sharper relief his insight that this divine Christ is to be found and even adored in other human beings (RB 53.7). **His incarnate presence is not limited to Jesus of Nazareth,** but remains among us in the monastic leaders, the sick, the guest, the poor, a list so inclusive as to signify Christ's presence in all whom one meets.
>
> —*www.lighthousetrailsresearch.com/warren.htm*
> and *www.basilica.org/meditationgrp.htm*

---

94. Ibid., p. 89.

❋   ❋   ❋

Rick Warren states: "Meditation is simply focused thinking" [95] . . . while he simultaneously endorses Richard Foster via his *pastors.com* resources in his appendix 2 resources.[96] Here is how Richard Foster defines meditation:

Richard Foster in his book, *Prayer: Finding the Heart's True Home*, speaks of the practice of "breath prayer," in which a Christian-sounding word or phrase is repeated over and over again like a mantra. Rick Warren promotes Richard Foster's 2002 (25th Anniversary Edition) of *Celebration of Discipline* on his *pastors.com website,* which seems to portray a more biblical definition of Christian meditation:

> Christian meditation, very simply, is the ability to hear God's voice and obey his word. . . . It involves no hidden mysteries, no secret mantras, no mental gymnastics, no esoteric flights into the cosmic consciousness.
> —Richard Foster, *Celebration of Discipline*, 2002, p. 17

But Foster's 1978 edition of *Celebration of Discipline* gives an entirely different and contradictory definition of Christian meditation:

> Christian meditation is an attempt to empty the mind in order to fill it.
> —Richard Foster, *Celebration of Discipline*, 1978, p. 15

Richard Foster opens his 25th Anniversary Edition chapter on meditation with a quote from Carl Jung, a known occultist whose ideas are also promoted in Rick Warren's *Purpose Driven Life* book. Richard Foster still promotes the same false teachers in his current edition as he does in his 1978 edition. These include Carl Jung disciples Agnes Sanford and Morton Kelsey (a trained Jung analyst). Richard Foster also quotes and/or lists as valuable contemplatives such universalists

95. Ibid., p. 90.
96. Ibid., p. 324.

as George Fox and Thomas Kelly, as well as pantheists such as Julian of Norwich, John of the Cross, Madame Guyon, and Meister Eckhart. Finally, Richard Foster promotes Shalem Prayer Institute founder Tilden Edwards who states: "This mystical stream [contemplative prayer] is the Western bridge to Far Eastern spirituality." Rick Warren should not knowingly give five stars to Richard Foster's book as a good spiritual resource on his *pastors.com* website.

For a more complete study on Richard Foster's teaching that Rick Warren promotes, please refer to a documentary I wrote, **"Spiritual Formation, Richard Foster, and Renovare: Renovare Analyzed for Biblical Soundness and Found Wanting"** (*www.cephas-library.com/ purposedriven/renovare_errors_in_renovare_analysed_and_discussed_ part_1_of_2.html*).

In his *Critical Issues Commentary,* Bob DeWaay has written an informative article which discusses Richard Foster, entitled "Contemporary Christian Divination" (July/August 2004) which can be found at *www.twincityfellowship.com/cic/downloads.php.*

For other excellent resources which discuss Richard Foster's teachings, visit these web sites:

> *www.lighthousetrailsresearch.com/richardfoster.htm*
> *www.thenowage.org*
> *www.withchrist.org/MJS/renovare.htm*
> *www.seekgod.ca/renovare.htm*
> *www.cephasministry.com/new_age_richard_foster.html*

While a growing number of evangelical Christians and Christian leaders do, in fact, promote and believe that Richard Foster's teaching is biblically solid, there is great concern over his examples of astral travel technique, summoning down a spirit and calling him Jesus, and praying and meditating with vain repetitions. Richard Foster also promotes Buddhist sympathizers Thomas Merton and Henri Nouwen.

For Thomas Merton:

. . . Foster considers Thomas Merton's book *Contemplative Prayer* "a must book" . . . and credits his [Merton's] books as being filled with "priceless wisdom for all Christians who long to go deeper in the spiritual life."

Merton expressed views such as "I see no contradiction between Buddhism and Christianity. . . . I intend to become as good a Buddhist as I can."

—Ray Yungen, *A Time of Departing* (Lighthouse Trails Publishing, 2002), p. 75

Like Richard Foster, Rick Warren quotes both John of the Cross (see page 88 above) and Henri Nouwen:[97]

What Did Henri Nouwen Really Believe?

Did Nouwen believe Jesus was the only way to God?

"Today I personally believe that while Jesus came to open the door to God's house, all human beings can walk through that door, whether they know about Jesus or not. Today I see it as my call to help every person claim his or her own way to God" (from *Sabbatical Journey*, Henri Nouwen's last book).

A Time of Departing, Ray Yungen (Lighthouse Trails Publishing, 2002) speaks on Henri Nouwen:

"The doctrines (instructions) of demons (no matter how nice, how charming, how devoted to God they sound) convey that everything has Divine Presence (all is One). This is clear heresy, for that would be saying Satan and God are one also. If what Henri Nouwen proclaimed is true when he said, 'We can come to the full realization of the unity of all that is,' then Jesus Christ and Satan are also united. That, my friend, is something only a demonic spirit would teach!"

Did Nouwen believe all is one?

"Prayer is soul work because our souls are those sacred centers

---

97. Ibid., p. 108.

where all is one, . . . It is in the heart of God that we can come to the full realization of the unity of all that is" (from *Bread for the Journey*), "a place for everyone in heaven" (*Life of the Beloved*, p. 53), "to become the Beloved, we must claim it." Nouwen says we are all the chosen ones (*Life of the Beloved*).

Is Nouwen accepted by evangelicals?

"Many pastors and professors are greatly attracted to his [Nouwen's] deep thinking. In fact, one of his biographers revealed that in a 1994 survey of 3,400 U.S. Protestant church leaders, Nouwen ranked second only to Billy Graham in influence among them" (*A Time of Departing*, p. 61).

—www.lighthousetrailsresearch.com/nouwen/htm

Rick Warren quotes Henri Nouwen again on page 269.

❇   ❇   ❇

Rick Warren: "My friend Gary Thomas . . . In his book *Sacred Pathways*. . . ." [98]

(This book Rick Warren also promotes on his *pastors.com* web site.) So what does *Sacred Pathways* have to teach? Mr. Warren is promoting pantheism, monasticism, contemplative prayer, and ascetics both in this book as well as through Gary Thomas:

Gary Thomas Biography

Gary L. Thomas is a writer and the founder and director of the Center for Evangelical Spirituality, a writing and speaking ministry that integrates Scripture, church history, and the Christian classics. He has served as a campus pastor and is an **adjunct faculty member at Western Seminary in Portland, Oregon**, where he teaches on spiritual formation.

—*www.garythomas.com/gary/index.html*
and *www.letusreason.org/BookR12.htm.*

The following review pertaining to Gary Thomas' teaching, recom-

---

98. Ibid., p. 102.

mended by Rick Warren, is excerpted from **Let Us Reason Ministries:**

> In Gary's book *Sacred Pathways,* He quotes Carl Jung favorably, *"Carl Jung developed four profiles to describe human nature. . . . Combinations of these four profiles can create sixteen different personality types, and the Myers Briggs test is designed to separate these types"* (*Sacred Pathways,* by Gary Thomas, p. 21). Psychologist Carl Jung is not a good source for any Christian to turn to as he received his information from a "spirit guide" named Philemon. During Jung's traumatic breakdown, on the brink of suicide "Philemon" became his "spirit guide." Jung says, *"Philemon represented a force which was not myself. . . . It was he who taught me psychic objectivity, the reality of the psyche."*
>
> In *Sacred Pathways,* pp.184–5,6 Thomas where he suggests the use of "Dancing Prayer," not bodily movements, but we are to image in our minds dancing with God and allowing Him to lead. Then He gives instructions on "Centering Prayer." Quote: *"Choose a word (Jesus or Father, for example) as a focus for contemplative prayer. Repeat the word silently in your mind for a set amount of time (say, twenty minutes) until your heart seems to be repeating the word by itself, just as naturally and involuntarily as breathing. But centering prayer is a contemplative act in which you don't do anything; you're simply resting in the presence of God."*
>
> Clearly a mystical approach not a Biblical one. This repeating words is what is called a mantra, it does not matter if one uses a Biblical name or word. We are not to be combining eastern mysticism with our practice of Christianity. Warren also mentions contemplative prayer in his book without defining it.
>
> On his website *"My wife, Kay, recommends this book! In it, Nouwen divides the life of ministry into five categories: teaching, preaching, pastoral care, organizing, and celebrating"* Sabbatical Journey Creative Ministry (Doubleday, 1991).
>
> —*www.letusreason.org/Popteac23.htm*

❋ ❋ ❋

Paul Yongi Cho, another Global Church Growth Movement leader, is endorsed and promoted by both Robert Schuller and Rick Warren on his *pastors.com* website.

※ ※ ※

Rick Warren: "Philip Yancey has wisely noted . . ." (p. 107).

Philip Yancey may be wise, but it is the wisdom of this world that he is teaching. He often quotes Carl Jung favorably in *Unhappy Secrets,* and pantheistic New Age psychologist M. Scott Peck (from *The Road Less Traveled*)! He was the editor of *Reality and the Vision* by Karen Mains, still another Jung disciple who is a Renovaré board of reference member. Philip Yancey is also a prominent defender of Alcoholics Anonymous and the Twelve-Step program (see chapter eight on Celebrate Recovery and more information on the Twelve-Step program). One article containing the actual quotes of Philip Yancey's aberrant teachings and his belief in psychology is written by Pastor Gary Gilley of Southern View Chapel entitled "The Pain, The Pain," which appeared in *Think on These Things* (September 2000). A copy can be accessed at *www.rapidnet.com/~jbeard/bdm/exposes/yancey.htm* and *www.lighthousetrailsresearch.com/yancey.htm.*

※ ※ ※

Rick Warren also promotes psychologist **Larry Crabb** on his *pastors.com* website. Larry Crabb is a major player and was a speaker at Rick Warren's Purpose Driven conferences and the 2004 congress in Boston. This alliance is indisputable (see *www.congress2004.org/groupleaders.asp*). As an integrationist who believes you can integrate psychology with biblical counseling based on Scripture, Crabb states that psychological counseling is a catalyst to biblical counseling. I refer you to other ministries which have researched and exposed his false teaching: *www.lighthousetrailsresearch.com/larrycrabb.htm* and *www.rapidnet.com/~jbeard/bdm/exposes/crabb/.*

> The Christian spiritual journey must extend beyond mere doctrinal orthodoxy to passionate faith, said psychologist and author Larry Crabb.
>
> —*www.pastors.com/article.asp?ArtID=4296*

In an article refuting "dream therapy," the following website discusses Larry Crabb's view of Freud.

> Crabb's own words best define his Freudian model—from *Understanding People:*
>   "Freud is <u>rightly credited</u> with introducing the whole idea of *psychodynamics* to the modern mind. The term refers to <u>psychological forces</u> within the personality (**usually unconscious**) <u>that have the power to cause</u> behavioral and emotional disturbance. He taught us to regard problems as *symptoms* of underlying *dynamic processes* in the psyche" (p. 59, italics his, underlines added).
>   Crabb further says, "I think Freud was correct . . . when he told us to look beneath surface problems to hidden internal causes" (p. 61). While Crabb does not agree with all that Freud taught, and even sees errors in his theories, he contends that "the error of Freud and other dynamic theorists is *not* an insistence that we pay close attention to unconscious forces within personality" (p. 61, italics his). In spite of Freud's strong criticism of Christianity, Crabb says, "I believe that [Freud's] psychodynamic theory is both provocative and valuable in recognizing elements in the human personality that many theologians have failed to see" (*Understanding People*, pp. 215–216).
>   —*www.rapidnet.com/~jbeard/bdm/exposes/crabb/crabb.htm*

The "unconscious" was a core doctrine of both Freud and Jung.

Earlier this year I wrote an e-mail directly to Larry Crabb, specifically asking him if he supports the theories of the subconscious of Freud and/or Jung. In his response he simply maintained his stance that psychotherapy is a catalyst to biblical counseling. Larry Crabb's recommended reading list includes Philip Yancey and contemplative mystics discussed in this book such as Henri Nouwen, Basil Pennington, Teresa of Avila, and Eugene Peterson. Source: *www.gospelcom. net/newway/literature/recommended_books.htm*

For more information on what the "unconscious" is according to Freud and Larry Crabb, visit: *www.rapidnet.com/~jbeard/bdm/Letter/v3n1-1.htm.*

✳   ✳   ✳

Rick Warren quotes Mother Teresa: "It's not what you do, but how much love you put into it that matters." [99]

I realize that even most evangelical Christians virtually define being a saint by comparing themselves to Mother Teresa. Nevertheless we are to still judge her teaching. In this regard, for proof that her teachings are heretical, I direct you to one of a host of valuable discernment ministry web sites that articulate her positions. Here are just two quotes from Mother Teresa, but I invite you to read the entire document:

> When "Mother" Teresa died, her longtime friend and biographer Naveen Chawla said that he once asked her bluntly, "Do you convert?" She replied, "Of course I convert. I convert you to be a better Hindu or a better Muslim or a better Protestant. Once you've found God, it's up to you to decide how to worship him" ("Mother Teresa Touched Other Faiths," Associated Press, 9/7/97).

> The April 7–13, 1990, issue of *Radio Times* tells the story of "Mother" Teresa sheltering an old Hindu priest. "She nursed him with her own hands and helped him to die reconciled with his own gods."
> —*www.rapidnet.com/~jbeard/bdm/exposes/teresa/general.htm*

And regarding the promotion of Mother Teresa:

> To laud Mother Teresa without mentioning her stand on the Gospel is a denial of the Gospel. Here is what Mother Teresa thought of the Gospel: "I love all religions. . . . If people become better Hindus, better Muslims, better Buddhists by our acts of love, then there is something else growing there." **She upheld that there are many ways to God: "All is God—Buddhists, Hindus, Christians, etc., all have access to the same God"** (12/4/89 *Time*, pp. 11, 13). While we can agree to love all religions and people there is a vast

---

99. Ibid., p. 125.

difference as accepting them as valid. Mother Teresa told everyone no matter what their religion: "If in coming face to face with God we accept Him in our lives, then we are converting. We become a better Hindu, a better Muslim, a better Catholic, a better whatever we are. . . . What God is in your mind you must accept" (from *Mother Teresa: Her People and Her Work,* by Desmond Doig, [Harper & Row, 1976], p. 156).

—*www.deceptioninthechurch.com/ditc11-4.html*

Rick Warren again quotes Mother Teresa: "Holy living consists of doing God's work with a smile." [100]

I am not saying that we won't often be smiling in doing God's work as we express the joy of the Lord. But that is not really the heart of holy living. Obeying Christ's commandments and teachings . . . that is holy living. That is holiness! David, Jeremiah, Jonah, Paul, and even Jesus all despaired unto death, but Scripture does not record that they had a smile on their face (and I seriously doubt that you saw a smile on their faces during their trials), yet they were doing God's work.

"DAY 25 – Transformed by Trouble" begins on page 193

Rick Warren stated on page 185 the importance of replacing lies with truth, yet he quotes and endorses the teaching of **Madame Guyon.** [101]

So, who was she and what did she teach? Guyon was a Catholic mystic (one more endorsed by Rick Warren). She said: "Here [the contemplative state] everything is God. God is everywhere and in all things" (*www.lighthousetrailsresearch.com/richardfoster.htm*).

For more information on her aberrant teaching read: G. Richard Fisher's "The Mindless Mysticism of Madame Guyon," *The Quarterly Journal,* Vol. 17, No. 1, pp. 4, 12–15 (see *www.pfo.org/mguyon.htm*).

---

100. Ibid., p. 231.
101. Ibid., p. 193.

Chapter Seven

How to Worship

Rick Warren: "Try praising God without using the words praise, hallelujah, thanks, or amen." [102]

Try telling this to Frederick Handel who penned the "Hallelujah Chorus" which extensively uses the word **"Hallelujah"** over and over, yet this choral piece is considered one of the most inspired works ever written. And how about the Four Creatures in Revelation 4:8 who *never stop* saying one phrase:

> And the four beasts had each of them six wings about him; and they were full of eyes within: and they rest not day and night, saying, Holy, holy, holy, Lord God Almighty, which was, and is, and is to come.

Following Rick Warren's instructions of trying to praise God without using the word "thanks" is a big problem if someone wants to obey Paul's command in *all* **things to give thanks**, for this is the will of God for you who are in Christ Jesus:

> **Giving thanks always** for all things unto God and the Father in the name of our Lord Jesus Christ.
>
> —Ephesians 5:20

> **In every thing give thanks:** for this is the will of God in Christ Jesus concerning you.
>
> —1 Thessalonians 5:18

---

102. Ibid., p. 104.

As for not using the word **amen**, are we now being asked to try not ending a prayer with the word Jesus used when giving us instructions how to pray when He gave us the Lord's Prayer? Even in the Old Testament, fourteen times we read: "And **all** the people shall say, **Amen.**"

This is just one more example of Mr. Warren contradicting his own teaching, because he simultaneously promotes a number of mystics who, in fact, do use these very words over and over in repetitive mantras to reach an altered state of consciousness.

❇ ❇ ❇

Rick Warren: **"You have heard people say, 'I can't make it to the meeting tonight, but I'll be with you in *spirit.*' Do you know what that means? Nothing. It's worthless!"** [103]

So let's see if the apostle Paul thought being with you in spirit only was "worthless."

> And this I say, lest any man should beguile you with enticing words. For though I be absent in the flesh, **yet am I with you in the spirit**, joying and beholding your order, and the stedfastness of your faith in Christ.
>
> —Colossians 2:4–5

So do we listen to Rick Warren's beguiling and enticing words, or do we listen to the apostle Paul who spent most of his ministry absent in the flesh from all of the churches he birthed and/or where he conducted his ministry? We spend most of our time *not* in assembly with other believers. We are therefore usually not physically with them when we pray for them. Paul was constantly praying for all of the churches where he could not physically be present. To be present in body is certainly valuable and of course we are to not forsake the assembling of one another. But if a believer can't be there physically, but is praying, don't call it "worthless"!

❇ ❇ ❇

---

103. Ibid., p. 105.

Rick Warren: "Matt Redman, a worship leader in England, tells how his pastor taught his church the real meaning of worship. To show that worship is more than music, he banned all singing in their services for a period of time while they learned to worship in other ways." [104]

Does this sound like good advice, when at the meeting of Jesus and His disciples it is recorded:

> And when they had **sung an hymn**, they went out into the mount of Olives.
>
> —Matthew 26:30

Does this sound like Paul's advice regarding singing in Ephesians 5:19?

> Speaking to yourselves in psalms and hymns and spiritual songs, **singing** and making melody in your heart to the Lord.
>
> —Ephesians 5:19

or

> Let the word of Christ dwell in you richly in all wisdom; teaching and admonishing one another in psalms and hymns and spiritual songs, **singing** with grace in your hearts to the Lord.
>
> —Colossians 3:16

or

> **Sing** unto the LORD, O ye saints of his, and give thanks at the remembrance of his holiness.
>
> —Psalm 30:4

or

> What is it then? I will pray with the spirit, and I will pray with the

---

104. Ibid., p. 106.

understanding also: I will **sing** with the spirit, and I will **sing** with the understanding also.

—1 Corinthians 14:15

or

Saying, I will declare thy name unto my brethren, in the midst of the church will I **sing** praise unto thee.

—Hebrews 2:12

or

Is any among you afflicted? let him pray. Is any merry? **let him sing** psalms.

—James 5:13

So does this sound like good advice to be telling the saints to not sing in order to learn how to worship? **Singing is *part* of how we worship.** No sooner does Rick Warren give this example of a particular congregation not singing to learn how to worship than he contradicts himself in the book, advising us to sing a new song. No wonder people are confused!

❈   ❈   ❈

Rick Warren: "The most common mistake Christians make in worship today is seeking an experience rather than seeking God." [105]

If this is true, then why does the "E" in his SHAPE program stand for "experience"? (See chapter ten in this book). Why does he endorse Nicky Gumbel and his Alpha Course from which the Toronto Blessing originated? For a complete exposé documentary on the Alpha Course, I refer you to the book, *Alpha—the Unofficial Guide Overview* by Elizabeth McDonald and Dusty Peterson (St. Matthew Publishing, 2002). Note particularly their appendix E for the list of Nicky Gumbel's false teachings. (See also *www.users.globalnet.co.uk/*

---

105. Ibid., p. 109.

-emcd/index.htm and www.deceptioninthechurch.com/AlphaBrochure. pdf

Mr. Warren later describes how we can improve our gift(s) of the Holy Spirit with practice, i.e., by experience. So, first he demotes the value of experience, and then he promotes it. Which is it? Once again, no wonder people are confused.

Finally, I would like to include the words of Jesus Christ regarding what true worship is, as well as what He describes as worship the Father does not hear.

> But the hour cometh, and now is, when the true worshippers shall worship the Father in spirit and in truth: for the Father seeketh such to worship him.
>
> —John 4:23

If Rick Warren wishes us to worship in a manner that the Father seeks, he must first begin by telling the truth about what the Bible really teaches, which extensively he has not done.

> But in vain they do worship me, teaching for doctrines the commandments of men.
>
> —Matthew 15:9

Rick Warren's unbiblical burdens of his covenants (such as the one at the beginning of his book) and the ones that he makes members of his church sign, and then recommends that other churches follow his lead, could not be a more perfect example of commandments of men. So for Rick Warren to enforce these covenants puts us all in great peril of having our worship be in vain.

Chapter Eight

Celebrate Recovery Program

"DAY 26 – Growing through Temptation" begins on page 201
"DAY 27 – Defeating Temptation" begins on page 209

Rick Warren promotes his **Celebrate Recovery program,** which he says is based on the Beatitudes, but in reality is based on Alcoholics Anonymous' Twelve-Step program. Mr. Warren states: **"Revealing your feeling is the beginning of healing."** [106]

How you "feel" is the foundation of psychological counseling and more proof that his Celebrate Recovery program is based on Bill Wilson's AA Twelve-Step program. No, this is more feelings-based gospel vs. comparing our feelings and behavior to Scripture and then repenting! Rick Warren attempts to convert or sanctify the Twelve-Step program into Eight Principles of the Beatitudes.

The very "spiritual disciplines" that Rick Warren recommends in his appendix 2 promote the very false teachers in this commentary that promote teachings that are not taught in the Bible!

Rick Warren's *"Celebrate Recovery"* Seminar Review
by James Sundquist
Rock Salt Publishing

The title banner on Rick Warren's Celebrate Recovery web site reads:

"What can you do when preaching a sermon is not enough?"

---

106. Ibid., p. 213.

I am still picking myself up off of the floor with this statement which is the promotional banner of Rick Warren's recovery seminars! Can you imagine walking up to Jesus after He just delivered the Sermon on the Mount and telling him . . . that was very nice, but your sermon was not *enough.*" I say *enough* of Rick Warren's teaching. I would remind Rick Warren of two scriptures which warn about adding and subtracting from God's Word, and the last verse of Revelation which was given to the apostle John. Which of Paul's sermons would you say to Paul were not enough? Or Peter, saying "to whom else should we turn . . . you have the words of Eternal Life."

I read the eight principles of Celebrate Recovery and the corresponding Scriptures. . . . I can't see how they go together, plus the scriptures themselves are taken from a corrupt translation. Since when does the word "blessed" now mean "happy"? Right before Jesus ascended into heaven he "happied" his disciples? At one point in the history of language, happy may have had more of a context of blessing, but to use that word now with all of its self-consumed, self-indulgent meaning . . . what a misleading term to use for the word "blessed" in today's vernacular.

. . . Happiness is recovery? Then ultimate happiness is never possible because you are *always* in a perpetual state of recovery. And assuming that your problem is a real disease vs. imaginary, why would you want to be restored to the old man, if as a New Creation, all things become new and the old man has passed away?

Rick Warren tells us that his Celebrate Recovery program is biblically-based. But all of the compromised translations we are told are also biblically-based. Rick Warren tells us that Celebrate Recovery is based on the Beatitudes, when in reality it is based on the foundation of Bill Wilson's Twelve-Step program. This program is anything but Christian, particularly because, by Bill Wilson's own admission, Wilson considers occultist, evolutionist, necromancer Carl Jung who practiced divination to obtain his theory of psychology, his co-founder. Rick Warren creates the impression that it is adhering to the principles of Christ that brings about recovery, while the Bible teaches that it is the Person of Christ that brings about repentance and sanctification. *So this is what the Sermon on the Mount has come to?*

Because Rick Warren's Celebrate Recovery and his Eight Principles are based on the Twelve-Step program, it would be most illuminating to include excerpts from my response letter to the director of the Twelve-Step program at Willow Creek Church, the other major pillar of the Church Growth Movement which promotes virtually the same philosophy as Rick Warren. (By the way, Lee Strobel, who endorses Rick Warren's book and is now a pastor at Rick Warren's church, was a pastor at Willow Creek Church.)

Dear [director of 12-Step program at Willow Creek Church],

. . . To clearly answer your question about my interest in the Christian 12-Step program you are offering at Willow Creek is the urgency of what I view as a clear and present danger to the church today, that is the promotion of Carl Jung and psychology.

From what I can tell from your e-mails, you appear to have very good intentions in leading this program. My mission is to try to convince you whether or not your programs are truly biblical.

We need to do as Isaiah commands: 'Shall we not inquire of our Lord,' not diviners and astrologers. It is not a matter of what we want to do for the Lord that we think will help people, but what the Lord requires of us. Or as the Psalmist puts it, "from whence cometh our help?" Our help comes from the Lord!

"[A Song of degrees.] I will lift up mine eyes unto the hills, **from whence cometh my** *help*. My *help* **cometh from the** Lord, which made heaven and earth" (Psalm 121:1–2).

The New Testament reaffirms who our true helper should be when the Holy Spirit Himself is referred to as our helper (Paraclete in Greek).

Isaiah records: "And when they shall say unto you, Seek unto them that have familiar spirits, and unto wizards that peep, and that mutter: should not a people seek unto their God? for the living to the dead? To the law and to the testimony: if they speak not according to this word, it is because there is no light in them" (Isaiah 8:19–20).

Later in this letter I will share the scriptural reasons why as a Christian, I am responsible to the Lord to expose false teaching. So part of the reason I must write you is because I am biblically commanded and mandated to do so. I am somewhat astonished that you would still ask the question why I would inquire about why you are teaching the 12-Step program conceived by Bill Wilson, after I supplied you with the incontrovertible comprehensive proof that Bill Wilson in no sense could be considered Christian. His own statement (and step) states, "whatever or whomever you deem that higher power to be" so that any higher power is acceptable in his eyes . . . that would include Satan himself who masquerades as an angel of light (I have come to "help" you). But Isaiah says that the Lord says, "I will share my glory with *none* other."

Your argument for defending the 12-Step program (and the common argument used by Christians and church leaders) is that we will just substitute Bible verses for the steps and just say that Jesus endorses it or has signed off on it. But devising a man-made system, then simply calling it Jesus does not make it Jesus. That is not how we test the spirits to see if they be of God.

One of the very best ways to see if something is of the Lord is to ask the questions: Where did these ideas come from? Who is the author? What did the author believe about Jesus? What did the author believe about other false prophets (in this case, what did Bill Wilson think of Carl Jung's ideas)? If Bill Wilson were truly of the Lord, he would have exposed Carl Jung who practiced the occult, necromancy, astrology, and believed in evolution. Carl Jung was an enemy of Christ. Carl Jung derived much of his psychology from a demon . . . a spirit guide named Philemon . . . from his own testimony. So what was Carl Jung, whom Bill Wilson admired, doing consulting the dead? And worse, what are Christians doing using the information that Carl Jung obtained from practicing magic arts by consulting the dead? But what does 12-Step founder Bill

Wilson do? He calls Carl Jung a co-founder of Alcoholics Anonymous. So Christians should not be promoting AA or Bill Wilson's 12-Step program, but rather renouncing it. They should be running from it!

Christian [recovery] programs such as **Celebrate Recovery** all are branches off of the same AA thornbush that Bill Wilson founded. Don't Christians ever ask, "Where did that idea come from? Who is Bill Wilson? Did he fear the Lord?" Without that, he did not even have the beginning of wisdom! Many Christians have the idea that they can use a man-made system replete with pagan and occultic content and simply say that Jesus is the "Higher Power." Since when did the Lord ever bless or borrow from any pagan system or religion, science falsely so-called, or principles of this world to put his seal of approval on it? This is another Jesus . . . a conjured Jesus. Besides, Jesus is not a string of principles we follow, he is a Person we follow. He is not a "higher power." He is the highest! "Glory to God in the Highest!" And He is all powerful!!

Carl Jung, whom Bill Wilson admired so much, also believed in an Aryan Jesus. Do you have any idea what this "another Jesus" is that Paul would have said that Carl Jung follows? The answer is that Carl Jung's (another Jesus) ideas about Jesus were derived from Aryan pagan mythology. . . .

Did Carl Jung inquire of the Lord, or did he inquire of familiar spirits? Did he fear the Lord? So what business does Bill Wilson have in claiming Carl Jung as a co-founder . . . that is, if Bill Wilson and his program are Christian? More importantly, what business does a Christian have in saying that there is any light in them? Isaiah asks why God's people are seeking the answers from the dead. Jesus asked a similar question: "Why seek ye the living among the dead?" Today I ask the same question: Why are Christians seeking help from consulting with the dead or from those who consulted with the dead? Why are not Christians asking what God requires of us? Why do they continue to seek counsel from the ungodly? Why are they using the scrolls of someone who received their blueprints from the dead. The early Christians in the Book of Acts did not think this was a good idea! They burned the scrolls containing magic arts!

But what is the church doing today? They've turned psychology and the 12-Step program into a billion dollar industry . . . and if we oppose them, they claim it is we who have lost our way! It is we who are forced out of the church. Believe me, I can document families that were removed from their church because they rightfully opposed Rick Warren and Bill Hybel's teachings and programs as unbiblical.

"Finally, brethren, whatsoever things are true, whatsoever things are honest, whatsoever things are just, whatsoever things are pure, whatsoever things are lovely, whatsoever things are of good report; if there be any virtue, and if there be any praise, think on these things" (Philemon 4:8).

So what is pure about ideas drawn from paganism, astrology, divination, necromancy, evolution, as that is precisely where Carl Jung got his ideas, from his own testimony? The Lord calls all of these an abomination. The church now calls it "help for the hurting!"

It is amazing to me that Christians would be so passionate in saying that there is no such thing as Christian astrology, Christian paganism, Christian New Age, Christian Eastern meditation, Christian atheist communism, Christian Naziism, Christian divination, Christian Baal worship, Christian necromancy, Christian evolution (i.e., that Christ descended from an ape), and Christian numerology. But as soon as you oppose psychology, personality profiling, and 12-Step programs as not being Christian, some Christians oppose you even to the point of removing you from the church . . . even though personality profiling and the 12-Step program are derived from many of these very same doctrines of demons. These Christians just don't get it. Jesus could not be more clear when He stated that you can't get figs from a thornbush.

"Ye shall know them by their fruits. **Do men gather grapes of thorns, or figs of thistles?**" (Matt. 7:16).

"For every tree is known by his own fruit. **For of thorns men**

do not gather figs, nor of a bramble bush gather they grapes" (Luke 6:44).

The apostle James agrees: "**Can the fig tree, my brethren, bear olive berries? either a vine, figs?** so can no fountain both yield salt water and fresh" (Jam. 3:12).

But Christians following Carl Jung or his disciple Bill Wilson think you can. They argue, "**Don't throw the baby out with the bath water.**" Where in the Scripture is that teaching? And even if true, what about Bill Wilson who says other higher powers are OK too (this is the baby)? No, you should throw out the baby and the bath water. This bath water allegory is quite well known, but it is not found in Scripture. Nevertheless, if we are going to employ it, it must still be harmonized with the Bible. So the parallel is that somehow that the "baby" is the good, that we should keep and the "bath water" is the bad that we should throw out. In this example, the baby is not the Bible, but psychology teaching. So the idea is that we can integrate the baby (psychology) with the Bible. A better allegory is the fig tree or thorn bush, which is in the Bible. But where in the Bible is there one single precedent for the Lord sanctifying, integrating, adding unto any other religion or philosophy in the Bible? Did He take the best (the baby) out of the Mystery Religion of Babylon? Did he borrow from Molech? Ashteroth? Baal? Anything from sun worship in Egypt? Here is Jeremiah's answer to the idea that we can just take the good things from the teachings of false prophets or teachers (keep the baby . . . throw out the bath water):

"Behold, I am against the prophets, saith the Lord, that use their tongues, and say, He saith. Behold, I am against them that prophesy false dreams, saith the Lord, and do tell them, and cause my people to err by their lies, and by their lightness; yet I sent them not, nor commanded them: therefore **they shall not profit this people at all, saith the Lord**" (Jer. 23:31–32).

Did Paul borrow from any of the Greek pagan philosophies or religions? The answer is absolutely *no!* Paul did not borrow from any of them! So, let's see what Paul thought about integrating ideas from the world's wisdom of philosophy and psychology: "But to preach the gospel: not with wisdom of words, lest the cross of Christ should be made of *none effect"* (1 Cor. 1:17).

Well maybe Paul left it out for us to add. Let's see what he says about that idea: "And these things, brethren, I have in a figure transferred to myself and to Apollos for your sakes; that ye might learn in us not to **think of men above that which is written**, that no one of you be puffed up for one against another" (1 Cor. 4:6).

Paul said in Acts 20:26–27: "Wherefore I take you to record this day, that I am pure from the blood of all men. For I have not shunned to declare unto you **all the counsel of God.**"

So, what counsel did Paul leave out?

So what scriptural authority are you using to integrate, add, or sanctify Bill Wilson's 12-Step program? Isn't this a classic case of changing the names of the guilty to protect the guilty?

Now more specifically to answer your question as to why I am inquiring. My basis for inquiry regarding teaching is always based on believing that the Bible is our ultimate and final authority. So my inquiry to you is the same question that Ezekiel would ask, that Isaiah would ask, that the apostle Paul would ask and commands us to ask. But also, it is the Scripture that tell us what we are to do about it, i.e, we must go beyond informing. We must warn, guard the sheep, expose false teaching, and rebuke false teaching. We can't agree to disagree about the "nuances" as you call them. We are commanded to contend for the faith once and for all delivered to the saints. How do we expose the deeds of darkness, and reprove them, if indeed such deeds are purely subjective . . . who is to judge? Here are the scriptures:

"This witness is true. Wherefore **rebuke** them **sharply**, that they may be sound in the faith" (Titus 1:13).

"A man that is an heretick after the first and second admonition reject" (Titus 3:10).

Does this Scripture sound like "debating over nuances" to you?

"Now I beseech you, brethren, *mark* them which cause divisions and offences contrary to the doctrine which ye have learned; and avoid them" (Rom. 16:17).

Does this Scripture sound like "debating over nuances" to you?

"Beloved, believe not every spirit, but try the spirits whether they are of God: because many false prophets are gone out into the world" (1 John 4:1).

Does this Scripture sound like "debating over nuances" to you?

"Now the Spirit speaketh expressly, that in the latter times some shall depart from the faith, giving heed to seducing spirits, and **doctrines of devils**" (1 Tim. 4:1).

Once again, one of the surest ways to establish whether something is a doctrine of the devil is to inquire where an idea came from and what does the person teaching it believe about Jesus? The second sure test is if *any* of the ideas of this person are specifically prohibited in the Bible or even called an abomination. That is how we know that Carl Jung and Bill Wilson's teachings do not line up with Scripture. So instead of promoting them, we need to repent of believing their ideas. But we must also doubly repent if we are teaching and promoting their ideas. A teacher is held to a stricter accounting. And anyone who stumbles the least one of these my children, Jesus says of them it would be better to have a millstone tied around their neck and tossed into the deepest sea! And there is a third test like unto the first two. This test is not whether something is subjectively determined to be helpful or pleasing to the Lord. This was Saul's argument for using some of the plunder for a "helpful" and "pleasing" sacrifice to the Lord. Saul justified in the same manner that you are justifying the 12-Step program . . . and he did the same thing: he wrapped his idea in the Lord's Name and brought forth the sacrifice in the Name of the Lord and for the Lord. But God rejected his offer in saying that "obedience is better than sacrifice." In the end, Saul's disobedience cost him his life. See 1 Samuel 13; also see 1 Samuel 28 where Saul visits the witch of Endor and practices divination and necromancy in bringing up

Samuel. (Carl Jung practiced exactly the same thing when he conjured up the demonic spirit guide Philemon.)

Hebrews 3 reiterates this exact same point about obedience in saying that *no one* entered God's rest who was disobedient! The Lord destroyed a whole generation. So my question for you is: "Is the 12-Step program obeying the Lord . . . even though it is wrapped in the language of Zion?" Do you really believe that you can enter God's rest, if there is anything disobedient in the 12-Step program? I have proved with the Scriptures above in testing the ideas of Wilson and Jung (as have many God-fearing scholars that I have sent you) that no one would be obeying the Lord that is following this man-made model of works! You can't borrow Bill Wilson's ideas, then call them sanctified before the Lord! And if it is not sanctified, it is disobedience. So your proposition that this is a biblical model completely collapses. You cannot simply construct an edifice on top of a false foundation, and because you call it Christ too by substituting Scriptures, that this is pleasing to the Lord. Bill Wilson's "12-Step" house is not built by the Lord.

"Except the LORD build the house, they labour in vain that build it: except the LORD keep the city, the watchman waketh but in vain" (Ps. 127:1).

Some of your arguments for the 12-Step program and again the one commonly used is:

"The 12-Step program works and thru it, I learned about Christ and gave my life to Him, at which point my drinking stopped and living began."

My question for you is, how did people with a drinking problem for the last nineteen hundred years come to Christ who did not have the 12-Step program? The Bible says "faith cometh by hearing" . . . Scripture. There is not another way. And there is not a way that combines two ways into one. I stopped drinking about seventeen years ago without the 12-Step program. It took *one* step: I repented!! But that should not be a surprise . . . and there is nothing special about me, as the Scripture says God is not a respecter of persons. *Everyone* is required to do it the same way . . . whether it was at the time of Jonah and the city of Nineveh, the time of Jesus, the time of Paul, or today! So there is *one* step to stop and then sanctification begins, which once again only the Holy Spirit can do via his Scriptures. Sanctification (not even mentioned in Bill Wilson's 12-Step program) is a life-long process that uses the *entire Bible. All Scripture* . . . not a mere twelve verses that even Bill Wilson did not use. Where in any of Bill Wilson's teaching is the concept of sanctification? And subsequent to salvation there is no biblical justification for the order of the 12 Steps. Where are the other thousands of verses of Scripture in the 12-Step program?

"All scripture [not just 12 verses for 12 steps] is given by in spiration of God, and is profitable for doctrine, for reproof, for correction, for instruction in righteousness: That the man of God may be perfect, throughly furnished unto all good works" (2 Tim. 3:16–17).

So, if a man of God is made perfect with the Scripture alone, what does adding Bill Wilson's 12-Step program add? The above Bible verse teaches that a man is now "throughly" furnished. The 12-Step program suggests that he isn't. All Scripture enables a man to do *all* good works. So what is lacking in *all?* Doesn't all mean all? What good work does the 12-Step program enable us to do that Scripture is deficient or anemic in its ability to do this everything? Isn't it amazing that all of the martyred and perse-cuted saints and all those Christians, all over the world, for nearly two thousand years, somehow managed to achieve everything the 12 Steps are purportedly able to do but *without* the 12-Step pro-gram? This would apply to the majority of Christians throughout the world even today who have never heard of the 12-Step pro-gram ("Christian" or non-Christian version). Somehow all of these Christians were made perfect with Scripture alone (*Sola Scriptura* . . . what the whole Reformation was about)! Somehow they were **thoroughly furnished!** Somehow they were able to do **all good works.** That is, until the 12-Step program came along. Right? Of course not! Then this scripture no longer applied or only partially applied, or was integrated with a Jesus version. It is a good thing too, because we might never have found Jesus to follow and obey were it not for this program.

Another common argument: "We believe in the program and have Willow Creek's blessing for doing what we are doing. Does any of the rest matter except for those that like to debate the nuances?"

The issue here is not whether you have Willow Creek's blessing, but whether you have the Lord's blessing. The Lord's blessing is not determined because even a large number of people feel blessed or "experience" a blessing, or a burning in the bosom. The criteria for blessing must first meet the litmus test of Scripture. It is objectively determined, *not* subjectively determined. And there is not "the rest of the matter." Once an idea does not meet scriptural criteria, we don't even get to "the rest." Secondly this is not a matter of debating "nuances." It is a matter of sound doctrine. It is a matter of another Jesus. It is a matter of another gospel. Paul would not say it does not matter. He would say, "Let those who preach another gospel be eternally condemned" (Gal. 1:9). That is unless they repent! In the last two documents, and in this letter I sent you, it is clearly demonstrated how the 12-Step program does not line up with the plumb line of Scripture.

Now there is another major problem with the 12-Step program, whether or not it is somehow "Christian," that was not addressed in the earlier documents I sent you. That has to do with **church discipline**. This is very crucial, because it determines whether or not Jesus or the apostle Paul would endorse or sign off on this program. I addressed this issue in my article entitled: "Sinners Anonymous!"

Sinners Anonymous—Is This a Biblical Model?

I was curious why the word "anonymous" is in Alcoholics Anonymous, particularly since anonymous groups are pillars in the PDC/CGM theology through such programs as Celebrate Recovery. So I went to the AA web site and found out. Something seemed rotten in the State of Denmark, but I could not quite put my finger *on it. I knew the CGM/PDC has a host of anonymous programs in its churches and curriculum, including a sexaholics anonymous type of program. There are several problems I have with the program in general, biblically speaking, such as we are "powerless." Would a sex offender say he is powerless to obey God? Or if he has a victim mentality, would he say, "I just can't help myself from molesting children"? These issues, including the concerns over "a higher power" are well known and addressed already. But the "anonymous" issue stuck in my craw. This was not as easy to discern, as there are issues of sin in our lives which could remain anonymous, or at least known to only those involved in the offense (both the perpetrator and the victim[s] and to one or more who are spiritual to help lead them to repentance.) But here is the major breakdown with "anonymous" regarding what the Bible says about it. First, I cannot find anywhere in the Bible where it recommends putting all of the people with the same problem in a targeted group where they can commiserate and help each other "recover." If you have seven pedophiles in the church, do you create a class and put them all together? Doesn't 1 Corinthians 15:33 read, "Do not be deceived: bad company corrupts good morals." Does it say put them in the same group? Or do you mark each and every one of them to identify them and then separate them out from the flock (and each other)? The Bible teaches that you would surround each one with good examples and the spiritually mature. Another glaring problem I see is that the anonymous charter gives a type of diplomatic immunity, whereby the individual **never** has to be exposed publicly, or before the congregation according to Matthew 18 or Ephesians 5, unless the individual chooses to do so. And this anonymity is supported and defended by the "anonymous" charter. So, for example, if a brother in the church (whether a member or not) were confronted for sexual adultery or fornication, was confronted by one or more other brothers or sisters (still note, no group of other like offenders), and then the elders, if he or she still has not repented (still no group), and then before the entire congregation (still no group of like offenders), the biblical procedure of church discipline is preserved. Finally, should the brother or sister not repent, removal from that local Body of Christ should be biblically* *exercised and mandated. But even then, after this sinner is turned over to the other "higher power," Satan himself, there is still a pathway of restoration left open for this fallen brother or sister to return to the church. But this person must still repent and once restored demonstrate the fruit of his or her repentance. But with the "anonymous" model or charter, such as a Sexaholics Anonymous type group that is promoted by a host of PDC/CGM programs, the person committing these ongoing acts could cling to the pre-agreed arrangement and charter position of remaining "anonymous." Who could then pierce this veil of unbiblical protection? This person could remain sexually anonymous . . . and active, and repent publicly only at his or her own behest, and remain so forever. If someone were to confront him or her, this person could say, "But you told me I could remain anonymous, and besides the charter permits me to remain anonymous . . . and you can't violate my anonymity and confidentiality!" Should any who is wise among them decide to act biblically, they would violate the "anonymous" charter, and the person in this group would easily be able to challenge any person who broke this confidence. Of course, were a brother to decide to act biblically in this example, he would be branded intolerant, unforgiving, and insensitive to Harry or Mary's felt needs! So sin in the body, or such leaven could continue to work until the entire lump is leavened with impunity.*

So let us examine more thoroughly if, in fact, the Bible really does support the idea of "anonymous" groups within the ongoing body life of the church as well as it pertains to the procedure for church discipline.

Does "anonymous" sound like what Jesus meant in Matthew 18:17: "And if he shall neglect to hear them, **tell it unto the church**: but if he neglect to hear the church, let him be unto thee as an heathen man and a publican"?

Is "anonymous" what Paul meant in *Ephesians 5:11* when he writes: "And have no fellowship with the unfruitful works of darkness, but rather **reprove** them."

Is "anonymous" what Paul meant in *1 Timothy 5:20* when

he writes: "Them that sin rebuke *before all,* that *others* also may **fear.**"

Is "anonymous" what Paul meant in *1 Corinthians 5:1–11:* "It is reported commonly that there is fornication among you . . . when ye are gathered together [i.e., in the church]. . . . To deliver such an one unto Satan **[in other words *remove* him from the church]** for the destruction of the flesh. . . . Your glorying is not good. Know ye not that a little leaven leaveneth the whole lump? . . . But now I have written unto **you not to keep company [or does it say form a fornicators anonymous group and keep them in the church?**], if any man that is called a brother be a fornicator, or covetous, or an idolater, or a railer, or a drunkard, or an extortioner; with such an one no not to eat."

Paul writes in: *2 Corinthians 13:1:* "This is the third time I am coming to you."

In the Old Testament:

Every matter must be established by the testimony of **two or three witnesses** (Deut. 19:15).

Does "anonymous" sound like what Ezekiel meant in *Ezekiel 33:6:* "But if the watchman see the sword come, and blow not the trumpet, and the **people be not warned**; if the sword come, and take any person from among them, he is taken away in his iniquity; but his blood will I require at the watchman's hand."

No, sinners-anonymous groups have no place in church life because there is simply no foundation for it biblically. (Plug any word you want in front of the word anonymous . . . see "anonymics anonymous" below.) In terms of conversation and story-telling in anonymous or Celebrate Recover groups, Scripture warns us not to speak about what these people do in private, except in the context of church discipline or counseling. The inverse of this is what we are to speak:

"Speaking to yourselves in psalms and hymns and spiritual songs, singing and making melody in your heart to the Lord" (Eph. 5:19).

"Let the word of Christ dwell in you richly in all wisdom;

teaching and admonishing one another in psalms and hymns and spiritual songs, singing with grace in your hearts to the Lord" (Col. 3:16).

"Is any among you afflicted? let him pray. Is any merry? let him sing psalms" (Jam. 5:13).

"Finally, brethren, whatsoever things are true, whatsoever things are honest, whatsoever things are just, whatsoever things are pure, whatsoever things are lovely, whatsoever things are of good report; if there be any virtue, and if there be any praise, think on these things" (Phil. 4:8).

Finally, the Bible does not speak of rounding up a group of like, or targeted sinners that I can recall, except to destroy them, e.g., the earth swallowing up the murmurers and God slaughtering the company of false prophets. It is a person who is more spiritual, one who first goes to the fallen brother to gently restore him or her. The only time a group appears is when the many who are spiritual go to the *one* brother or sister to confront. The next group is the congregation. But it is always a process of putting the sinner in good company, not bad company with more bad company to corrupt their morals even further. There is absolutely *no* model in Scripture for this "group think." The only example I can possibly think of is a hospital . . . and you could argue that the church is a hospital of sinners. But carefully note that no one goes to the hospital to hang around and get well from someone else with the exact same disease. It is the doctors and nurses and equipment they surround themselves with, but these are all *well people,* and medically trained staff, all of whom would be disqualified in an Anonymous or Celebrate Recovery group, *right?*

If the church uses AA or any one of its many 12-Step hybrids, why don't they call "alcoholics" what the Bible calls it: "drunkards." The Bible does not *once* call the abuse of alcohol a disease! It never once calls a drunkard a victim, though there certainly are victims of drunkards, such as car accident victims and battered wives. And even if the higher power is Jesus (as though Jesus could be a force vs. a Person, as though Jesus can be summoned up . . .

that is pure sorcery), it is of no value, because the prayer is asking the higher power for something Jesus would never ask us to pray. He never told us to pray that we recover from being a nonexistent victim. He never told us to pray that we recover from having a nonexistent disease. He never told us to pray that we recover from being born a drunk. He would never ask us to pray a prayer that we are powerless to obey, when He already told us that obedience is *always* an option over disobedience (Rom. 1:20–21 says that *none* are with excuse). He never told us to pray that we will always be in a perpetual state of being a "recovering alcoholic," but never be *free* or delivered. He never told us to pray that we recover when He already told us to repent. I did a search for the word recovery throughout the entire Bible. It always meant either property or land being recovered, or recovering from a physical disease, so that recovery meant being restored to a previous state of being healthy physically. Never once did it refer to behavior or recovering from what comes out of the heart of man. Never!!

"Be careful [anxious] for nothing; but in every thing by prayer and supplication with thanksgiving let your requests be made known unto God. And the peace of God, which passeth all understanding, shall keep your hearts and minds through Christ Jesus" (Phil. 4:6–7).

If we do this how does this leave any room or any need for AA, . . . PDC, CGM, SHAPE, temperament tests (based on theories of occultist and atheist Carl Jung), or Celebrate Recovery? Note further that the peace of God exceeds understanding, or leaning unto your own understanding. So at best, even with hidden knowledge of ourselves revealed to our understanding, we are still left with only *our* understanding which can *not* release the peace of God. So our hope of peace is crippled on both counts and can never walk if gleaned from any form of psychology or anonymous group.

Now I could not help but wonder what would happen if someone in a recovery group *did* violate the anonymity agreement of confidentiality. Would they be kicked out? Are you kicked out of the membership of just the group, or the group and the church?

Can you be a member of the group without being a member of the church? Assuming the worst, and they are kicked out for violating anonymity, do they go form a separate Celebrate Recovery group and entitle it:

Anonymics Anonymous
(a group of people who are struggling with keeping their mouths shut)
When you join this group you vow to keep everything said in the group confidential, the only way you are kicked out is if you gossip . . . three times and you're out. I have never heard of such a group, and if it did ever exist, it could only last a nanosecond, as who could keep their mouths shut any longer? Now, do I have any takers? Imagine standing up before the group and announcing, "I am a recovering anonymic," then tell your story about your history of telling these strangers all the names and places of people you know things about, but I just can't help myself telling you about them. Then another anonymics victim stands up and says, "That's nothing, you should hear about all of the people I have talked about, and after you just stood up and gave your testimony, I just could not help myself and had to stand up to tell my story, too!" What is really great about this group, is that everyone in here has a story to tell . . . no one in here who does not struggle with keeping anything in confidence. . . . Now I take it when everyone has reached a state of recovery, the testimonies will dwindle and their testimonies will be shorter, eventually, the group will have no members.

Strange Fire in the Theater
So much for casting down vain strongholds of imagination! Anyone who yells fire in a crowded theater has done a favor to everyone by warning them to evacuate immediately. However, if they discover there is no fire and he yells fire on a future occasion, no one would listen, thinking the man is a fool. So one day there was a real fire . . . and he yelled fire. Of course, no one listened and only the fool was saved . . . everyone else burned to death in the theater. To-

day we have a different twist on this story. Today we have a raging strange fire in the theater (church), but *no one* is yelling fire and no one is evacuating. No one is sounding an alarm on His Holy Hill! In fact, multitudes more are actually crowding into the theater to hear the strange fire and recruit more multitudes, even going into the highways and byways to compel people to come into this feast of strange fire . . . like myriads of moths drawn to the flame. But in the end there will be only dead spiritual carcasses, but you who are truly redeemed will hear the voice of the Good Shepherd, and you will listen to him who with a still small voice is speaking to your heart that there is a fire in the theater, but it is not God's fire of Pentecost, but strange fire, and you will flee the theater, hating even the garments that have been singed and scorched, abhorring the smell of the smoke of the strange fire in the garments. But praise the Lord, you will be saved out of it . . . that is if you obey the voice of the Lord and flee and don't look back!

Kindest regards in Christ,
James Sundquist

❆   ❆   ❆

Rick Warren opposes a code of silence, yet he supports AA-based Celebrate Recovery which champions anonymity.[107]

After Rick Warren opposes a code of silence, then he says: "What is shared in your group needs to stay in your group." What group? There is certainly a season in which only two or more people are exposed to the truth in the case of confronting a brother, whereby the whole congregation does not need to be apprised of every sin in the body. But that is only if the brother or sister repents and only if the offender does not affect the entire church. Matthew 18 would be impossible to fully carry out regarding church discipline if we were to take Rick Warren's advice. There can be no code of silence with respect to false teaching. So it is difficult to tell where Rick Warren stands since, once again, he contradicts himself.

---

107. Ibid., pp. 147, 150.

Chapter Nine

Regarding Prophecy

Rick Warren: "That is why Jesus talked more about money than he did about either heaven or hell." [108]

Try simply doing a word search on "money," "heaven," then "hell." Answers: Money occurs sixteen times in the New Testament . . . and this not always Jesus speaking, except in the sense that Jesus is the author of the entire Word. The word "heaven" appears 144 times in the Gospels alone, and this does not even include all of the references to heaven in the Book of Revelation . . . remember it is Jesus speaking in this book where it occurs fifty-six times. So what about the occurrences of the word "hell" in the Gospels alone? "Hell" appears fifteen times, plus four in Revelation. But this is not the only term used for hell. "Lake of fire" is also used, which occurs four times. "Outer darkness" occurs four times. So let's add the total number of times Jesus refers to heaven and hell in the Gospels and the Book of Revelation. The total is: 223 where Jesus talks about heaven and hell, compared to sixteen times he talks about money. In fact, in some cases Jesus does not separate money from his discussion of heaven, as the whole point is to contrast the love of riches to heaven. The parables about money are also about the Kingdom of heaven. And this does not even include the importance of the topic addressed in the rest of the New Testament. So, for Rick Warren to make such a statement that the Lord talked more about money than he did about "either" heaven or hell is totally irresponsible and poor scholarship on his part! As a teacher he

---

108. Ibid., p. 267.

is held to a stricter accounting (Jam. 3:1), and you can't help but question his credibility about everything else that Rick Warren teaches in this book. It is amazing to me that (to my knowledge) none of his congregation caught this error, none of his editors at Zondervan caught this error, none of the tens of thousands of pastors who use his book in their church caught this error, and none of millions of Christians who read his book caught this error and a host of others in his book, for that matter.

☒   ☒   ☒

Since Warren has such a low view of prophecy, I can't help but wonder why he included it in his list of gifts under his SHAPE program.

Rick Warren: "When the disciples wanted to talk about prophecy, Jesus quickly switched the conversation to evangelism. . . . If you want Jesus to come back sooner, focus on fulfilling your mission, not figuring out prophecy." [109]

No, Jesus did *not* quickly switch the conversation to evangelism; He continued on the very same theme and even warned His disciples three times to not be deceived about what was going to take place in prophecy. His telling them that it was not for them to know only applied to the day and the hour. And Jesus does not even make that statement until He was much further into His discourse in Matthew 24.

Preaching prophecy is central to our mission because it is part of Scripture, in fact a great part of Scripture. Fulfilled prophecy is what distinguishes Judeo-Christianity from all other religions. Prophecy is the crown jewel of our faith! The Bible itself is comprised of thousands of prophecies: those fulfilled and those yet to be fulfilled. It is how we identify false prophets, because prophecy must come to pass 100 percent.

Rick Warren thinks prophecy is a distraction, and he goes even further by doing violence to Luke 9:62. Here he suggests that anyone

---

109. Ibid., pp. 285–286.

who is distracted by preaching prophecy is not fit for the Kingdom of God. Let's take a closer look at **Luke 9:62:**

> And Jesus said unto him, No man, having put his hand to the plough, and looking back, is fit for the kingdom of God.

This has nothing to do with being distracted from teaching prophecy so you can evangelize. If anything, this scripture is about prophecy! In fact, prophecy is looking forward, and if anything Jesus is saying the opposite of what Rick Warren teaches, that any one who does not look forward (prophecy) is the one who is not fit for the Kingdom of God. Even when Christ again appeared to His disciples in Acts 1, performing miracles between His resurrection and His ascension, Christ was talking about prophecy because He was talking to them about the Kingdom of God, exactly what He did when He spoke to them in parables prior to His crucifixion. The parables were about the Kingdom of God, and they were about the distant future, which is prophecy. In fact it was that very discussion (which Rick Warren calls a distraction) that gave birth to the question about when Christ will restore again the kingdom to Israel. The Lord was not rebuking them for asking about prophecy, particularly because the Lord himself thought it important enough to be talking about it right before His ascension. He was simply telling them that they did not need to know the time or season.

After Christ ascended, He appeared to two of His disciples on the road to Emmaus. Jesus did not even discuss evangelism in this discourse, but spent the entire account telling them how He was the fulfillment of prophecy from the beginning of time *beginning with the prophets!* It is obvious that Jesus did not think teaching prophecy was a distraction! In fact, it was fulfilled prophecy that Jesus wanted these two disciples to not be sad about, but joyful (see Luke 24:13–32).

Also see:

> To whom also he shewed himself alive after his passion by many infallible proofs, being seen of them forty days, and speaking of the

things pertaining to the kingdom of God: . . . And he said unto them, It is not for you to know the times or the seasons, which the Father hath put in his own power.

—Acts 1:3, 7

Did the apostle Paul think talking about prophecy was a distraction? Here is what the apostle Paul says about prophecy:

This charge I commit unto thee, son Timothy, according to the prophecies which went before on thee, that **thou by them mightest war a good warfare."**

—1 Timothy 1:18

Now this is an amazing statement by Paul. He not only didn't think prophecy wasn't a distraction, but actually tells Timothy that prophecy helped Timothy be a better warrior for Christ, as in spiritual warfare.

And to the church in Thessalonica: "Despise not prophesyings" (1 Thess. 5:20).

So, if prophecy is a distraction, why did the apostle Paul say to not hold it in contempt, and even charged them to have this letter read to all the brothers? (see 1 Thess. 5:27)

How does Rick Warren reconcile his statement (that prophecy is a distraction) with 1 Peter 1:10–11 *which declares the glory of prophecy?*

Of which salvation the prophets have enquired and searched diligently, who prophesied of the grace that should come unto you: Searching what, or what manner of time the Spirit of Christ which was in them did signify, when it testified beforehand the sufferings of Christ, and the glory that should follow.

—1 Peter 1:10–11

In other words, they studied and taught prophecy. Daniel studied the prophecy of Jeremiah to determine if the prophecy was fulfilled and if the seventy years of captivity had come to and end.

Abraham looked forward to the day of Christ, and *that's prophecy!*

If prophecy is a distraction, we should not be paying attention to the last several chapters of Ezekiel, all of Zechariah, and major portions of the other major and minor prophets, because they *all* have to do with prophecy!

Jesus Christ himself gave us the Book of Revelation, wherein He tells us that anyone who reads, hears, and heeds the **prophecy** of this book would be blessed!

> Blessed is he that readeth, and they that hear the words of this prophecy, and keep those things which are written therein: for the time is at hand.
>
> —Revelation 1:3

If we were to take Rick Warren's advice, it would also refute Paul's passage in 2 Timothy that **ALL** Scripture is profitable!

> **All scripture** is given by inspiration of God, and is profitable for doctrine, for reproof, for correction, for instruction in righteousness.
>
> —2 Timothy 3:16

If we were not to discuss prophecy we would have to virtually remove a large percentage of the entire Bible, including the major and minor prophets, many sections of the Book of Acts, and the entire Book of Revelation. We can't pick and choose which passages in the Bible we want to communicate to a lost world vs. which ones we want to eliminate or never discuss! You can't claim to preach Jesus Christ, but then fail to preach what Jesus Christ preached and commanded us to preach!

It is wrong for Rick Warren to suggest that Christians who obey Jesus Christ's own words (prophecy) are distracted and not fit for the Kingdom.

If prophecy is distracting and makes us unfit for the Kingdom, then how do we know to gather together that much more often, as we see the day of our redemption drawing near (Heb. 10:24–25)? If we have no prophetic knowledge of what events and circumstances need to take place and what prophecy still needs to transpire, then how would we even know when the day of our redemption is near, even at the door?

And Rick Warren calls prophecy a distraction? **This is an unbelievable statement!** This is a recipe for being deceived! And it wars against the Great Commission of evangelism that he professes is necessary, because it is the warnings of what is going to happen on the earth that is in prophecy that we must tell the world! All this certainly explains, in part, why so much false teaching is now prevalent in Rick Warren's church, because false teaching and false teachers are also a great part of prophecy.

Chapter Ten

The SHAPE Program

Purpose Four Section:
"You Were Shaped for Serving God"

"DAY 29 – Accepting Your Assignment" begins on page 227
"DAY 30 – Shaped for Serving God" begins on page 234

Days 30 and 31

This chapter will first discuss the definition and complete description of what Rick Warren's SHAPE program actually is before we respond to what is contained about it specifically in *The Purpose Driven Life*. Rick Warren talks in general about what SHAPE is in his two chapters (days 30 and 31). But for a complete understanding of what his SHAPE program is, we must first go to his website and other churches which use it or variations of it for its description. We must see and understand the actual SHAPE questionnaire itself (which is not in the book), not simply a reference to it. One of the biggest problems I discovered was that there are many different versions of SHAPE, otherwise known as *Discovery 301 Class*. And though they have much in common, there are many glaring differences in the various hybrids or offshoots. So you are left with the question: "Will the real SHAPE program please stand up?" Anyone trying to figure out which SHAPE is the true vs. counterfeit currency must be left completely baffled. To obtain one version of the SHAPE questionnaire itself, you must go to Rick Warren's website (*www.saddlebackfamily.com/ministry/images/ discoverytool.pdf*), or obtain it from his Saddleback Church directly.

But there are many other versions online as well, as you will see.

It is a supreme irony that Rick Warren would tell you that you need his book, *The Purpose Driven Life*, to find your purpose, but then leave out a key diagnostic ingredient to finding your SHAPE . . . the questionnaire itself . . . which Rick Warren requires prospective members of Saddleback Church to fill out in order to find their overall SHAPE. Mr. Warren seemingly contradicts himself. On the one hand he tells us that we will find our purpose at the end of his forty days. Then he tells us we can't find our purpose until we find our SHAPE. But prospective members can't find their actual SHAPE (according to him) until they take the SHAPE questionnaire. In fact, you can't even take the SHAPE test if you are a member of Rick Warren's church until you take Class 101 and 201 as prerequisites. So, one can't help but wonder why he would tell us in his book we can find our SHAPE just by reading his book, which has neither Class 101 nor Class 201, let alone the SHAPE questionnaire itself. So one reading *The Purpose Driven Life* would be woefully insufficient to find their true purpose, even according to Warren's own schematic. You really can't know your purpose even at the end of forty days, because if you are very careful to note, there is a very important footnote #14 (Rick Warren's own footnote) which states, "which includes a Shape identification tool" (see page 332), at the end of Day 31 (page 248). This questionnaire tool is, again, nowhere to be found in *The Purpose Driven Life*. This is very confusing.

The SHAPE questionnaire contains some disturbing elements, which reveal Rick Warren's underlying philosophy. These are so important that we are going to include critical excerpts to some of the various SHAPE questionnaires in this book. Once this has been completely laid out, we can then go back to his quotes in chapters thirty and thirty-one and comment on his statements. We devote extensive commentary to the "P" (Personality) in his SHAPE program. Once we comment on this, we will better understand his personality theory and test and how he integrates it into his church membership covenants.

Here is a more detailed analysis of Rick Warren's SHAPE program which is the actual questionnaire referred to in *The Purpose Driven Life* book, Day 31, footnote 14 (Warren's footnote).

For reference you may access one implementation of Rick Warren's SHAPE questionnaire at the website for the First United Methodist Church in Mineola, Texas: *http://ourworld.compuserve.com/homepages/bojo/station3_1.htm,* which states:

> **"What is S.H.A.P.E.?**
>
> Pastor Rick Warren at Saddleback Valley Community Church in Mission Viejo, CA, coined the acronym S.H.A.P.E. in his best selling book *The Purpose Driven Church.* As we've applied it here, it is a holistic and integrating concept of God's activity in calling forth people for ministry. S.H.A.P.E. is a way of looking at how we are equipped by God for ministry that says, "God can use all of you, not just the 'holy parts.'"

Each point of this SHAPE questionnaire is outlined, followed by a response. The next chapter goes into more extensive detail and documentation on the Carl Jung connection to Rick Warren's personality profile. But first let's look at the other letters of Rick Warren's SHAPE program.

Here is what Rick Warren's SHAPE acronym stands for:

* *Spiritual gifts*—God-given abilities to do Kingdom work
* *Heart*—Areas of passion or burden in your life
* *Abilities*—Skills you have developed or acquired
* *Personality*—Your natural bent
* *Experiences*—Both good and bad

Spiritual Gifts

Even though we may desire a gift of the Holy Spirit, I can't find one single scripture that instructs us how to find our gift. Anything we do in Christ is not through strengths, but is perfected in weakness.

I can't find one single scripture or historical account that says finding our gift was ever a problem for believers (believers have found their spiritual gifts without the SHAPE program).

I can't find one single scripture which uses a subjective balance of weighing our strengths and weaknesses to determine our gift(s) of the Holy Spirit (refer to "balancing" in chapter eleven).

I can't find one single scripture that instructs us to come up with a numerical value or rating system for the gifts of the Holy Spirit.

I can't find one single scripture that instructs us to use what even the proponents of profiling concede are imperfect tools to calibrate or calculate or determine a perfect gift(s) of the Holy Spirit.

But I *can* find a scripture that confirms that a gift of the Holy Spirit arrives *already* perfect: "Every good gift and every perfect gift is from above, and cometh down from the Father of lights, with whom is no variableness, neither shadow of turning" (Jam. 1:17).

Where in the Scripture does it say to practice your gift in the Holy Spirit in order to develop it as SHAPE tells us?

Where in the Scripture does it say, as SHAPE states: ". . . There may be some pitfalls along the way" in developing or determining your gift of the Holy Spirit. The acquiring or determining of the gifts of the Holy Spirit do not have any pitfalls. Jesus Christ is the Author and Finisher of our salvation and He who has begun a good work in us will complete to the day of perfection . . . and He does this completely without a SHAPE profiling test cunningly devised by man!

Where does it say in Scripture the following ideas proposed in SHAPE?

My experiences have influenced my interest in the following people [to determine my gift in the Holy Spirit].

—SHAPE

My experience might have nothing to do with how God directs me after becoming born again, or even what gift of the Holy Spirit I might acquire!

SHAPE states: "People that know you well may be able to shed some light for you as well," and "As we said, the best way to discover your Spiritual Gifts is through other people, by testing, and by exercising your gifts."

Like Job's friends, they were useless!! The Holy Spirit will tell your friends the gift of the Holy Spirit you have before he tells you?

SHAPE states:

> Using the results of the Spiritual Gifts Assessment questionnaire on the following pages, list your top three Spiritual Gifts.

We are going to depend on a man-made and invented questionnaire to determine our top three gifts? And who decided it should be three? Maybe it is one. Who does the ranking and what scripture ranks our spiritual gifts?

SHAPE states:

> Using the response sheet below, write your response to each statement in the block whose number corresponds to that number statement in the Spiritual Gift Assessment. Add the numbers in each column and write in the block marked "T". Assess your gifts matching the letter at the bottom of the row with the Spiritual Gift Assessment Key.

Assess your gifts matching the letter at the bottom of the row with the Spiritual Gift Assessment Key . . . say what? Did all those Christians for two thousand years have this assessment key? We determine our gift of the Holy Spirit by adding up a score? This sounds more like numerology prohibited and condemned in the Bible than it sounds like scriptural authority!

SHAPE (also known as Discovery Class 301) lists the following 19 Spiritual Gifts:

Spiritual Gift Assessment Key

A = Administration
B = Apostleship
C = Craftsmanship*
D = Creative Communication*
E = Discernment

F = Encouragement
G = Evangelism
H = Faith
I = Giving
J = Helps
K = Hospitality*
L = Intercession*
M = Knowledge
N = Leadership*
O = Mercy
P = Prophecy
Q = Shepherding
R = Teaching
S = Wisdom

(Note: Healing, Speaking and interpreting Tongues, Miracles are not included in the Spiritual Gift Assessment because their presence tends to be self-evident.)

Since when does the Bible make this distinction between evident and non-evident gifts of the Holy Spirit?

Tongues are mentioned on the list of the Rick Warren SHAPE questionnaire on Saddleback Church's own website (*www.saddleback-family.com/ministry/images/discoverytool.pdf*), but Warren's definition of tongues there states: "The ability to pray in a language understood only by God." But this is neither the definition nor primary function of tongues in the New Testament commencing with Pentecost. Tongues were languages understood by those nations who spoke other languages but understood the tongues in their own native language. Acts 2:9–11 even lists the nations. And as to function, tongues were primarily a sign to unbelievers and were directed at unbelievers as the primary audience, not to God.

> Wherefore tongues are for a sign, not to them that believe, but to them that believe not: but prophesying serveth not for them that believe not, but for them which believe.
>
> —1 Corinthians 14:22

And even when an interpretation was given in the church later, after Pentecost, it was so men could understand the tongue or language. If the primary audience was God, *no* interpretation would be necessary. This is just one more of a host of examples where Rick Warren does not rightly divide the truth.

Does this list above sound accurate to you? Only one problem. The above version of SHAPE has added five gifts of the Holy Spirit (See the asterisks [*] above) that are not even listed in the New Testament (examples: craftsmanship and creative communication). Then they left off "serving." I compared the spiritual gifts list for three different churches using the SHAPE Discovery Profile and they are not even in agreement. The lists are not consistent. Compare them for yourself.

Now let's look at the list of spiritual gifts that the Scriptures record:

> For to one is given by the Spirit the word of wisdom; to another the word of knowledge by the same Spirit; To another faith by the same Spirit; to another the gifts of healing by the same Spirit; To another the working of miracles; to another prophecy; to another discerning of spirits; to another divers kinds of tongues; to another the interpretation of tongues. . . . And God hath set some in the church, first apostles, secondarily prophets, thirdly teachers, after that miracles, then gifts of healings, helps, governments, diversities of tongues.
>
> —1 Corinthians 12:8–10, 28

> Having then gifts differing according to the grace that is given to us, whether prophecy, let us prophesy according to the proportion of faith; Or ministry, let us wait on our ministering: or he that *teacheth*, on teaching; Or he that *exhorteth*, on exhortation: he that *giveth*, let him do it with simplicity; he that ruleth, with diligence; he that sheweth *mercy*, with cheerfulness.
>
> —Romans 12:6–8 (italicized words are additions to those made in 1 Corinthians 12:8–10,28)

And he gave some, apostles; and some, prophets; and some, evangelists; and some, pastors and teachers; For the perfecting of the saints, for the work of the ministry, for the edifying of the body of Christ: Till we all come in the unity of the faith, and of the knowledge of the Son of God, unto a perfect man, unto the measure of the stature of the fulness of Christ.

—Ephesians 4:11–13

So, doesn't "perfecting" mean perfecting? What is lacking in perfect? And doesn't "fullness" mean fullness? The church possessed all of these tools for two thousand years *without* any SHAPE test. So why does it need it now?

Being confident of this very thing, that he which hath begun a good work in you will perform it until the day of Jesus Christ.

—Philippians 1:6

Looking unto Jesus the author and finisher of our faith. . . .

—Hebrew 12:2

So, who is doing the work? The Lord began it, continued it, and finished it without SHAPE tests. And He performed this work for every saint that ever lived in the last two thousand years *without* SHAPE!

Finally, Proverbs 3:5–6 should seal the doom of this SHAPE program or any clone of it.

Trust in the LORD with all thine heart; and lean not unto thine own understanding. In all thy ways acknowledge him, and he shall direct thy paths.

SHAPE is effectively teaching:

JESUS CHRIST + PSYCHOLOGY =
THE PERFECTING OF THE SAINT(S)

The church was not deficient for nineteen hundred years because it did not possess the secret knowledge and keys to one's personality and diagnostic tools through the SHAPE test. All of the martyred and persecuted saints throughout the ages had everything they needed to be fully equipped to do the work of the ministry, including the ability to figure out what gift of the Holy Spirit they had.

This whole idea is a reproach to every saint that ever lived and an insult to the sufficiency of Christ. The twenty-first century saints now have tools which were unavailable to the rest of the body of Christ for the duration of the first twenty centuries? How did the first twenty centuries of the church manage to get by without these tools? How could they possibly even know that they might be mistaken? Did they simply stumble into the truth of the right gift for them? How would even the twenty-first century Christian know with certainty that the personality profile produced the right result, since it relies on fallen man, the old man, the old creation, perhaps even false memory syndrome, or a spirit guide they called Jesus? Imagine that the Christian used this flawed test, based on the fatal attraction of what's in it for me, or even for noble purposes such as the gift of healing, but then in fact, it was determined that it was a mistake? But by then you may have already given false hope to millions of victims such as the fraudulent faith healers.

The apostle Paul said:

> For I determined not to know any thing among you, save Jesus Christ, and him crucified.
>
> —1 Corinthians 2:2

Why did Paul say: "But God forbid that I should glory, save in the cross of our Lord Jesus Christ, by whom the world is crucified unto me, and I unto the world" (Gal. 6:14), when he could have said, "You should glory in the Lord Jesus Christ plus psychology, since you need both to become whole, sanctified, and perfect"? Or, "There is so much good in the Greek pagan religions in all of the Greek-speaking nations where I started churches, that we must integrate the best of these religions into Christianity! Just think of how this will help the Church Growth Movement!"

But what does Paul really say?

> O Timothy, keep that which is committed to thy trust, avoiding profane and vain babblings, and oppositions of science falsely so called.
>
> —1 Timothy 6:20

> Beware lest any man spoil you through philosophy and vain deceit, after the tradition of men, after the rudiments of the world, and not after Christ.
>
> —Colossians 2:8

The apostle Paul admonishes us:

> All scripture is given by inspiration of God, and is profitable for doctrine, for reproof, for correction, for instruction in righteousness: That the man of God may be perfect, throughly furnished unto all good works.
>
> —2 Timothy 3:16–17

He did not say, "almost perfect," "nearly furnished," and "many good works," because it is impossible to be perfect, thoroughly furnished, and perform all good works *without* a personality profile and without a gift diagnosis from at least one of the host of psychology contradictory programs available which combined with faith will produce the perfecting of the saint!

Again, Paul warns of fables and myths (regarding integrating them into the Gospel):

> As I besought thee to abide still at Ephesus, when I went into Macedonia, that thou mightest charge some that they teach no other doctrine, Neither give heed to fables and endless genealogies,

which minister questions, rather than godly edifying which is in faith: so do.

—1 Timothy 1:3–4

or

For the time will come when they will not endure sound doctrine; but after their own lusts shall they heap to themselves teachers, having itching ears; And they shall turn away their ears from the truth, and shall be turned unto fables.

—2 Timothy 4:3–4

and

According as his divine power hath given unto us all things that pertain unto life and godliness, through the knowledge of him that hath called us to glory and virtue.

—2 Peter 1:3

Something else which stands out in Scripture as to how we find our gift. Note that the gifts of the Holy Spirit are *all* given by God's grace via the Holy Spirit. They are not ascertained by taking a man-made test any more than you could take a man-made test to see if you are born again or to obtain a dream. The Lord distributes and informs each individual directly and according to His good pleasure, "dividing to every man severally as he will" (1 Cor. 12:11), *not as we will.*

Countless saints have been martyred unnecessarily because of their biblical stance of *Sola Scriptura.* Countless lives could have been saved had they simply said: "Scripture is good as far as it goes . . . but we must keep the best of our traditions, and we must leave room for mankind to improve on and refine the Scriptures."

The type of thinking in Rick Warren's SHAPE has turned the church into Big Brother. So now we have *Brave New Church,* run by profiling and transforming the gifts of the Holy Spirit into a commodity which is integrated into a corporate management computerized dictatorship, whose records of each member will be already completed for the government and ultimately the one-world government. Imagine the nightmare prophetic fulfillment of George Orwell's *1984* or Aldous Huxley's *Brave New World*. Berit Kjos gives us a glimpse of this diabolical programming going on in public schools, which she exposes in her great book *Brave New Schools*. But in my wildest imagination, I would never have dreamed of a dystopian *Brave New Church* . . . which Rick Warren started locally, has expanded nationally, and now has plans for taking globally. This Brave New Church is the futuristic vision of Rick Warren and will be made up of Brave New Christians. I would never have believed that the government did not initially impose this system on the church, but the church itself gleefully created and implemented it, all on its own, and would do so in the Name of Jesus Christ and even claim it was with the help of the Holy Spirit!

SHAPE states:

> You have now completed the S.H.A.P.E. Discovery Workshop. You have explored how God has SHAPE'd you for ministry through your spiritual gifts, heart, abilities, personality, and experience.

SHAPE further states:

> This summary page will help you capture the essence of what you learned and will help you toward the next step, a ministry mentoring consultation.

Does it have to be a ministry mentor (no biblical precedent), or can it be an elder? What if the mentor knows nothing about SHAPE, can we seek counsel from someone else? Someone even outside of this local church? Ministry mentoring consultation? Where is the concept of "mentoring" in the Bible? I can find discipling, but not mentoring. The concern here is that a blind guide would lead a host more blind into the ditch! And remember when you have finally taken this supposedly reliable test to find God's shape for your life, it is then conformed to the vision of the pastor for that church. How do you know that his vision is biblically sound, particularly when it is built on the vision of SHAPE itself which we are demonstrating is fatally and biblically flawed. And also remember that the mentors who are interviewing you after you take the test are also trained in SHAPE, and have as their mission conforming you to the vision of the pastor of the church. These mentors are trained guides . . . but trained in what? Psychology whose worldview is antithetical to Christianity? This is not a mutual testing of the spirits to see if they be of God, but a unilateral interrogation which *must* conform to the vision of the pastor. It is not set up so that both parties can go through materials as good Bereans to see if these things be true in conformity to Scripture.

> Let them alone: they be blind leaders of the blind. And if the blind lead the blind, both shall fall into the ditch.
>
> —Matthew 15:14

Experience
SHAPE asks:

> Which of the elements of experience do you feel were most influential in determining who you are?

I don't know how many more umpteen times I am going to hear the word "experience" as a major determining factor where we learn God's direction for our life, gleaned mainly from our own subjective, carnal, fallen, corrupted nature! Where have I heard the word "feel" before? This is wonderful . . . we get to trust our feelings for determining "who we are"! (It occurs thirteen times in the SHAPE profile test document.) Since when do subjective feelings determine our spiritual gifts?
SHAPE states:

> Discovering our unique S.H.A.P.E. helps us see more clearly how God is calling us to minister in His world.

And for those millions of saints that lived the last two thousand years who did not take this test, did they see less clearly how God was calling them to minister, including the millions of martyred and persecuted saints? This test which, by their own words, may not be reliable and might need improving, will help them see more clearly what the Bible by itself can not do?

SHAPE states:

> Picture this scenario: You are putting together a 100,000 piece puzzle. The day comes when you are finally finished only to discover that one piece is missing!!!

So, I did 99.999 percent of the puzzle by myself, and the rest of the body of Christ comes together to help me figure out the .001 percent?

SHAPE states:

> Although the puzzle is 99.99% complete, it will never look like the picture on the box. So it is with the Body of Christ. God needs each of us.

God needs us?

SHAPE states:

> . . . Every part of us: "From him the whole body, joined and held together by every supporting ligament, grows and builds itself up in love, as each part does its work" (Eph. 4:16).

As determined, defined, and refined by the SHAPE test? If you are going to use this analogy, it is Christ who is the head of the body, so He is the one who does the thinking and completing the puzzle . . . and it's 100 percent of the puzzle. The leg, the heart, the toe, the kidney do *nothing* to compute the design of the finished puzzle.

SHAPE states:

> To discover your S.H.A.P.E. is to discover where God is calling you to do His work in the world.

How then did all of those Christians discover God's calling for two thousand years without SHAPE? And how do you know with assurance that this even is His work? If the Lord does not build the house, the workers labor in vain!

SHAPE states:

> Once you have discovered your S.H.A.P.E., God asks you to continue the development process

What development process? Under whose guidance? SHAPE mentors? There are more levels and courses we must take?

Now that we have explained the complete SHAPE questionnaire itself, which technically is not in Rick Warren's *Purpose Driven Life* book, we may now refer back to the two chapters in his book in which he describes his SHAPE program. I also refer you to the next chapter on personality which addresses more statements in the SHAPE program on Mr. Warren's own church website as well as other SHAPE questionnaires available online. Here are some of the quotes in chapters thirty and thirty-one of his book, followed by my commentary.

Heart ("H" in SHAPE)

Rick Warren explores the heart from many angles, including, as he states:

> Your heart represents the source of all your motivations—what you love to do and what you care about most.

> Your heart reveals the *real* you . . .

> . . . God has given each of us a unique *emotional* "heartbeat." . . .

> Another word for heart is *passion.*

> How do you know when you are serving God from your heart? The first telltale sign is *enthusiasm.*

The second characteristic of serving God from your heart is *effectiveness.*[110]

Certainly, it is true that a Christian may have such qualities as passion and enthusiasm for their faith. But Rick Warren omits the most important description of the nature of the heart of man as described in Scripture:

> The heart is deceitful above all things, and desperately wicked: who can know it?
>
> —Jeremiah 17:9

What is implied in Rick Warren's description of the heart is that it is some vast reservoir of something good . . . creating the impression that the heart of man is basically good. This may not have been his intent, but without the above scripture from Jeremiah, both believers and non-believers are left without the whole truth and nature of the heart of man.

Apparently, according to Rick Warren, you can know the "real you" just by studying your heart. No, the Holy Spirit and the Word of God reveals your true nature. The heart is simply where it comes from. And there is another problem with the term "real you."

The "real you" is an idea set up by psychologists, showcased in such personality profiles as the Enneagram. See article on the Enneagram at: *www.abrahamic-faith.com/James/Part%20X%20Enneagram%20Profiling%20vs.%20Scripture%20Documentary.html* which compares the teaching of the "true self" to the "false self" and why it too does not conform to Scripture. Richard Foster, who is promoted by Rick Warren, also promotes the Enneagram on his own website for the Renovare organization. Contemplative prayer mystic leader Thomas Keating (who is held in high regard by Richard Foster), promotes the idea of the true self vs. the false self. But this is not an idea or comparison based on Scripture. The reality is that the Bible reveals to us what we need to know about the heart!

---

110. Ibid., p. 237–239.

Finally, regarding "enthusiasm" and "passion" as a determining factor for serving God from your heart, Rick Warren on the one hand seems to indicate that serving God should be done passionately, not dutifully, without needing rewards or applause or payment. And yet on the other hand Mr. Warren does not qualify the zeal, but states that it is a determining factor. However, the Israelites as described by the apostle Paul had both enthusiasm and passion. But this zeal was misdirected:

> For I bear them record that they have a zeal of God, but not according to knowledge.
>
> —Romans 10:2

"DAY 31 – Understanding Your Shape" begins on page 241

Abilities ("A" in SHAPE)

Rick Warren stated on page 75 in *The Purpose Driven Life* that "there are no unspiritual abilities, just misused ones." Then on page 242 he states that there are both "natural" and "spiritual" abilities. Well if all abilities are spiritual (i.e., no unspiritual abilities) then it logically follows that all "natural" abilities are spiritual. This is clearly a contradiction on Warren's part and totally confusing. Then he goes on to tell us on page 242 that "natural abilities . . . are just as important . . . as your spiritual gifts." Even if we are able to sort out all of the confusion here of what Warren really means, he would still be wrong. Spiritual ability must always be more important than natural ability and reign supreme over it. If this were not true, then non-believers who also have the very same natural abilities as believers would have to be viewed in the church as important as Christians. There is not a single scripture to support Warren's glaring error in doctrine here, but there are plenty of Scripture examples to prove that spiritual abilities exceedingly outweigh natural abilities in importance. For example, are we to suggest that performing miracles, signs, and wonders as we see described in the Book of Acts as equal in importance to natural abilities? The Bible says that the natural man understands not the things of the Spirit, as the following scripture verifies:

But the natural man receiveth not the things of the Spirit of God: for they are foolishness unto him: neither can he know them, because they are spiritually discerned.

—1 Corinthians 2:14

So, it is incomprehensible that man's abilities he possesses in the natural could be compared to the spiritual man's abilities in importance! Who would dare suggest what Rick Warren has proposed? Warren further states on page 242 that "every ability can be used for God's glory." But every ability can't be used for God's glory (such as sorcery, necromancy, etc.). In the Book of Acts, Simon the Sorcerer had ability to soothsay but he clearly should not have used it for the church when he became a Christian. Rick Warren on the next page (page 243) uses 1 Corinthians 12:6 (TEV) to try to prove that every ability can be used for God's glory. But a careful examination of 1 Corinthians 12 shows that Paul is referring to spiritual gifts, not natural abilities. Rick Warren then goes on and gives a list of natural abilities that this scripture is supposed to support, such as baking, farming, fishing, needlework, etc. Certainly these abilities could be performed for the glory of God. But they are not spiritual gifts. Mr. Warren also stated under his definition of "abilities" that, "Your abilities are the natural talents with which you were born" (Source: *www.saddlebackfamily.com/ministry/images/discoverytool.pdf*). Now it is true some of us were born more athletic than others, but you weren't born a cook or a weapons maker, you are trained to be one. So he is in error on several counts.

❋ ❋ ❋

Rick Warren: "What I'm able to do, God wants me to do." [111]

Really? Moses was not able to speak, as he had a speech impediment, yet God told him to speak. Many great singers get saved, but that doesn't mean God wants them ministering as a singer in the church, particularly because they may not have shed the worldly or seductive techniques they acquired and used so effectively in the world.

111. Ibid., p. 243.

Besides this, Scripture records that we are perfected in our weakness
. . . not necessarily our ability.

> And he said unto me, My grace is sufficient for thee: for my strength
> is made perfect in weakness.
>
> —2 Corinthians 12:9

God's mission for how you should serve may have nothing to do with
your ability!

✖   ✖   ✖

**Rick Warren: "God doesn't waste abilities. . . . New members
are told, 'Whatever you're good at, you should be doing for your
church.'" 112**

Rick Warren certainly needs to qualify what he means by this,
which he doesn't do. So, if I am a good bookie or gambler, I should do
that for the church? If I was a psychotherapist in the world teaching
ideas in psychology which contain worldviews antithetical to Christianity, God forbid I should now counsel God's sheep! Rick Warren
seems to imply that just because a man is trained and good at even a
noble profession such as being a CPA, that he should be the accountant for the church. Maybe God wants him to be an accountant for a
bank, so he can make the necessary income to take care of his family
and even give to the church financially. God may want him to be an
usher at church. Musicians may have had great abilities in the world
and also learned its devices how to be a good entertainer, but would
not want to bring these abilities to the church. They would rather
serve in other ways. I have known Broadway and pop singers who
bring their licks and styles to the altar, and I am offended, not blessed,
by their entertaining rather then ministering to the body.

✖   ✖   ✖

**Rick Warren: "Today there are many books and tools that can help
you understand your personality so you can determine how to use
it for God." 113**

---

112. Ibid., p. 244.
113. Ibid., p. 246.

Even though Rick Warren's personality theory is part of his overall SHAPE program, we are devoting the entire next chapter to the "P" in SHAPE because it clearly demonstrates the connection to Carl Jung and contains what may be the clearest and most present danger to the church of all of his teachings.

❊　❊　❊

Rick Warren: "Using your shape is the secret of both fruitfulness and fulfillment in ministry." [114]

This is a most astonishing statement for those of us Christians who have not taken the SHAPE test to discover the secret to a fulfilling ministry! The fact remains, you can't really know your SHAPE (according to Warren) until you take this profile. You still have not determined it even at the end of forty days. So even after finishing this book, you could not fully know your SHAPE. Then you have to take this profile to become a member at his church. This tool is not optional! The tool is *not* in his book, it is in his tapes and the curriculum of his Discovery 301 Class which you must order from him in order to do as the title says, "Discovering Your Shape for Ministry." You haven't discovered your SHAPE until you take this tool!

We have already discussed *Experience* (the "E" in SHAPE) above when we commented on the SHAPE questionnaire used at First United Methodist Church in Mineola, Texas.

Conclusion

Rick Warren states in his SHAPE Profile: "Not only did God shape you before your birth." This is a very troubling statement, particularly since, you can't even possess the "S" in SHAPE, or Spiritual Gifts, until your *rebirth*. Even Rick Warren concedes this point. But if this is true, you can't be shaped at or before your birth. At the very most you could only be incomplete in possessing "HAPE," but not "SHAPE" when you are born. In Christ Jesus you are a new creation and all things become new.

---

114. Ibid., p. 248.

Jesus Christ in the Gospels, and the apostles Paul, John, Peter, and Jude, warned of deception in the last days because of the very philosophy that *new* or secret information was needed which was different from or in addition to the Scriptures, prophecy, and instructions already given to the saints. So with this in mind, I remind you of the following scripture:

> Beloved, when I gave all diligence to write unto you of the common salvation, it was needful for me to write unto you, and exhort you that ye should earnestly contend for the faith which was once delivered unto the saints.
>
> —Jude 1:3

This faith is for the Christians of *all* nations, all people, all generations, for all time.

> In all thy ways acknowledge him, and he shall direct thy paths.
>
> —Proverbs 3:6

> He restoreth my soul. . . .
>
> —Psalm 23:3

> For the word of God is quick, and powerful, and sharper than any twoedged sword, piercing even to the dividing asunder of soul and spirit, and of the joints and marrow, and is a discerner of the thoughts and intents of the heart.
>
> —Hebrews 4:12

Chapter Eleven

Personality Profiling

In the last chapter we discovered in general what Rick Warren's SHAPE program is as well as an in depth look at what he means by the S, H, A, and the E in SHAPE. The S in SHAPE refers to Spiritual Gifts that can only be possessed by a believer, as even Rick Warren asserts, meaning that only the "new man" can possess them. However, the Heart, Abilities, Personality, and Experience (the H,A,P,E in SHAPE) could apply to believers as well as non-believers. The impression is created that there is an attempt to combine the attributes of the new man (the S in SHAPE) and the old man (the H,A,P,E in SHAPE) in what Rick Warren describes as a "custom combination of capabilities." When Jesus warned us against putting new wine into old wineskins (the old man) . . . the wineskins did not burst right away, but after a season. Much, if not all, of Rick Warren's SHAPE (HAPE) is the old wineskin. So the only thing that is going to happen is that eventually, Warren's SHAPE wineskin is going to burst!

By now many of you must be asking, "If some of the teachings behind the other letters in Rick Warren's SHAPE are faulty, then how can we trust the teaching behind the remaining letter (P") in his SHAPE acronym?" Well you would be right! You can't trust it, and we will prove why! The individual letters of SHAPE as well as any value of combining all of the letters cannot be biblically defended. Even if four out of the five letters in SHAPE could be biblically defended, but one is in error, it corrupts the entire acronym. A little leaven leaveneth the *entire* lump. A little strychnine in the stew poisons the entire stew, no matter how excellent and fresh the meat, potatoes, and vegetables.

Once again I must point out that the actual personality profile questionnaire (the P in SHAPE) is not in Rick Warren's *Purpose Driven Life* book. Rather he gives a general description of it. In order to obtain the actual personality profile questionnaire that you take and fill out (and determine your score), you must do the same thing you did to obtain the SHAPE questionnaire. The personality questionnaire is a questionnaire within a questionnaire, in that it is embedded in the SHAPE questionnaire (the P in SHAPE). You may access one website's adaptation of it online at: *www.unl.edu/navs/resources/shape. pdf* or directly from Saddleback Church.

But before I go into detail to describe how Rick Warren's personality profile is based on Carl Jung's theories of personality, it would be very instructive to give you the background of how Carl Jung's psychology of personality found its way into evangelical Christianity. This can best be described in the following article on Myers-Briggs Temperament Indicator (MBTI), which will also clearly reveal where Rick Warren got his ideas for his personality profile embedded in his SHAPE questionnaire. We have received special permission to reprint this excellent article. We invite you to read it. It may be found in appendix C at the end of this book and documentary. It may also be accessed online at *www3.bc.sympatico.ca/st_simons/arm03.htm*

As to the validity of the Myers-Briggs Temperament Indicator, as well as the abridged version known as the Keirsey-Bates Temperament Sorter, for determining your personality temperament, please refer to the following research article: "Measuring the MBTI . . . And Coming Up Short" at *www.work911.com/cgi-bin/links/jump.cgi?ID=4014.* The following quote summarizes Dr. Pittenger's findings:

As noted above, the Myers-Briggs™ instrument generates sixteen distinct personality profiles based on which side of the four scales one tends toward. Technically, the instrument is not supposed to be used to spew out personality profiles and pigeonhole people, but the temptation to do so seems irresistible. Providing personality tests and profiles has become a kind of entertainment on the Internet. There is also a pernicious side to these profiles: they can lead to discrimination and poor career counseling. Employers may hire, fire, or assign personnel by personality type, despite the fact that the MBTI® is not even reliable at identifying one's type. Several studies have shown that when retested, even after intervals as short as five weeks, as many as 50 percent will be classified into a different type. There is scant support for the belief that the MBTI® would justify such job discrimination or would be a reliable aid to someone seeking career guidance (Pittenger 1993).

—Source: *http://skepdic.com/myersb.html*

In answer to the question as to whether Rick Warren's personality profile integrates the teachings of Carl Jung (in terms of the MBTI and the Keirsey-Bates), there are at least three places online which feature the actual SHAPE Discovery test (and at least three variations of the test . . . but both variations invoke Jung's terms: Introvert/Extrovert and Thinker/Feeler). These websites will be listed later in the chapter.

Rick Warren, in talking about the P component in *The Purpose Driven Life*, uses the same terminology coined by Carl Jung. Rick Warren contrasts Introvert/Extrovert and Thinker/Feeler . . . exactly the terminology and meaning promoted and intended by Carl Jung.[115] It is well-documented both by Carl Jung himself as well as by reputable scholars that Carl Jung obtained his personality theory by divination, necromancy, Taoism, astrology, paganism and evolution (refer to appendix C). My own correspondence with the Jung Institute in Zurich, Switzerland, confirms this. There is no question that Jung's personality theory and books constitute magic arts. Christians have no business drawing from his magic arts to minister or teach Christians to follow. It is so surprising that Rick Warren would utilize Jung's terms in order for Christians to plug this into their personality evaluation.

---

115. Ibid., p. 245.

Believers should be aware of what the Bible says regarding *divination*:

> There shall not be found among you any one that maketh his son or his daughter to pass through the fire, or that useth divination, or an observer of times, or an enchanter, or a witch, Or a charmer, or a consulter with familiar spirits, or a wizard, or a necromancer. For all that do these things are an abomination unto the LORD: and because of these abominations the LORD thy God doth drive them out from before thee.
>
> —Deuteronomy 18:10–12

Here is the *Merriam-Webster Dictionary* definition of *divination*:

> The art or practice that seeks to foresee or foretell future events or **discover hidden knowledge** usu. by the interpretation of omens or by the aid of supernatural powers.

What follows is an excerpt from a more comprehensive SHAPE profile, otherwise known as *Discovery Class 301*. It can be found at First United Pentecostal Church's website that uses it. The complete profile is posted at: *www.firstchurch.ca/pdf/Ministry%20301.pdf.*

The following excerpt from the SHAPE (Discovery 301) questionnaire is absolute proof of the Carl Jung rooted personality profile, or the "P" in Rick Warren's SHAPE program Discovery 301 Class. (This version of the SHAPE questionnaire is approximately 68 pages).

Class 301 – Discovering My Ministry—Page 46

It's obvious that God has not used a "cookie cutter" to stamp out people in a process of uniformity. He loves variety—just look around! There are no "right" or "wrong" temperaments. Rather, we need opposites in personality types to balance the church. Although there are many fine (and detailed!) personality assessments available, for the purpose of your ministry profile, we want you to consider just five aspects . . .

HOW DO I SEE MYSELF?

Extroverted			Introverted		
3	2	1	1	2	3
extreme		mild	mild		extreme

Thinker			Feeler		
3	2	1	1	2	3
extreme		mild	mild		extreme

Routine			Variety		
3	2	1	1	2	3
extreme		mild	mild		extreme

Self-Controlled			Self-Expressive		
3	2	1	1	2	3
extreme		mild	mild		extreme

Cooperative			Competitive		
3	2	1	1	2	3
extreme		mild	mild		extreme

Note in particular that your personality traits are scored. These traits were derived from Carl Jung's practice of divination. The numbers assigned above were not originally used by Carl Jung (though Carl Jung practiced astrology, numerology and Ouija boards). The numbers were later introduced by Myers-Briggs, who codified these traits. Again we see numbers assigned to the Discovery 301 Class questionnaire, as seen above. Numerology is practicing or ascribing numerical values to hidden knowledge (including personality), not limited to predicting the future. Using this chart as though these numbers have some spiritual significance for a Christian is why this is numerology (a form of divination) which the Bible forbids.

Every SHAPE questionnaire adaptation online we have discovered (for which the churches credit Rick Warren's SHAPE program) uses the personality profiling derived from Carl Jung.

Another example is the First United Methodist Church in Mineola, Texas, which uses and adapts Rick Warren's SHAPE and specifically his personality profile. They state:

List your Kiersey-Bates personality type from the test:

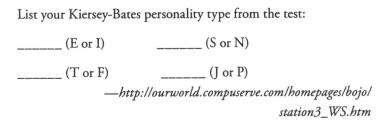

_____ (E or I)   _____ (S or N)

_____ (T or F)   _____ (J or P)

—*http://ourworld.compuserve.com/homepages/bojo/*
station3_WS.htm

In this Jung-based personality profile, E stands for Extrovert, I stands for Introvert, S stands for Self-Expressive, N stands for Intuitive, T stands for Thinker, F stands for Feeler, J stands for Judging, and P stands for Perceiver.

If you visit the above site, you will see Warren's SHAPE questionnaire, but you will also note references to the Keirsey-Bates Temperament Sorter.

A visit to Keirsey's own website should remove any doubts that the Keirsey-Bates Temperament sorter is completely Carl Jung-based to the core, which they state by their own affirmation: *http://keirsey.com/.* (I have also confirmed this via e-mail with Keirsey's son whose father developed the profile). Similarly the Myers-Briggs website will authenticate the Carl Jung connection: *www.myersbriggs.org/about_mbti.basics.cfm.*

❀   ❀   ❀

Now let's continue our examination of what Rick Warren discusses in *The Purpose Driven Life* regarding discovering your Personality (the P in your SHAPE).[116]

As fruit falls close to the tree, we can observe Rick Warren's teachings on personality being manifested throughout the world. Under the "P" in many different SHAPE sites conceived by Rick Warren, and adapted by a host of churches (see: *http://host73.hppc.org/hppweekly.nsf/hppweekly/03.24.02/$file/03-24-02.pdf* [Highland Park Presbyterian Church, Dallas, Texas, where Purpose Driven Life series are conducted] and *www.firstchurch.ca/pdf/Ministry%20301.pdf*

---

116. Ibid., p. 245.

[First Church in New Brunswick, Canada]), SHAPE states: **"Where does my personality best suit me to serve?"**

Then they quote 1 Corinthians 2:11 (LB), which says:

> No one can really know what anyone else is thinking or what he is really like, except that person himself.

Note even in the erroneous Living Bible paraphrase, "what he is really like" would actually be what comes out of his heart. Often a person's personality is observed by others. And even if the Living Translation were correct, there is nothing in it that would automatically tip us off how it would be used to show us how we are to best serve in the church.

Now let's look at this verse in the King James Version:

> For what man knoweth the things of a man, save the spirit of man which is in him? even so the things of God knoweth no man, but the Spirit of God.
>
> —1 Corinthians 2:11 (KJV)

Psychologists think man is body, soul, and personality. The above scripture is describing "spirit." It is important to note that we all have unique personalities as different as a fingerprint, or as star differs from star in glory. But "spirit" and "personality" have completely different meanings.

> And the very God of peace sanctify you wholly; and I pray God your whole **spirit and soul and body** be preserved blameless unto the coming of our Lord Jesus Christ.
>
> —1 Thessalonians 5:23 (KJV)

Statements on Rick Warren's Website

On Rick Warren's Saddleback Church website also note, under the personality profile you fill out, that you must list "traits" and "types."

These are definitely psychology theory terms and this is determined by taking the Jung-based personality profile questionnaire.

Personality ("P" in S.H.A.P.E.)

Rick Warren: "For instance, two people may have the same gift of evangelism, but if one is **introverted and the other is extroverted,** that gift will be expressed in different ways."

So where is one biblical precedent that a single spiritual gift was expressed in a different way because one Christian was supposedly introverted while another was extroverted?

> Woodworkers know that it's easier to work with the grain rather than against it. In the same way, when you are forced to minister in a manner that is "out of character" for your temperament, it creates tension and discomfort, requires extra effort and energy, and produces less than the best results. This is why mimicking someone else's ministry never works. You don't have their personality. Besides, God made you to be you! You can learn from the examples of others, but you must filter what you learn through your own shape.
>
> Like stained glass, our different personalities reflect God's light in many colors and patterns. This blesses the family of God with depth and variety. It also blesses us personally. It feels good to do what God made you to do. When you minister in a manner consistent with the personality God gave you, you experience fulfillment, satisfaction, and fruitfulness.
>
> —*The Purpose Driven Life* by Rick Warren, pp. 245–246

The example of a woodworker is a natural ability, not a supernatural gift, so Warren's example cannot even be applied.

❋   ❋   ❋

Rick Warren: "It's obvious that God has not used a cookie cutter to stamp out people in a process of uniformity. He loves variety; just look around. **And there is not a "right" or "wrong" temperament. We need opposites to** *balance* **the church. The personality** *traits* listed below are grouped in four couplets each with two opposing tendencies."

What Does the Bible Have to Say About "Balance"?

Balancing or reconciling opposites is another concept of personality theory drawn directly from Carl Jung's invoking Taoism's yin and yang (female, male). Jung's terms for yin and yang were "animus" and "anima," which Jung described as "psychological bisexuality." In other words, he believed that all human beings are bisexual. Jung compounded his perversion by promoting evolution in this very personality theory by believing that these male/female archetypes were derived from when humans were animals. But there is no reconciliation or balancing of male/female opposites because God created man and then woman as separate entities ("male and female he created them") and even condemned any attempt by man to blur this line or create an appearance of blurring or crossing the line such as androgyny.

The apostle Paul records:

> For this cause God gave them up unto vile affections: for even their women did change the natural use into that which is against nature: And likewise also the men, leaving the natural use of the woman, burned in their lust one toward another; men with men working that which is unseemly, and receiving in themselves that recompence of their error which was meet.
>
> —Romans 1:26–27; see also Deuteronomy 22:5 in the Old Testament where even cross-dressing was condemned

The boundaries between male and female, in fact, are so clearly drawn by God that God even condemned the fallen angels who left their former or natural estate to have sexual relations with women producing the giant Nephilim offspring.

The apostle Peter records:

> For if God spared not the angels that sinned, but cast them down
> to hell, and delivered them into chains of darkness, to be reserved
> unto judgment; And spared not the old world, but saved Noah the
> eighth person, a preacher of righteousness, bringing in the flood
> upon the world of the ungodly; And turning the cities of Sodom
> and Gomorrah into ashes condemned them with an overthrow,
> making them an ensample unto those that after should live un-
> godly.
>
> —2 Peter 2:4–6

The Book of Jude records what happened to these angels as well as
how God judged Sodom and Gomorrha for committing androgynous
acts:

> And the angels which kept not their first estate, but left their own
> habitation, he hath reserved in everlasting chains under darkness
> unto the judgment of the great day. Even as Sodom and Gomorrha,
> and the cities about them in like manner, giving themselves over
> to fornication, and going after strange flesh, are set forth for an
> example, suffering the vengeance of eternal fire.
>
> —Jude 1:6–7

So it could not be any clearer what God says about such personality
theories and Jung's perverted ideas of anima and animus. I am not
suggesting that Rick Warren is promoting literal androgyny. But by
invoking Jung's concepts of psychological and personality profiling,
he is certainly endorsing and implementing his spiritual androgyny.
So it is a wonder that Mr. Warren himself did not likewise condemn
Jung's false teaching, instead of promoting his wolf's personality theory in the sheep's clothing guise of Christianity.

When Evil Is Good?

Jung thought the process he called individuation would result in the
reconciliation of good and evil. And the idea and method of the yin-

yang is nothing more than a Chinese form of divination taken directly from the *I-Ching*. But the Bible teaches that good will *never* be reconciled with evil.

Here is how Isaiah the prophet describes this:

> Woe unto them that call evil good, and good evil; that put darkness for light, and light for darkness; that put bitter for sweet, and sweet for bitter!
>
> —Isaiah 5:20

This is exactly what Carl Jung has done by attempting to merge good with evil. But you might say: "But doesn't the Bible talk about a need for balance?" Yes! But the word is used only eight times in the Bible and its primary and recurring theme and application refers to not cheating in scales, fair wages, and to administering justice. It has everything to do with right vs. wrong, not "there is no right or wrong answer!" And it certainly has nothing to do with personalty typing. Here is the proof:

> A false balance is abomination to the LORD: but a just weight is his delight.
>
> —Proverbs 11:1

> Divers weights are an abomination unto the LORD; and a false balance is not good.
>
> —Proverbs 20:23

❋　❋　❋

Rick Warren: "Your personality will affect how and where you use your spiritual gifts and abilities."

Show me one scripture to back up this statement. Since you allegedly have the same personality before and after you are born again, how does your personality affect how and where you use your spiritual gifts that you can't even possess until you become a Christian or new creation? The personality of the natural man does not understand the things of the Spirit. The Lord gives spiritual gifts as He deems appropriate. The idea that the personality from the old man or nature could have influence over the spirit is frightening. In fact, completely different personalities could and did use various spiritual gifts in an identical way without the personality having any impact whatsoever on the operation of the gifts.

❋ ❋ ❋

Rick Warren: "When you minister in a manner consistent with the personality God gave you, you experience fulfillment, satisfaction, and fruitfulness."

So personality is the template and requirement for achieving fulfillment, satisfaction, and fruitfulness? Well if this is true, you can do this without even being born again . . . just follow your natural bent or personality! No, our fruitfulness is based on how much we are plugged into the Vine (Jesus) and the Vine Dresser (Jesus). Fruitfulness is fruit of the Spirit, not the personality.

Many Christians and apostles had completely different personalities yet often had the exact same ministry, e.g., whenever they were sent out or went out two by two. But you could not get personalities which were more contrasting that Paul, Peter, and John. You could make an argument that Paul's ministry was different in that it was to the Gentiles, but what does that have to do with personality? You could argue that other apostles carried out their ministry to different geographic areas, but what does that have to do with personality?

There are at least two different temperament categories circulating among churches which use Rick Warrens' SHAPE program. Some have five temperament categories and some have four. On Warren's SHAPE questionnaire on his own Saddleback Church site he left out Jung's Thinker/Feeler even though he mentions it in his *Purpose Driven Life* book when he discusses SHAPE. The profile shown previously in the chapter which assigns numerical values to the temperaments does list Thinker/Feeler. So are there four couplets or five couplets? This is very confusing and unstandardized. And what is the biblical basis for either four or five, let alone requiring them to be balanced? And what does "balanced" mean? Balanced in the individual or balanced in the church or both? Why not ten couplets or forty or ten thousand? Are there only four temperaments because paganism teaches that there are only four? Because Carl Jung teaches that there are four?

On the personality questionnaire on Rick Warren's site he also forces a choice of one or the other, e.g., you must choose Extrovert or Introvert. And just like Jung's personality theory, everyone is either an Extrovert or Introvert. So a person taking the profile is forced into a choice of only two options. What if he doesn't see himself as either, even assuming these terms are valid? The terms themselves set up straw man arguments in which we are led to assume or believe that the premise for Warren's opposites and the ones he drew from Jung are even correct. What if a person taking this test feels he needs seventy times seven couplets to choose from and can't be straitjacketed into Rick Warren's four choices of personality couplets? The Discovery 301 curriculum shown above states that God is not a cookie cutter, yet this is precisely what Warren does in his four personality couplet choices. The only difference is that instead of one cookie cutter mold, he offers us four or five mold choices. But even if a person believed in Jung and Warren's idea of reconciliation of opposites, he might reject totally the four or five personality choices Warren proposes and subjectively select his own criteria or couplets. The fact is there are no absolute truths (or right or wrong) in this framework, but the Bible requires adherence to absolute truth.

From Rick Warren's Discovery 301 Class (otherwise known as SHAPE) questionnaire, we read:

"PLUGGING IN MY PERSONALITY
  Please remember to record your responses on your S.H.A.P.E. profile.
  Instructions: Circle one or the other
  "I tend to . . ."

Be Extroverted		**Be Introverted**
I prefer interacting with many people and gain energy from being part of a variety of activities.	or	I prefer interacting with only a few people and gain energy from quiet reflective time. I am a good listener.

Be Self-expressive		**Be Self-controlled**
I am more open and verbal about my thoughts and opinions. I enjoy sharing these with other people.	or	I tend to keep my thoughts and opinions to myself.
Prefer Routine		**Prefer Variety**
I am more comfortable being involved in activities where I clearly know what is expected of me. I like closure and completion before starting something new.	or	I am more fulfilled by tasks that change and maybe even have some surprises. Finishing one task before starting another is not crucial.
Be Cooperative		**Be Competitive**
As I work with others, I easily see their point of view. I like being part of a team effort.	or	I like a sense of challenge. It increases my effort and helps me overcome the obstacles.

—Source: *www.saddlebackfamily.com/ministry/
images/discoverytool.pdf*

Are These Opposites?

The most obvious and baffling question that strikes me and stands out upon reading this chart is the fact that I was expecting to see genuine "opposites" or antonyms in the titles or headings of all four of Warren's personality couplets. Assuming they are legitimate terms to begin with, introverts and extroverts are opposites. Routine vs. variety could be opposites, though that is arguable. But I don't think it is abundantly obvious that self-expressive is the opposite of self-control or that cooperative is the antonym of competitive. It is easy to see that black is the opposite of white, that sweet is the opposite of sour, that thick is the opposite of thin, that high is the opposite of low, that shiny is the opposite of dull. Two couplets in the chart could qualify as opposites. But to say that self-expressive is the opposite of self-control, or that cooperative is the opposite of competitive is like saying a basketball is the opposite of a potato, unless there is some kind of esoteric abstract way of interpreting these as symbols or archetypes, in which case who then determines their true meaning or application? If anything, these two allegedly opposite characteristics show things in common. For example, a person on a basketball team who is very spirited or has *esprit de corps* is one who has **both** traits of being cooperative and competitive. (What the potato and a basketball have in common is that they are both round to a certain degree). A good preacher might have **both** self-control and be self-expressive. Opposites indeed may attract, but they may be just as likely to repel or neutralize.

Introverted vs. Extroverted

There could not be a more glaring link between Jung and Warren than this Introvert/Extrovert personality typing comparison. This should drive a stake right into the heart of Rick Warren's SHAPE profile! Virtually any first-year psychology major in college, let alone a person with a Masters in psychology or counseling should immediately recognize Warren's Introvert/Extrovert terms as Carl Jung terminology for personality profiling. A discerning Christian should reject this personality theory drawn from Jung's practice of divination from these two terms in Jung's intended meaning and application!

Regarding Warren's definition of introvert, does he mean by "quiet reflective time" one who practices Richard Foster's definition of meditation? And even if Warren means a biblical sense of meditation, this would once again qualify as a good trait. But why wouldn't or couldn't extroverts (according to Warren's definition) also practice a quiet reflective time before the Lord? Warren forces us to choose "one or the other."

Self-Expressive vs. Self-Controlled

There are other problems with being confined to the choices Warren gives you in his personality profile. Christians would understand the term "self-control" as a fruit of the Spirit. Unlike Warren's contention that there is no right or wrong to temperament traits, self-control is very much a RIGHT trait. Its opposite is not self-expressive but one *without* self-control, or one who is licentious or lawless. And why does one have to choose between self-expressive and self-controlled under Warren's schematic. Why can't a person be both? Warren defines them as opposites . . . but this is very confusing because his titles don't even match some of his definitions. Christians could and should keep opinions to themselves with things which pertain to gossiping, but they should be very verbal with their thoughts about false teaching such as the foundation and theory of this very occult/pagan-based personality theory and very much carry out Matthew 18 to expose it or any other false teaching. In this case both opposites should apply and both traits would be a "right" trait, not "there is no right or wrong temperament trait" to your personality, as Rick Warren would have us believe.

Competitive vs. Cooperative

Now it is quite remarkable that Rick Warren would say in his personality profile that there are no right or wrong answers regarding the opposite personality traits he postulates that a person must possess (so that whether you are competitive or cooperative, either answer would be acceptable), yet he contradicts himself when he states on page 158 in his *Purpose Driven Life* (on which I commented earlier).

Rick Warren quotes Matthew 5:9 (MSG): **"You're blessed when you can show people how to cooperate instead of compete or fight. That's when you discover who you are and your place in God's family."**

Wait a minute, I thought competing was just as viable an option for your personality trait as cooperating? So if we follow Rick Warren's direction we should never choose "competitive" on his profile if we truly want to be blessed.

Regarding Competitive vs. Cooperative, all Christians should be like Paul to compete for the prize of the high calling of God, but there is no need to be competing with each other, at least spiritually since all Christians get the same prize of salvation.

One may ask the question: "Christians are not supposed to compete against each other are they? Isn't that self-seeking?" Some kinds of competition within the body of Christ are actually healthy. For example, canvassing or having a search committee to find a teaching elder or pastor is competitive in order to discover who is approved to function as an elder. A church choir may require auditions which are competitive. Every time you apply for a job you are competing, and if you apply for a job in a ministry you are competing with other Christians. So does this mean your are not blessed because you are competitive vs. being cooperative, according to his quotes of Matthew 5:9 (MSG)? These personality couplets by Rick Warren are supposed to be opposites. So wouldn't the opposite of cooperative be uncooperative or rebellious? And wouldn't uncompetitive be the opposite of competitive? The problem is that the same person in the choir would have been both a competitive and cooperative person . . . he or she had to compete to get in the choir, but would have to be cooperative to be in this group. But if we adhere to Rick Warren's schematic, he would have us not only believe that cooperative is the polar opposite of competitive, but that we must choose between the two. But we could be both cooperative and competitive simultaneously. So they aren't necessarily opposites, if at all. And what biblical precedent would even require this dialectic?

Routine vs. Variety

Regarding preferring Routine vs. Variety, I might prefer routine with respect to liturgy, but want variety in what I cook and when I am on vacation. I might want to complete some kinds of tasks in life before starting something new such as college or military service, but I am constantly beginning new writing projects before I finish others and have several going on at the same time which are at various stages for a host of different reasons. A person might prefer having a variety of types of jobs such as postal worker and softball coach, but want a routine for some of the individual missions in life such as the route he takes to deliver the mail. So it is nearly impossible to make an absolute choice or choices that Warren has postulated. I could not in good conscience even take such a personality profile because of all of its internal problems as well as the poor if not impossible fit to my unique personality. This personality schematic should be rejected by its poor logic and confusion alone, let alone its occultic foundation, rendering it unbiblical.

Another huge problem with his list of opposite personality traits, even assuming they could rightfully be ascribed to any or all people, is how do we know that the choices we are forced to make in this test apply for all time to a given person? (See the above-referenced article on the problems accurate measurements in the Myers-Briggs Temperament Indicator. For example, 50 percent of those taking the test had a different personality result only weeks later.) I could be cooperative this week but competitive next week. I could be cooperative at a picnic, family gathering, or church activity or ministry, but be competitive at church softball games or Bible quizzes. Or I could change again when I got married . . . got a job, had kids. All of one's traits could be in a constant state of flux throughout your life. And again assuming these criteria can be even applied to a schematic, how is Warren so certain that the same personality traits are automatically applied to a person after they are born again as they were before they were born again? Jung devised his terms like Introvert/Extrovert and Thinker/Feeler for what he deemed a "normal" individual. So what is an abnormal person? What personality profile would Rick Warren advise that we give an abnormal person? And how and where did he acquire the criteria or empirical data?

Now let us assume for the moment that all of Warren's definitions of his personality traits are legitimate and that there really are only four or five couplets to choose from and that his couplets truly represent polar opposites. Let us also assume that we know how we are balanced and that we even know what normal means. There still remains at least one more major hurdle to even begin to qualify his personality theory to perform any real road test. That is, how does Warren determine that his couplet choices are equally weighted? After all, to balance a scale, don't you need to have equal weight on both sides? And if the weights aren't equivalent, you must add or subtract weight from one side so that the scales balance. For example, the value of a professional sports figure is determined by supply and demand and how much he is worth to a given team or the sport in general if he or she is not in a team sport. Judging in ice skating, for example, uses weighted scores. So to use this analogy, how do we know that Introvert weighted value is worth 50 percent and Extrovert weighted value is worth 50 percent? Why wouldn't Introvert personality type weigh in at 75 percent and Extrovert 25 percent? Then let us assume that Warren has it right with each of his four or five menu-driven couplets and that each of the couplets is properly weighted. How do you then weigh each couplet choice against the weighted value of another couplet? For example, how would you know that choosing Introvert over Extrovert would weigh in equally to the next couplet of Self-Expressive vs. Self-Controlled? Do all four or five couplets weigh equally? The fact is, Warren doesn't know, he doesn't supply any empirical data to back up his claims, and he gives misapplied scriptures to support his personality schematic. The bottom line is that his personality schematic is absurd and preposterous at best and occultic at worst.

Forced Choices and Church Discipline

Now if an attendee of Rick Warren's Saddleback Church does not complete this profile they can't become a member of his church. That is still another most troubling attribute of his SHAPE questionnaire. Should the attendee take the profile, then they meet with an advisor, mentor, or church leader in charge of this program at the church for an interview to evaluate their profile to "plug" them into the "right" ministry. How is this advisor going to evaluate, let alone enforce these impossible choices in the personality profile to complete the SHAPE test for a person's service and purpose determination for God?

Finally, even if these traits were all verifiable and, in fact, do exist in bipolar pairs, so what? What could they possibly tell us about the leading of the Holy Spirit, or how to obey Christ's commands? If somehow we even needed this secret information about our personality, wouldn't God supply all our needs because we first sought the Kingdom of God? And how does this information contribute to our sanctification?

In a dialogue I had with Erik Rees, who is one of the pastors administrating SHAPE at Rick Warren's own church, Erik Rees flatly denies any connection of Rick Warren's SHAPE to Carl Jung, in spite of the terms taken right from Rick Warren's book[117] that Carl Jung either coined or developed into his personality theory: Introvert, Extrovert, Feelers, Thinkers.

In my appeal to Saddleback Church, I inserted other useful Jung terms for context and clarity (but the main terms that Rick Warren uses I retained). Here is the e-mail I received back from Pastor Erik Rees at Saddleback:

> SHAPE is originated by Pastor Rick Warren, our senior pastor . . . not Carl Jung. There are NO connections between the two and there is absolutely no reason to try to connect them." 10/19/2004
> —Erik Rees
> Pastor of Ministry & Small Group Leadership Development
> Saddleback Church
> 1 Saddleback Parkway
> Lake Forest, CA 92630
> 949-609-8301
> *erikr@saddleback.net*
> *www.saddlebackfamily.com/ministry*

Here is my response to him:

> Dear Erik,
> I don't know why you simply can't tell the truth about Carl Jung's connection to Rick Warren's SHAPE.
> Here is **Carl Jung's own glossary** of just some of the terms or temperament profiling you have in your SHAPE program and in Rick Warren's Purpose Driven Church which I sent you and have printed out. And this is just the tip of the iceberg. These ideas and many others are also integrated into the 12-Step program. If it were not for the 12-Step program, there would be no such thing as Celebrate Recovery.
> *Ego*: Freud's term for the aspect of the "psyche" that processes

---

117. Ibid., p. 245.

a person's "conscious" perception of reality. In a healthy person, it also controls the "id," so that satisfaction occurs only in socially acceptable and/or personally meaningful forms, and decides when to obey or disobey the "superego."

Introvert: Jung's word for the "type" of person who normally adapts to new situations by focusing "psychic" energy inwardly (e.g., through self-reflection and inner experience). (Contrasts with "extravert.")

Extravert: Jung's word for the "type" of person who normally adapts to new situations by focusing "psychic" energy on the external object (e.g., by being immersed in a social life). (Contrasts with "introvert." Also spelled "extrovert.")

Feeling: One of the four basic "personality" functions in Jung's theory of "types." A rational process whereby judgment is based on a thing's *value*. (Contrasts with "thinking.")

Personality: An individual person's unique "conscious" and "unconscious" ways of adjusting to the environment and organizing his or her life. For Jung, personality is the expression of a "Self."

Self: The inner core of a person's "personality." For Jung, "Self" refers to a person's *whole* "personality" and represents the ultimate goal of the "individuation" process.

Soul: The non-physical aspect of human nature, believed by Plato and many others to be immortal. Philosophers often identify it with the mind, treating it as a "thinking" substance. Theologians often associate the soul with the "spirit." (See "anima" and "psyche.")

Thinking: One of the four basic "personality" functions in Jung's theory of "types." A rational process whereby judgment is based on what a thing *is*. (Contrasts with "feeling.")

Type: Jung's term for the natural tendency of a person's "psychological" disposition, as determined by the way he or she deals with "psychic" energy (as either an "extravert" or an "introvert") and by the person's dominant function (i.e., either "thinking," "feeling," "sensation," or "intuition"). A person's type is especially noticeable by observing how he or she copes with new or stressful situations. Subsequent theorists have shown how Jung's theory defines 16 distinct types.

Unconscious: The aspect of a person's "psyche" consisting of everything that is not easily accessible to the immediate field of awareness. Freud relates the unconscious primarily to the "id," though the "ego" and "superego" are also partially unconscious. Jung gives the unconscious both a personal aspect (unique to each individual) and a collective aspect (shared by all humans). (Contrasts with "conscious.") (*www.hkbu.edu.hk/~ppp/dow/dowglos. html*).

Kindest regards in Christ,
James Sundquist

So, it is nothing short of astonishing that Saddleback would deny any connection to Carl Jung in their SHAPE personality profile. Many of the authors that Rick Warren recommends and/or quotes such as Richard Foster and Gary Thomas consistently are quoting and endorsing the teaching of Carl Jung.

Here is another church that uses Warren's SHAPE profile: *www. firstchurch.ca/pdf/Ministry%20301.pdf.*

This is the longest Rick Warren SHAPE questionnaire I have found to date. It is sixty-eight pages long.

Other Pagan Influences to Warren's Personality Theory

Rick Warren goes on to suggest that "Peter was a sanguine," "Paul was a choleric," and "Jeremiah was a melancholy." This is based on the Greek pagan ideas of four humors, the fourth being "phlegmatic." Rick Warren offers no scripture to prove this, and even if he did, it would have to presume that the Greek pagan philosophy and mythology on which it is based (which Paul opposed) were true. Rick Warren goes on to say that "There is no 'right' or 'wrong' temperament for ministry" . . . the exact terminology used in all of the psychological personality profile tests. But the word "phlegmatic" means sluggish, lazy, slothful, or sluggard. Definition of *phlegmatic* in **Webster Dictionary**: "Not easily excited to action or passion; cold; dull; sluggish; heavy; as, a phlegmatic person."

If being a sluggard is neither right nor wrong, then why are there six proverbs which describe it as a wicked trait vs. a righteous trait? If it is neither a positive or negative quality, then why is the word "slothful" used fifteen times throughout the Old and New Testaments?

Chapter Twelve

Judgment and Separation

"DAY 17 – A Place to Belong" begins on page 130

As you approach the end of this book, many of you may be asking questions like: "How could we not have known?" or "How could we have been so deceived?" And from all of the host of appeals coming into our ministry, many are now asking the same question: "What should we do now? Is it too late?" Regarding what you should do, the word is *flee!* Now, I would recommend that you warn as many of your brothers and sisters in Christ at your church and elsewhere, as well as your pastors and elders that they too might heed the warning. But this should take place swiftly and you should not linger long. Scripture is clear when it compares spiritual harlotry to literal harlotry in saying that we are to flee fornication. So, if we are to flee literal fornication, we must likewise flee spiritual fornication. We should flee just as fast as Joseph fled Potiphar's wife . . . not even worrying about losing a coat in the process. Proverbs 7 gives us a great graphic picture of this "strange woman." Revelation 17 also gives us a clear picture of the Mother of Harlots, and though it would also apply to literal harlotry, the force of these passages is spiritual harlotry.

Rick Warren says: The body of Christ is to "admonish each other." [118]

Yet Rick Warren himself refuses correction, having been admonished by a number of ministries. He invites you to e-mail him in his

---

118. Ibid., pp. 134–135.

book, but he has never once responded to my appeals by e-mail. It is ironic that he would advise that if you know people who have wandered from the truth to go after them (he quotes the Book of James), yet when God-fearing brothers take his advice to go after him, he refuses to respond! He touts the spiritual protection of godly leaders. But what protection can his false teaching provide? What protection is he providing with the false teachers he endorses and promotes and does not mark as false teachers, such as I and many others have documented in this commentary. What protection is provided by his working directly with Dr. Robert Schuller, who has redefined the foundational doctrines of the apostles once and for all delivered to the saints, such as "sin" and "hell"? (See resources on Schuller at the end of this document).

❋   ❋   ❋

Rick Warren: "God warns us over and over not to criticize, compare, or judge each other. . . . Whenever I judge another believer, four things instantly happen: I lose fellowship with God, I expose my own pride and insecurity, I set myself up to be judged by God, and I harm the fellowship of the church." [119]

Many have asked what problems I had with any of Rick Warren's specific purposes. Well, I don't even agree with his first purpose. In fact, we don't even have to proceed past Mr. Warren's Purpose One, which is: "You Were Planned for God's Pleasure," because it is found nowhere in Scripture. So if somehow, you have gotten this far in his book and still have not rejected it outright, this should give you grounds. We do find God's purpose for man in the following scripture, and note that there is only one purpose, not five.

> Everyone who is called by my name, Whom I have created for my glory; I have formed him, yes, I have made him"
>
> —Isaiah 43:7

This statement is under his Purpose Three section, "You Were Created

---

119. Ibid., pp. 163–164.

to Become Like Christ." Except for the connotation that the Word of Faith Movement gives this phrase that we can become gods and can do what God does, I can agree that we are to be conformed to His image and will be like Him when Christ returns. But if we are to be like Christ, we must obey Him and His Scripture. Teaching untruths are not in obedience to God.

Yes, there are scriptures that teach us not to judge, but Rick Warren is leaving out the scriptures that *do* teach us to judge and how to judge. Rick Warren's teaching that we are not to criticize or judge each other (that you and I can "agree to disagree") does not conform with a host of scriptures, commanding us to correct, admonish, reprove, rebuke, and in some cases even rebuke sharply.

Ezekiel's watchman passage applies to a righteous man, not just to Ezekiel. We can "agree to disagree" with nonessentials such as diet and days of the week; however, we can't agree to disagree about fundamental doctrine. We are commanded to contend for the faith once and for all delivered to the saints. If these deeds are purely subjective, then how are we to obey God's Word, thereby exposing and reproving the deeds of darkness? And if we don't follow God's Word in this matter, then what person is it who can judge?

Here are some of the scriptures that collide with Rick Warren's advice:

This witness is true. Wherefore **rebuke** them **sharply**, that they may be sound in the faith.

—Titus 1:13

A man that is an heretick after the first and second admonition reject.

—Titus 3:10

Now I beseech you, brethren, *mark* them which cause divisions and offences contrary to the doctrine which ye have learned; and avoid them.

—Romans 16:17

Does this scripture sound like, "It's the devil's job to blame, complain, and criticize members of God's family," as Rick Warren advises?

> Beloved, believe not every spirit, but try the spirits whether they are of God: because many false prophets are gone out into the world.
>
> —1 John 4:1

Again, does this scripture sound like, "It's the devil's job to blame, complain, and criticize members of God's family," as Rick Warren states?

> Now the Spirit speaketh expressly, that in the latter times some shall depart from the faith, giving heed to seducing spirits, and **doctrines of devils.**
>
> —1 Timothy 4:1

I don't know how many times I have heard the expression, "Don't criticize what God is blessing," in defense of Rick Warren's teachings and movement. This presumes, of course, that Warren's teachings and movement are indeed being blessed of God! Defending Mr. Warren by using the above expression also has a distinct way of silencing any who would speak out against him!

However, we have a clearly different example in Scripture. The apostle Paul criticized Peter because he was clearly in the wrong, and Paul acted righteously in opposing him. According to Warren's warning (above) Peter should not have experienced further blessings, and Paul would suffer because he judged and criticized Peter! And we know by God's Word that neither of these things is true.

Furthermore, Paul did not expose his pride or lose fellowship with God. He did not set himself up to be judged by God. And he certainly did not harm the fellowship of the church by opposing Peter, Hymenaus, and Alexander, and many others whom he named, as Rick Warren confesses were his consequences for acting in the same manner. Paul's criticism not did not harm the church, but safeguarded the church, as he opposed these men *publicly* before the whole church that *all* might fear the Lord.

Upon inquiring of the various ministries and individuals who have challenged or opposed Rick Warren's teaching, I learned that these Christians (who were simply trying to be good Bereans in searching the Scriptures to see if these things be so) have often been accused of: attacking a brother or sister in the Lord, bashing, smearing, touching God's anointed, not following Matthew 18, etc. It is getting to the point that even with the meekest and gentlest and kindest of voices you cannot and dare not correct or reprove a Christian leader.

I am desperate to know if there is ever *any* situation in which these people think that correcting, opposing, and rebuking is *not* harmful.

Furthermore, it does *not* mean those who obey God by correcting a church leader are like the devil, the accuser of the brethren, as Rick Warren suggests. Rather, they are actually helping these leaders and the church.

Regarding guilt by association, I am sure you are familiar with the doctrine of separation. Simply put, it is that we are not to form alliances with ungodly counsel and known false teachers such as Robert Schuller. (See resource on Schuller at the end of this book.) We are not to be co-laborers or teachers with them, as Warren is doing, but rather expose and reprove them and separate from them so we do not share in their sins. But it is not just guilt by association, it is guilt by identification, guilt by promoting them, guilt by quoting a number of false teachers who all share the same heresies (the Catholic mystics I named, many of whom repeatedly also quote and endorse Carl Jung, for example), it is guilt by never giving any disclaimer to their well-known false teachings which permeate their books, it is guilt by being confronted with promoting these false teachers, and still not repenting or disclaiming them. Paul repeatedly teaches on guilt by association and the Old Testament backs it up with its teaching on unholy alliances. The Scripture warns us that the wrong companions will corrupt good character (1 Cor. 15:33).

I do know of examples of people being kicked out of churches because they simply opposed Warren's teaching (we are talking about God-fearing families). I can produce the transcript of a church even using Matthew 18 to remove them. I can document another brother who was kicked out of a Rick Warren Bible study because he simply brought his King James and pointed out time after time where the Bible study collided with both the text and the doctrines of the apostles. I also refer you to the article where 165 members were ousted from their church for opposing Rick Warren's Purpose Driven Life program (see page 194).

❈   ❈   ❈

Rick Warren: "When you're busy serving, you don't have time to be critical." [120]

Aren't you serving when you critique and test a prophecy? Aren't you serving while being critical when you need to rebuke or even rebuke harshly, which the apostle Paul said would sometimes be necessary? Isn't a Christian who is a discerner of spirits serving? How do you test the spirits to see if they are of God without being critical if they are not of God? Mr. Warren also talks about practicing your gifts in order to get good at them. Are we then to imagine getting the Holy Spirit gift of discerner of spirits in which a prophecy is 10 percent accurate at first, then with practice we get it up to 30 percent, or even 90 percent? Of course not. A prophecy must be 100 percent accurate immediately, or it is to be deemed *not* of God. Wasn't even Paul critical of Peter when he opposed him? Was Paul not serving the church even then?

❈   ❈   ❈

Rick Warren quotes Romans 14:4 (GWT): "Who are you to criticize someone else's servant." [121]

The correct word here should be "**judge**." But if you carefully examine this passage, you will see that Paul is speaking about judging another man's servant because of his diet. There are a host of other passages in which Paul instructs us how to judge things within the church. Isn't Matthew 18 a process of church discipline, which requires making judgments about a brother? Of course, no man can judge another man's eternal destiny; that is up to God. And isn't it

---

120. Ibid., p. 268.
121. Ibid., p. 268.

somewhat hypocritical of Rick Warren to admonish his readers to not criticize a brother while he has built his whole "New Reformation" on criticizing the methods of a host of other Christians and denominations in this book, in his preaching, and in his *Purpose Driven Church* book?

❉ ❉ ❉

Rick Warren: **"It is not our job to defend ourselves against criticism."** [122]

Of course it is, particularly when it is an issue of false teaching or promoting false teachers. The apostle Paul commended the Bereans for making sure what he was saying could be found in the Scripture. He even invited the Galatian church to oppose him if he preached another gospel. Paul was always defending himself against those who opposed him, many of whom were his own Hebrew people. And don't we as Christians need to be always **ready** to **give** a **defense** to everyone who asks for the reason of our hope in Christ Jesus (1 Pet. 3:15). Using Rick Warren's logic, Jesus would not have defended himself against His critics for wasting the costly ointment that Mary put on Jesus' feet (John 12:1–8). Read the account to see whether or not Jesus defended himself against this criticism.

Finally, isn't Rick Warren unrighteously judging another Christian when he first assesses whether or not they can even become a member of his church, and when he later removes them from membership if they fail to participate in his plans?

One of the best articles I have ever read that refutes Rick Warren's position that Christians should not judge Christians is entitled "Is It Right to Judge?" by *Franklin C. Buling,* with a quote at the end by **Horatius Bonar.** We are grateful to the Fundamental Evangelistic Association for giving us permission to reprint this article:

Is It Right to Judge ?

THIS QUESTION—"IS IT RIGHT TO JUDGE?" is one that puzzles many sincere Christians. A careful and open minded study of the Bible makes it clear that concerning certain vital matters, it

---

122. Ibid., p. 268.

is not only right but a positive duty to judge. Many do not know that the Scripture commands us to judge.

The Lord Jesus Christ commanded, "Judge righteous judgment" (John 7:24). He told a man, "Thou hast rightly judged" (Luke 7:43). To others, our Lord asked, "Why even of yourselves judge ye not what is right?" (Luke 12:57).

The Apostle Paul wrote, "I speak as to wise men; judge ye what I say" (1 Corinthians 10:15). Again, Paul declared, "He that is spiritual judgeth all things" (1 Corinthians 2:15). It is our positive duty to judge.

False Teachers and False Teaching

"Beware of false prophets!" (Matthew 7:15) is the warning and command of our Lord. But how could we "beware" and how could we know they are "false prophets" if we did not judge? And what is the God given standard by which we are to judge? "To the Law and to the Testimony: if they speak not according to this word, it is because there is no light in them." (Isaiah 8:20). "Ye shall know them by their fruits" (Matthew 7:16), Christ said. And in judging the "fruits," we must judge by God's Word, not by what appeals to human reasoning. Many things seem good to human judgment which are false to the Word of God.

The Apostle Paul admonished believers, "Now I beseech you, brethren, mark them which cause divisions and offences contrary to the doctrine which ye have learned; and avoid them. For they that are such serve not our Lord Jesus Christ, but their own belly; and by good words and fair speeches deceive the hearts of the simple" (Romans 16:17–18). This apostolic command could not be obeyed were it not right to judge. God wants us to know His Word and then test all teachers and teaching by it. Notice also that it is the false teachers who make the "divisions," and not those who protest against their false teaching. And these deceivers are not serving Christ, as they profess, "but their own belly," or their own "bread and butter," as we would put it. We are to "mark them and avoid them."

"Come out from among them, and be ye separate, saith the Lord" (2 Corinthians 6:17, read verses 14–18), and "From such turn away" (2 Timothy 3:5). "Withdraw yourselves" (2 Thessalonians 3:6). "And have no fellowship with the unfruitful works of darkness, but rather reprove them" (Ephesians 5:11). "Abhor that which is evil; cleave to that which is good" (Romans 12:9). "Prove all things; hold fast that which is good" (1 Thessalonians 5:21). It would be impossible to obey these injunctions of God's Word unless it were right to judge! And remember, nothing is "good" in God's sight that is not true to His Word.

The Apostle John wrote, "Beloved, believe not every spirit, but try [test, judge] the spirits whether they are of God: because many false prophets are gone out into the world" (1 John 4:1). Again he wrote, "For many deceivers are entered into the world, who confess not that Jesus Christ is come in the flesh. . . . If there come any unto you, and bring not this doctrine, receive him not into your house, neither bid him God speed: For he that biddeth him God speed is partaker of his evil deeds" (2 John 7, 10–11). This Scripture commands us to judge between those who do, and those who do not bring the true doctrine of Christ.

Whenever a child of God contributes to a denominational budget that supports Modernist (liberal, compromising) missionaries or teachers, he is guilty before God, according to this Scripture, of bidding them, "God speed " in the most effective way possible. And he thereby becomes a "partaker" with them of their "evil deeds" of spreading soul damning poison. How terrible, but how true! Arouse yourself, child of God. If you are guilty, ask God to forgive you and help you never again to be guilty of the blood of souls for whom Christ died. When we are willing to suffer for Christ, we can readily see the truth of God's Word on this tremendously important matter. "If we suffer, we shall also reign with Him" (2 Timothy 2:12).

Misunderstood and Misused Scripture

One of the best known and most misunderstood and misapplied Scriptures is "Judge not" (Matthew 7:1). Let us examine the entire passage:

"Judge not, that ye be not judged. For with what judgment ye judge, ye shall be judged: and with what measure ye mete, it shall be measured to you again. And why beholdest thou the mote that is in thy brother's eye, but considerest not the beam that is in thine own eye? Or how wilt thou say to thy brother, Let me pull out the mote out of thine eye; and, behold, a beam is in thine own eye? Thou hypocrite, first cast out the beam out of thine own eye; and then shalt thou see clearly to cast out the mote out of thy brother's eye" (Matthew 7:1–5).

Read this again carefully. Notice that it is addressed to a hypocrite!—not to those who sincerely want to discern whether a teacher or teaching is true or false to God's Word. And instead of being a prohibition against honest judgment, it is a solemn warning against hypocritical judgment. In fact, the last statement of this Scripture commands sincere judgment—"Then shalt thou see clearly to cast out the mote out of thy brother's eye." If we take a verse or a part of a verse out of its setting, we can make the Word of God appear to teach the very opposite of what it really does teach. And those who do this cannot escape the judgment of God for twisting His Word (2 Peter 3:16). Let this be a warning to us never again to take a text of Scripture out of its context.

Many who piously quote, "Judge not," out of its context, in order to defend that which is false to God's Word, do not see their own inconsistency in thus judging those who would obey God's Word about judging that which is untrue to the Bible. It is tragic that so much that is anti-Scriptural has undeservedly found shelter behind a misuse of the Scripture just quoted. The reason the professed church of Christ is today honeycombed and paralyzed by satanic Modernism is because Christians have not obeyed the commands of God's Word to judge and put away and separate from false teachers and false teaching when they first appeared in their midst. Physical health is maintained by separation from disease germs. Spiritual health is maintained by separation from germs of false doctrine. The greatest peril of our day is not too much judging, but too little judging of spiritual falsehood.

God wants His children to be like the noble Bereans who "searched the Scriptures daily, whether those things were so" (Acts 17:11).

Romans 2:1–3 is also addressed to the religious hypocrite who condemned himself because he was guilty of the same things for which he condemned others. James 4:11–12 refers to an evil spirit of backbiting and fault finding, not to judging whether teachers or teachings agree or disagree with God's Word. The Bible never contradicts itself. To understand one portion of Scripture we must view it in the light of all Scripture. "No prophecy of the Scripture is of any private [isolated] interpretation" (2 Peter 1:20). "Comparing spiritual things [words] with spiritual" (1 Corinthians 2:13).

The "Wheat and Tares" parable of Matthew 13:24–30, 36–43, is much misunderstood. First of all, our Lord is talking about the world, not His Church—"the field is the world." He goes on to say that "the good seed are the children of the Kingdom; but the tares are the children of the wicked one" (Matthew 13:38). They are the two groups in the world; children of God—those who have received Christ (John 1:12), and the children of the devil—those who reject Christ (John 8:44). When any of the "children of the wicked one" get into the professed church of Christ, as they have always done, a definite procedure for God's children is set forth in His Word. First, it is their duty to tell them that they have "neither part nor lot" in Christ (see Acts 8:21–23 and context).

If the children of the devil do not leave voluntarily, as is generally the case, God's children are commanded to "purge out" (1 Corinthians 5:7) these unbelievers. But God's people have disobeyed His Word about this, and so unbelievers [and disobedient brethren—2 Thessalonians 3:6, 14–15] have gotten into control, as is now the case in most denominations. Therefore, those who purpose to be true to Christ and His Word are commanded to "come out from among them, and be ye separate, saith the Lord" (2 Corinthians 6:17), regardless of property or any other considerations. When we obey God's Word, we can trust Him to take care of all the consequences of our obedience.

Other Matters to be Judged

The immoral conduct of professed believers in Christ is to be judged. 1 Corinthians, Chapter 5, tells a sad story and closes with the Apostolic injunction, "Therefore put away from among yourselves that wicked person" (1 Corinthians 5:13).

Disputes between Christians concerning "things that pertain to this life" (1 Corinthians 6:3), should be judged by a tribunal of fellow Christians instead of going before unbelievers in the civil courts. The whole sixth chapter of 1 Corinthians makes clear God's plan for His people in this regard. And some startling truths are here revealed: First, "The saints shall judge the world." Second, "We shall judge angels" (1 Corinthians 6:2–3). Beloved, are we letting God prepare us for this high place?

We ought to judge ourselves. "Examine yourselves, whether ye be in the faith; prove your own selves" (2 Corinthians 13:5). "For if we would judge ourselves, we should not be judged. But when we are judged, we are chastened [child trained] of the Lord, that we should not be condemned with the world" (1 Corinthians 11:31–32). What a change and what a blessing it would be if we would judge our own faults as uncharitably as we do the faults of others—and if we would judge the failings of others as charitably as we do our own! And Christians could save themselves much chastening of the Lord if they would judge and confess and cease their disobedience to God. And, oh, how much dishonor and lack of fruit would our blessed Lord be spared!

Limitations of Human Judgment

Not scruples or conscience concerning matters of which the Bible does not directly speak. God forbids our judging our brethren concerning the eating of certain kinds of food, keeping of days, etc. Romans, Chapter 14, 1 Corinthians 10:23–33, and Colossians 2:16–17 cover this subject.

Not motives. See 1 Corinthians 4:1–5. Only God can see into the heart and know the motives that underlie actions.

Not as to whom are saved. "The Lord knoweth them that are His" (2 Timothy 2:19). We cannot look into anyone's heart and say whether or not they have accepted the Lord Jesus Christ as their personal Saviour, if they profess that they have. But we had better test ourselves according to 2 Corinthians 5:17: "If any man be in Christ, he is a new creature: old things are passed away; behold, all things are become new." If this change has not taken place, our profession is vain.

Two Elements in Judgment

The New Testament Greek word that is most often translated "judge" or "judgment" is "*krino.*" On the one hand, it means to distinguish, to decide, to determine, to conclude, to try, to think and to call in question. That is what God wants His children to do as to whether preachers, teachers, and their teachings are true or false to His Word. The Apostle Paul writes: "And this I pray, that your love may abound yet more and more in knowledge and in all judgment; that ye may approve things that are excellent" (Philippians 1:9–10). A wrong idea of love and lack of knowledge and judgment causes God's people often to approve things that are anything but excellent in God's sight. The epistle to the Hebrews tells us that mature believers, that is, those who are of "full age," are ". . . those who by reason of use have their senses exercised to discern both good and evil" (see Hebrews 5:11–14).

On the other hand, the Greek word "*krino*"—judge or judgment—means to condemn, to sentence, and to punish. This is God's prerogative for He has said, "Vengeance is Mine, I will repay, saith the Lord" (Romans 12:19).

Guard Against a Wrong Attitude

Christians should guard against the tendency of the flesh to assume a critical and censorious attitude toward those who do not share our opinions about other matters than those which have to do with Bible doctrine and moral conduct. Rather than "pick to pieces" our brethren in Christ, it is our privilege and duty to do everything we can to encourage their spiritual edification. We ought to love and pray for one another and consider ourselves lest we be tempted. Galatians 6:1.

A Final Word

If you are saved, my reader, let us not forget that "We must all appear before the Judgment Seat of Christ" (2 Corinthians 5:10). It will be well with those who are studying God's Word, walking in the light of it, living for Christ and the salvation of souls. It will go ill with those who have accepted Christ but who are living for the things of this world. If you are a mere professor of Christ, or profess nothing, my friend, may I lovingly remind you "That judgment must begin at the House of God; and if it first begin at us, what shall the end be of them that obey not the Gospel?" (1 Peter 4:17).

Delay not another moment to ask God for Christ's sake to forgive your sins. Surrender your heart and will to the loving Saviour who died for you and rose again. Make Him the Lord of your life. Happy and blessed will you be, now and forever.

—by Franklin C. Buling, MA

For there is some danger of falling into a soft and effeminate Christianity, under the plea of a lofty and ethereal theology. Christianity was born for endurance; not an exotic, but a hardy plant, braced by the keen wind; not languid, nor childish, nor cowardly. It walks with strong step and erect frame; it is kindly, but firm; it is gentle, but honest; it is calm, but not facile; obliging, but not imbecile; decided, but not churlish. It does not fear to speak the stern word of condemnation against error, nor to raise its voice against surrounding evils, under the pretext it is not of this world; it does not shrink from giving honest reproof, lest it come under the charge of displaying an unchristian spirit. It calls sin sin, on whomsoever it is found, and would rather risk the accusation of being actuated by a bad spirit than not discharge an explicit duty. Let us not misjudge strong words used in honest controversy. Out of the heat a viper may come forth but we shake it off and feel no harm. The religion of both Old and New Testaments is marked by fervent outspoken testimonies against evil. To speak smooth things in such a case may be sentimentalism, but it is not Christianity. It is a betrayal of the cause of truth and righteousness. If anyone should be frank, manly, honest, cheerful (I do not say blunt or rude, for a Christian must be courteous and polite); it is he who has tasted that the Lord is gracious, and is looking for and hasting unto the coming of the day of God I know that charity covereth a multitude of sins; but it does not call evil good, because a good man has done it; it does not excuse inconsistencies, because the inconsistent brother has a high name and a fervent spirit; crookedness and worldliness are still crookedness and worldliness, though exhibited in one who seems to have reached no common height of attainment.

—Horatius Bonar (1808-89)

Fundamental Evangelistic Association
P.O. Box 6278
Los Osos, California 93412 U.S.A.
Telephone 805-528-3534 : Fax 805-528-4971
—www.cnview.com/on_line_resources/is_it_right_to_judge.htm

[Reprinted by Permission by Fundamental Evangelistic Association]

Conclusion

In the end, it is not so much what I think the purposes of the church and what one's personal purpose should be; rather it is what Scripture says they should be. Please weigh Rick Warren's book in light of Scripture. I have devoted 272 pages to give you very precise details.

God's purposes are revealed in Scripture. God's purposes are worked out in our lives by His ordained means of grace (preaching of the Word being primary, see Acts 2:42), not by means of Warren's man-made techniques. If Warren's "purposes" are nothing more than basic truths of the Scripture then why do we need his method? Don't all people who are converted have the same basic purposes and are not those purposes fulfilled by God's ongoing work of grace by His ordained means? If so, then Warren's whole program is thwarting God's purposes by keeping people away from the means of grace, since it effectively crowds out the focus on the Bible in churches.

Finally, I conclude with the words of Scripture which were sent to me by a family who was caught in Rick Warren's snare in their church. This family was in this church for eleven years before being set free. "In all thy ways acknowledge him, and he shall direct thy paths" (Prov. 3:6).

"Thy paths" are both the church's purpose and our personal purpose. We can do both without Rick Warren's *Purpose Driven Life* book. And we can guard our hearts and minds against all of his false teachings and the false teachers, whom he promotes and works with by avoiding his book, by exposing the errors and heresies in the book, and by trusting completely the sufficiency of Scripture to find our personal purpose.

Two great scriptures in the Bible which affirm that Scripture alone (*Sola Scriptura*) will help you determine Christ's purpose in you are:

> Whereby, **when ye read, ye may understand** my knowledge in the mystery of Christ.
>
> —Ephesians 3:4

along with:

> According to the eternal purpose which he **purposed in Christ Jesus our Lord.**
>
> —Ephesians 3:11

So Paul was telling the saints in the early church they could understand the mystery of Christ and His purpose in them simply by reading the Scripture. That was the key. Rick Warren needs to focus on this key.

We are to worship the Lord in spirit and truth. In fact, if we don't tell the truth, Psalm 66:18 tells us that the Lord will not even hear us because we have regarded iniquity in our heart (falsehood is iniquity). So we should not be regarding Rick Warren. "If I regard iniquity in my heart, the Lord will not hear me" (Ps. 66:18).

I pray that everyone takes heed to these words and helps bring this Rick Warren campaign to a complete halt before it is too late!

Chapter Thirteen

Frequently Asked Questions by Pastors and Churches Using Rick Warren's *Purpose Drive Life* and SHAPE

You might be very surprised to know that most of the main issues raised in this book regarding Rick Warren's teachings have already been presented to various pastors of various denominations who have implemented his *Purpose Driven Life* book and campaign. But you may be even more surprised to learn that even after clearly documenting a host of his false translations, false teachings, and the false teachers he promotes, that even then these pastors would still try to defend him and simply refuse correction.

This chapter is devoted to presenting many of the rationalizations and excuses used by pastors to insist on continuing on the same present course. The same questions and reasonings kept coming up repeatedly. I have not included the letters of scorn, retaliation, and ridicule we have received, nor any of the names I have been called. I must hasten to add, however, that we have also received letters from many Christians who are very grateful bringing this truth to light regarding Rick Warren's teachings. We have endeavored to answer questions in light of Scripture and close every loophole that has come up. This is very important because readers are going to be faced with many of the very same questions and defenses were you to approach your own church or pastor, and you will need to be armed with the truth in order to give a good defense of the faith.

I know many of you might be afraid that you are going to hurt the pastor. But remember this, you will only be hurting him and your congregation if you remain silent. So in fighting the good fight of faith, just recall the apostle Paul's own words: "Am I therefore become your enemy, because I tell you the truth?" (Gal. 4:16).

Question or Comment

We are not presently using the SHAPE tests. We are putting them on the back burner, for now, so what's wrong with that?

Response

If you are offering the *Purpose Driven Life* book at all, you are promoting his SHAPE. SHAPE is the heart of his book and the schematic for finding your purpose in Warren's eyes. To remove SHAPE is like offering a hamburger to someone, then handing them just the buns . . . that is, if you think it is purely an accessory to his *Purpose Driven Life* book. But, in fact, it is not an accessory; it is the heart and soul of his philosophy and program. The meat of Warren's hamburger has Mad Cow's Disease. So whether or not you think you are withholding SHAPE because you are just offering the *Purpose Driven Life* book alone, they will nevertheless still be receiving SHAPE, and therefore still consuming the hamburger meat. And it is not just the "P" for the Personality Profile (in SHAPE) which is flawed, but Mr. Warren's theology behind the S, the H, the A, and the E (the rest of the SHAPE acronym) as you would see by going to that section of my commentary where it is described in detail.

As an example, SHAPE states: "Describe any experiences that have confirmed these spiritual gifts." Rick Warren seems to be implying that life experiences confirm our Spiritual Gifts. The word "experience" occurs twelve times in this test. Why are spiritual gifts tested by our subjective experience rather than testing the spirits against the objective Word of God? Are we to use our fallen and flawed memories to determine our perfect spiritual gift? Are these results supposed to be authoritative in addition to or above and beyond God's Word?

Pastors, are you proposing to offer the book to your congregation, and then remove or skip two chapters (i.e. Days 30 and 31) which specifically discuss SHAPE? Even if you were to do that, the philosophy in those chapters cannot be surgically removed from the book, as though the philosophies contained in them were not also permeated throughout the rest of the book. The cancer has already metastasized and is in the blood stream, the lymph nodes, and the major organs, etc.

> . . . Know ye not that a little leaven leaveneth the whole lump?
> Purge out therefore the old leaven, that ye may be a new lump, as
> ye are unleavened. . . . Therefore, let us keep the feast, not with
> the old leaven, neither with the leaven of malice and wickedness;
> but with the unleavened bread of sincerity and truth.
>
> —1 Corinthians 5:6–8

Even if you could somehow separate SHAPE and Celebrate Recovery from the book, Rick Warren's teachings in those programs make him a false teacher, so you can't then present this teacher or his teachings to your congregation. These programs (SHAPE and Celebrate Recovery) should not be put on the back burner, but directly into the fire, not unlike what the early Christians in the Book of Acts did.

❦   ❦   ❦

Question or Comment
Whether or not Warren is correct in stating what he states in his book, isn't his book still valuable to help us find our purpose?

Response
Stop right there! Play that sentence back again: ". . . whether or not Warren is correct"? If he is not correct with what he says the Bible is saying about each of his examples and characters drawn from the Bible, *then he is not telling the truth.* If he is not telling the truth about those passages, then he is a false teacher. There are times when any Bible teacher might make a mistake here or there, but that person should immediately correct himself when it is brought to his

attention. Warren has not been correctable. Whether something is true or false is what Christianity must be all about. Imagine repeating your statement about any prophet or teacher in the Bible ". . . whether or not Jeremiah's (or Peter's) statements are correct." There is no *not* correct. *It must be correct.* Anyone who professes to be a teacher, as Rick Warren is claiming to be, is held to a stricter accounting than Christians who are not teachers. So there is no room for introducing a teacher to your congregation who does not even teach the truth about the accounts of the forty-day biblical examples. You asked how God's purpose differs from Rick Warren's. Well, here is a perfect example. Rick Warren does not tell the truth, and God's purpose is to require him to!

A teacher must tell the truth, i.e., he must be correct in all statements about what the Bible actually says. And whether or not any errors are intentional, he must be subject to correction for those errors. To date, Rick Warren has refused correction in these matters. Furthermore, Erik Rees, his director of this program at his own church, Saddleback, has not correctly represented the connection of Carl Jung to Warren's personality profile and philosophy. The heart of orthodox Christianity is that Jesus is the Way, the *Truth,* and the Life. When Mr. Warren does not tell the biblical truth about his forty-day examples, and when he continues to promote them as though they were true, then he is acting totally contrary to the host of scriptures which condemn falsehood.

These glaringly obvious errors about the forty-day examples occur in his book even prior to Day 1 in his journey and they occur even before the page listing his covenant, which he signed with his name. Even a Christian who is not a scholar or pastor could easily detect these errors by being a good Berean and checking the facts of those forty-day examples.

※   ※   ※

Question or Comment
But have you personally witnessed any bad fruit coming out of *Purpose Driven Life?*

Response

Bad fruit has already occurred in many churches. Because you have introduced PDL to your congregation, there are people who already are very upset and who don't want to participate, and for very good biblical reasons. This is not a matter of simply disagreeing with a carpet color or the wattage of a light bulb in the sanctuary. There are plenty of biblical commentaries and study guides that you could use without causing any division or dissension. In fact, these have previously been used with your congregation.

There was a church that split, partly because there were two camps. One camp believed Scripture was sufficient for the churched and unchurched Harry and Mary, and the other camp insisted they had to follow Rick Warren's recipe. I have the transcripts of a trial of two families in a Baptist church in Minneapolis who were found guilty of opposing the leadership because the church was going fully *Purpose Driven Church*. When their church went PDL, these two families opposed Rick Warren's teachings and supplied the scriptural proof. The church pastor and elders then actually invoked Matthew 18 and held a trial. These families did not have a record of being divisive in this church, and this action against them was totally uncalled for. If anyone should have been brought before the congregation, it should have been the ones who introduced these destructive heresies, not the messengers who were deemed the enemies simply because they told the truth. For more insight in how Rick Warren teaches pastors how to deal with "resisters," I invite you to read Berit Kjos' article, "Dealing with Resisters" at *www.crossroad.to/articles2/04/4-purpose-resisters.htm*.

In case there remains any doubt what may happen to those who resist the Purpose Driven Life within a church which has launched this campaign, I invite you to read the following article entitled "165 members ousted from Gardendale Baptist" (in Corpus Christi, Texas on July 18, 2004). Source: *www.caller.com/ccct/local_news/article/0,1641,CCCT_811_3050141,00.html*.

The church office confirmed that they had launched Purpose Driven Life in the winter of 2004. And just as I have warned, members were removed because they did not swear absolute allegiance to the pastor (and his vision) and will not be restored to the church until they have signed another covenant of church unity—in other words, effectively the same covenant Rick Warren teaches and requires of his Saddleback Church members.

Another couple was forced out of their Reformed Christian Church near Cleveland, Ohio, one of whom was teaching a very good inductive Bible study to women and was asked to discontinue it because the church was going PDL/CGM. A friend of Pastor Bob Dewaay (in Minneapolis) was kicked out of his Bible study for simply pointing out what I did in verse after verse, because Warren's translations did not line up with Scripture.

I can name city after city around the U.S. where PDL *is* being forced on the church members, thanks to their pastors. In dismay, these Christians then look around their various cities for another church, only to discover that those churches have gone PDL, too.

You wanted a general observation. Well, in general, churches across the country are reading and implementing Rick Warren's book *without scrutiny*. They are like a deer caught in the headlights and are totally smitten. I find it rare that Christians are being good Bereans, regarding Warren's book. They are not even bothering to examine his textual errors against the facts of Scripture, which they might at least consider along with other books they teach in Sunday school.

Even more baffling is that thousands of pastors, who should know better, read the book and pass it right along to their congregations. These pastors should have caught all of Warren's glaring errors in his account of the forty-day examples, long before they even reached Day 1 in the book. In fact, these errors should be apparent to anyone who has read the Old Testament even once, let alone anyone who has taken any courses in Old Testament survey. Even more astonishing to me is that when I point out these errors to pastors, it still does not matter; they are going to proceed anyway! Rick Warren gets a free pass!

And now Rick Warren has become a judge on the Templeton Foundation Panel, and he will help determine what writer will receive the Templeton Foundation prize. That is certainly not good fruit (see:

www.letusreason.org/Curren40.htm).

Bad doctrine *is* bad fruit:

For the fruit of the Spirit is in all goodness and righteousness and *truth*.

—Ephesians 5:9

Ye shall know them by their fruits. Do men gather grapes of thorns, or figs of thistles? Even so every good tree bringeth forth good fruit; but a corrupt tree bringeth forth evil fruit. A good tree cannot bring forth evil fruit, neither can a corrupt tree bring forth good fruit.

—Matthew 7:16–18

This discussion in Matthew 7 leads here:

Therefore whosoever heareth these sayings of mine, and doeth them, I will liken him unto a wise man, which built his house upon a rock: . . . And every one that heareth these sayings of mine, and doeth them not, shall be likened unto a foolish man, which built his house upon the sand.

—Matthew 7:24, 26

It goes back to following the teachings of Jesus that are contained in the New Testament.

There is one more paramount concern that is related to bad fruit, but is very important because one might not witness any bad fruit for an extended season. And this concern is *consequences*. Whether or not there is any present bad fruit, there are still eternal consequences for promoting false teachers which you may not have to face until the Judgment Seat. Many Christians have tampered with Ouija boards, Enneagram, and horoscopes, and have used a similar argument or question you proposed: "Well, I tried these things and nothing bad happened to me. In fact, I even feel better." In other words, they did not experience any bad fruit . . . yet.

✖ ✖ ✖

Question or Comment
Since PDL (*Purpose Driven Life*) is an outcropping of PDC (*Purpose Driven Church*) and the center of that is Saddleback, what bad fruit have you personally seen coming from that church?

Response
This is an easy question to answer. One of their pastors, Erik Rees, is not telling the truth about the Jungian foundation in their personality profile. That PDL is an outcropping of PDC is hardly a very good credential. Robert Schuller, who is Rick Warren's mentor, endorses the PDC book. Given Schuller's endorsement alone, all Christians should flee for their lives from the foreword to that book. Mr. Warren has formed an unholy alliance with Robert Schuller, and Warren's participation in Schuller's Institute of Church Leadership serves to strengthen that false alloy. You say this is guilt by association, but I call it both the appearance of evil and the promotion of a clearly identified heretic!

How about the fact that Rick Warren has driven Bible preaching out of thousands of pulpits and Bible teaching out of thousands of Bible studies. I showed in my article that he tells people not to have Bible study and later tells them to study his book. How bad does it have to get? And now he is going to reform the worldwide church. Dr. Noah Hutchings of Southwest Church Radio, Pastor Bob Dewaay of the Twin City Fellowship in Minneapolis, many other discernment ministries, and I get calls or letters from all of the United States from people who cannot find a Bible preaching church now because Rick Warren's *Purpose Driven Church* and *Purpose Driven Life* have taken them over.

✖ ✖ ✖

Question or Comment
I'm sure there are dissenters that will disagree and leave Saddleback, so I'm not asking for their testimonies. I guess I'm asking from a broader perspective, how you personally have seen Saddleback Church as producing bad fruit.

Response

Bad fruit is not the only evidence of false teaching. False teaching can produce no fruit at all (whether good or bad) as we see in the scriptural example of Christ cursing the fig tree.

❊   ❊   ❊

Question or Comment

The paraphrases are generally attempts to reach a very specific demographic rather than a broad constituency. What's wrong with that?

Response

God is not a respecter of persons. And you have done no favors by offering one demographic an honest, accurate rendering and another demographic a false or distorted rendering. Every demographic should still get the same truth!!! Isn't it amazing that Paul used the same Hebrew Bible for the Old Testament to every demographic where he preached the Gospel, as well as the same Greek New Testament letters to every church in every city in every country he traveled . . . even telling them to exchange epistles with each other and read them to all the brothers.

❊   ❊   ❊

Question or Comment

Isn't there is a place for all of the Bible translations and/or paraphrases and, if used appropriately, valid uses in teaching people God's will for them from Scripture?

Response

Not if they have added to and subtracted from what the Scripture actually says and go beyond what is written . . . the very thing Paul opposed and other scriptures corroborate. And what do you mean by "used appropriately"? Isn't this a subjective test? Objective tests are what we use to determine what is "appropriate."

❊   ❊   ❊

Question or Comment

I have read both of Rick Warren's books, *Purpose Driven Church* and *Purpose Driven Life,* and I do not find that Warren has taught anything heretical.

Response

I find it inconceivable that you would not find anything heretical in either of Rick Warren's books when I have pointed out all of his false teachings, the false teachers he promotes, and the false translations he uses. In our correspondence you assert that the Greek and Hebrew meanings of words has changed. But you still seem to be rightfully clinging to meaning of heretic as the word is used in Greek in the New Testament. So I trust that you would agree that the word "heretic" should mean what the Bible says it means. It means exactly what it did when Paul penned the word. And the same false teachings that were current in Paul's day are the same false teachings alive and well today. Jesus said in Matthew 28:20:

> Teaching them to observe all things whatsoever I have commanded you: and, lo, I am with you **alway,** even unto the end of the world. Amen.

Would you agree that alway(s) always means always. There is no time when Jesus is not with us in spirit (though not physically). Jesus uses the Greek word *pas.* So even though you suggest that the Greek has changed, I would trust that you would also agree that Greek *pas* still means "always." Rick Warren has not observed all of the things Jesus has commanded in his teachings, as I prove in this book. And if he does not teach what the Bible says by repeatedly not telling the truth, departing from the truth is what constitutes being a heretic. Here is a perfect example which I have already described at the beginning of this book.

Rick Warren states: "**Whenever** God wanted to prepare someone for his purposes, he took forty days."

The word "whenever" is a virtual synonym for the word "always." There can be no exceptions. Therefore, there can *never* be a time when God did not take forty days to prepare someone for his purposes, that is if Rick Warren's statement constitutes absolute truth. In fact there is not even one time in Scripture when God took forty days to determine his purpose for a man. There is no example in Scripture to support this, and in all of the forty-day examples Rick Warren cites from Scripture do not bear record with the scriptural accounts themselves. What Rick Warren postulates would also have to be true and binding for Abraham, Paul, James, and every other person listed in the Bible. And why wouldn't Rick Warren give us a record or transcript in his book of when the forty-days transpired in Rick Warren's own life that God's purposes were determined for him? Forty days certainly were not the time frame God took for me to determine my purpose. Take a show of hands in your own congregation, or interview each member and ask them how many days, or even years it took for the planting and watering before God granted the increase or established their purpose.

Rick Warren compounds his error with another axiom of supposed absolute truth when he says: "The next forty days will transform your life" on the very next page (page 10 of his book). Telling the truth is a central core doctrine of orthodox Christianity. Anyone whose teachings do not line up with Scripture is a heretic. Rick Warren's teachings do not line up with Scripture, so this is what makes him a heretic. His book should be rejected even before you arrive at Day 1 in his *Purpose Driven Life* book, based on this fact alone.

Now, if you are suggesting that the meaning of the Greek word for heretic has changed, since you have postulated in our correspondence that the meanings of Greek and Hebrew words have changed over the centuries, then, indeed, we are in great trouble. How could we ever identify false teaching if the definition of heretic is so chameleon-like.

Since the English word "heretical" comes from the Greek word transliterated *hairetikos,* we ought to be able to do as you suggested; i.e., this Greek word is a "constantly changing and developing process as language constantly changes and develops." Therefore, we really can't say for certain what this word actually means, right? Now you might protest that of course this word means heretic. Well then, what mechanism did you use to decide that changing the meaning of this particular word is off-limits to change the meaning, while other Greek or Hebrew words are open game? By what or by whose authority? The mysticism Rick Warren promotes, the teachers he frequently quotes (which I describe in chapter six of this book), and the suggestions that we can gain secret information from God if we know the right technique, is indeed heretical. That in itself is enough reason to reject his book.

Here is a passage with the Greek word *heretick*, and note how accurate the KJV is in its rendering:

> A man that is an heretick after the first and second admonition reject.
>
> —Titus 3:10, KJV

A man [444] ανθρωπος (*anthropos*) **that is an heretick** [141] αιρετικος (*hairetikos*) **after** [3326] μετα (*meta*) **the first** [3391] ειζ (*mia*) **and** [2532] Κι (*kai*) **second** [1208] δευερο (*deuteros*) **admonition** [3359] voθεσι (*nouthesia*) **reject** [3868] παραιτεμαι (*paraiteomai*).

You seem to indicate that a heretic is a bad thing. But if you suggest that "language constantly changes and develops," how could we know for sure?

Heresy is also considered to be a teaching that is heterodox or that which is not orthodox.

> In Titus 3:10 a "heretical person" is one who follows his own self-willed "questions," and who is to be avoided. Heresies thus came to signify self-chosen doctrines not emanating from God (2 Pet. 2:1).
>
> — *www.apologeticsindex.org/h27.html*

> from the same as αιρετιζω—hairetizo [140]; a schismatic:— heretic (the Greek word itself).
>
> —Strong's Dictionary

So don't you think that if a church or the church in general is commanded by Paul to reject such a person, that we had better have a very clear and unchanging meaning to the word "heretic"?

If we follow Paul's advice to see if a teaching is in the Scripture and discover it is not only not in there, but completely different facts are recorded, then wouldn't this depart from the historic and commonly held beliefs? If something is not truth, does that not depart from orthodox Christianity?

❋ ❋ ❋

Question or Comment

I would not see him as being in the same league as a cult that claims to be Christian, but in fact warps the central doctrines to Christianity. I do not find Warren doing this.

Response

Rick Warren hasn't rejected such doctrines as the virgin birth and the resurrection of Jesus. But isn't telling God's truth a central doctrine? Isn't bearing false witness to a scriptural text a central doctrine to Christianity? Isn't teaching ideas that collide with Scripture a central doctrine? Isn't promoting known false teachers, whom the Body of Christ has already collectively and rightfully named as false teachers, a central doctrine? You do not see Warren in the same league as a cult, yet he is closely associated with Robert Schuller, who wrote the inside cover of *The Purpose Driven Church* book, which you do stand behind and state that PDL was an outcropping of this book. Well, Schuller has perverted most of the central doctrines of the faith. This fact is indisputable. Schuller, a co-laborer with Warren, states: "Unchristian strategy of attempting to make people aware of their lost and sinful condition" is "destructive to human personality" (Dave Hunt and T. A. McMahon, *The Seduction of Christianity*, p. 15, and *Christianity Today*, October 5, 1984). On sin, Schuller says, "Sin is an act or thought that robs myself or another being of his or her self-esteem" (Schuller, *Self Esteem*, p. 14). On hell, "a person is in hell when he has lost his self-esteem" (Schuller, *Self Esteem*, pp. 14–15). On Christ, "Christ is the Ideal One, for he was Self-Esteem Incarnate" (Schuller,

Self Esteem, pp. 14–15). Schuller would not even be disturbed if his grandchildren became Muslims. Schuller both invites Muslim clerics to preach and he preaches in Islamic centers. Don't these published teachings by this man qualify him as one who has warped the central doctrines of orthodox Christianity? Had Warren acted responsibly, he would have identified Schuller as a false teacher. And had he done so, he would never have obtained Schuller's endorsement and the glowing reports Schuller gives him.

Here is a source of just some of Schuller's quotes which confirm that he is a heretic: *www.myfortress.org/RobertSchuller.html.*

You should not even have gotten past *The Purpose Driven Church* book without rejecting it as soon as you read the inside cover of the book, let alone then move on to his "outcropping" (*Purpose Driven Life*).

Of course we can disagree on non-essentials such as diet and days, and Paul affirms this. But we cannot disagree on essentials such as telling the truth, not promoting false teachers, not completely changing the meanings of scriptural passages, and his teaching on prophecy. That is what renders Rick Warren a heretic, not your opinion or my opinion, but rather God's Word and the central doctrines of the faith contained therein.

❋   ❋   ❋

Question or Comment
We must recognize that there are going to be differences in peripheral doctrines amongst true believers but that does not negate our salvation.

Response
I never said that one is automatically lost (from their salvation) because they teach a false doctrine. Paul confirms this with his commentary on Hymenaus and Alexander. However, we are still to identify individuals whose teaching does not line up with Scripture; we are to mark them, and separate from them. We are not to join forces with them or import their teaching into the church, whether or not the doctrine is peripheral. Furthermore, I do not see how you can

think promoting Carl Jung and making statements in a published book about false teachers, as well as the false teachers he promotes on his *pastors.com* web site and in his *Purpose Driven Church* book, is all nothing more than a peripheral doctrine or teaching. These kinds of differences are *not* to be tolerated. The content of all Scripture and what is necessary for salvation and sanctification is not peripheral.

❋ ❋ ❋

Question or Comment
I do not find anywhere in Rick Warren's material that he states that "growth is the purpose of the church."

Response
As far as I know, this literal word-for-word sentence is not stated anywhere by Rick Warren. But as you should know from reading *Purpose Driven Church* and Rick Warren's leadership seminar materials, he lists method after method by which to grow the church. A reasonable person would construe that growth is a major purpose of Rick Warren's teaching by this statement regarding what happened to Saddleback Church the minute they changed the music: "Within a year of deciding what would be 'our sound,' Saddleback exploded with growth" (Rick Warren, *Purpose Driven Church*, p. 285). Warren's philosophy is built in great part on Peter Drucker's theories of growth. Two hundred fifty thousand pastors and church leaders from 125 countries attend Warren's seminars for the purpose of learning Warren's methodology. Obviously, pastors all over the country don't go to his seminars to shrink their churches. Rick Warren even states in the March 29, 2004, issue of *Time* magazine, page 56:

> The Purpose-Driven principles are like Intel chips, and they can be inserted into any congregation, whether it's a megachurch or a tiny one, Lutheran AME, Pentecostal or Baptist.

Contrary to Warren's teachings, it is not a principle that we follow, but a person (Christ). It is the Holy Spirit who should be inserted into a church, not an Intel chip. If it were truly the Holy Spirit inserted, he would convict churches of the great falling away, to the point of when Christ returns, will Christ find *the* faith on the earth?

Does that sound like church growth to you? A church might become healthier by becoming smaller and not by growing, because its pastor and members believe that being faithful to sound teaching (not to Warren's "principles of success") is the most important thing.

There is another troubling statement by Rick Warren in this magazine article:

I believe I have the key to meaning and purpose in life with God.

We don't already have the key within Scripture alone? Every Christian has the key! It is not the exclusive domain of one person in this present age, or any age! This reminds me of Roman Catholicism which teaches that only a Roman Catholic priest can administer the sacraments or tell us what the Bible already teaches us and only the pope is the vicar, or Christ's final and absolute authority in the church.

❈   ❈   ❈

Question or Comment
Doesn't Rick Warren consistently state that the purpose of the church is to live out the Great Commandment and the Great Commission (*PDC*, pp. 103–107; *PDL* becomes a personalized version of *PDC*, as can be seen in the fact that the same five church purposes in *PDC* are personalized in *PDL*).

Response
Rick Warren's good news is to accentuate the positive, which he learned in great part from one of his mentors, Robert Schuller, and others. But part of the biblical Great Commission is to also teach the wrath of God; i.e., the bad news and prophecy, which Warren thinks is a distraction.

The biblical Great Commission also teaches to *obey everything* Christ taught. One way we obey is to identify and mark false teachers and false teachings. Rick Warren does not identify Robert Schuller as a false teacher.

Another way we obey is to not introduce false teachers such as Richard Foster, Madame Guyon, Gary Thomas, and many others with *no warning labels* or *disclaimers* to unsuspecting Christians.

As to the Great Commandment (to love the Lord your God with all your heart and love your neighbor as yourself), if Rick Warren wants to live it out, telling the truth would be a good start. I hardly think that his not telling the truth throughout his book is a good way to love your neighbor as yourself.

※ ※ ※

Question or Comment
Rick Warren does believe that if people live out these two "greats" of Scripture that a typical side effect will be a growing church. I find it hard to disagree.

Response
Show me the scripture that says growth is a typical side effect. There is *no* such proof. It is the Lord always and alone who adds to the church (i.e., church growth . . . or shrinkage for that matter), not man-made methods and principles.

Noah did all the right things and got no recruits; i.e., no typical side effect. Jonah also did the right things and had 100 percent conversions in Nineveh.

Besides this, what a peculiar word to use for whom the Lord adds unto the church—to describe new Christians added to the church—to call them side effects. The term "side effects" usually has a negative connotation, such as what occurs when taking drugs, and one would far prefer no side effects at all in this case. If anything, taking Rick Warren's "spiritual drugs" will produce the most disastrous of side effects: " **There is a way that seemeth right unto a man, but the end thereof are the ways of death**" (Prov. 16:25).

※ ※ ※

Question or Comment
So, I think in assessing Warren, you have mistaken what he defines as the fruit of the obedience for the obedience itself.

Response

Obedience to what? Obedience to the Great Commandment and the Great Commission? If this is his passion, then he should not stray from Scripture by using erroneous translations and interpretations, and by promoting false teachers who themselves are also disobedient to the teachings of Scriptures. These false teachers whom Warren promotes are teaching things that ought not to be taught and are thereby ruining whole households of faith! My entire documentary catalogs how Warren has been in error regarding the teachings of Scripture. And I am not alone in reporting these things. Go to the end of the documentary, you will see the host of ministries that have rightly exposed his teachings.

✳ ✳ ✳

Question or Comment

You've not really defined the purpose for individual people or the church in your statement. You've referenced John 3:16. However, that really states only God's purpose in sending Christ, not our own personal purpose.

Response

That is true for the first half of the verse. But here is the whole verse, along with John 3:17:

> For God so loved the world, that he gave his only begotten Son, **that whosoever believeth in him should not perish, but have everlasting life.** For God sent not his Son into the world to condemn the world; but that the world through him might be saved.
>
> —John 3:16–17

How could anyone miss that the second half of the verse defines our personal purpose and eternal destiny? For if our personal purpose is everlasting life, these verses tells us how to secure it; we must believe in Him.

✳ ✳ ✳

Question or Comment

You also reference 2 Timothy 3:16–17 to define God's purpose in giving us Scripture, but again, how does that specify our own personal purpose?

Response

> All scripture is given by inspiration of God, and is profitable for doctrine, for reproof, for correction, for instruction in righteousness: That the man of God may be perfect, throughly furnished unto all good works.

Shouldn't our personal purpose include doctrine? Shouldn't our personal purpose include reproof? Shouldn't our personal purpose include correction? Shouldn't our personal purpose include instruction in righteousness? Now some might argue that Scripture is useful but not complete in determining our personal purpose. So, let's look at the next verse. Wouldn't being made perfect (from all Scripture) mean being made perfect? If we are being made perfect, wouldn't that mean our personal purpose is fully achieved? If we are thoroughly furnished, wouldn't that mean we have everything we need to achieve our personal purpose? If Scripture is profitable to furnish us unto *all* good works, what good work is lacking that can be provided by something outside of all Scripture so that we can "specify our own personal purpose," as you put it? Or to put it another way, aren't all good works what our personal purpose should be?

Doesn't all mean all? What work would you is suggest necessary to determine our personal purpose which is not identified or specified in all Scripture? What personal purpose would you propose which all Scripture is insufficient to identify? Second Timothy 3:16–17 does not directly give each of us our "own personal purpose." However, by referring to all Scripture, this very scripture tells us where to look to find our personal purpose . . . that is the rest of or *all* Scripture.

Paul reinforces this in all of the passages where he talks about sanctification, because that is the total process of our personal purpose between salvation and glorification. Paul says that this process is achieved by the watering of his Word. Peter agrees when he says:

According as his divine power **hath given unto us all things that pertain unto life and godliness,** through the knowledge of him that hath called us to glory and virtue.

—2 Peter 1:3

And how do we have the knowledge of Him? By studying and obeying His Scripture. And once again, doesn't all mean all? What is missing here to help us find our own personal purpose? Isn't our own personal purpose life and godliness?

More Questions Which Have Come in Regarding Rick Warren's SHAPE and Celebrate Recovery and Bill Hybels' Christianized Twelve-Step Program

Question or Comment
My experience in the church is that most people do not know their spiritual gifts, have no clue as to how to discover them, and no interest in discovering them, so we need Rick Warren's SHAPE questionnaire.

Response
Gifts of the Holy Spirit are revealed and given directly to a believer from the Holy Spirit by His grace. They can be confirmed and affirmed by the church, but they are not discovered by other men or any man-made or pagan-based system or test. We are commanded by Paul to eagerly desire the spiritual gifts (this presumes that those eagerly desiring spiritual gifts are, indeed, Christians). Now, you can also test the spirits to see if they are of God, as Satan is a great counterfeiter of gifts, but he is abysmal at producing the fruit of the Spirit. Finally, you don't discover the gifts. In accordance with Scripture, they are either already given to you when you believe (one or more), or you can pray for one or more of them. "You have not because you ask not." But again, I repeat: You do not discover your gifts any more than you discover that you are born again, or had a dream. You just know by (1) the inner witness of the Holy Spirit, (2) the testing of the

spirits, (3) the fruit of the Spirit, and (4) the Word of God.

As to having no interest in the gifts, according to God's Word it would be impossible for one to be a Christian and not have any interest in the gifts, because Paul commands us to seek them and use them for the building up and edification of the church. In fact, Paul's exhortation under the guidance of the Holy Spirit inherently presumes that a true believer will, indeed, be given the desire for spiritual gifts by the Holy Spirit, Himself. Paul's admonition is not to be (and should not be) confused with the man-made program of church growth . . . as in greater numbers, but rather Paul is referring to the growth and maturity of each individual in Christ. If a professed Christian, a true believer, has no interest in the gifts, they are simply being disobedient to God's Word. And besides this, they should not be interested in "discovering them." This would be a futile journey, or worse, divining

Question or Comment

There is virtually no teaching in the Bible on the subject of gifts of the Holy Spirit, therefore we need Rick Warren's book to help clarify.

Response

We are commanded in the Scripture to ***not*** go beyond what is written. There is some teaching on the gifts in the Bible, but there is absolutely no teaching in the Scripture on how to "discover your gift(s)." Anything there is to learn about the gift is revealed within the gift itself at and by the direction of the Holy Spirit who indwells each and every true believer. There is not a single scripture to support the idea that practicing a gift improves it. You either have it or you don't. Did the original apostles perform partial or imperfect miracles until they got them right? Besides, "imperfect miracle" is an oxymoron and unbiblical, as every good and perfect gift comes from the Father of Lights. A miracle suspends the laws of nature; that is why it is a miracle. Humans cannot suspend these laws, no, not even Christians. You practice an ability, but not a miracle!

❋ ❋ ❋

Question or Comment

People minister in churches when it is pretty apparent they have no special abilities. Preachers preach with no preaching gift, teach with no teaching gift, often have no evangelism gift, modest administrative skills and no administrative gift, a dislike of leading and no gift of leadership, and often no one else in the fellowship seems to have those gifts either, or is willing to step forward and do those tasks believing they have those gifts.

Response

It sounds like you are possibly mixing up gifts of the Holy Spirit with special abilities. A non-Christian can have the same special abilities as a Christian; in fact, oftentimes non-Christians will have ***more*** talents.

For example, the Scripture even says: "For the children of this world are in their generation wiser than the children of light" (Luke 16:8). And if the children of the world have given heed to seducing spirits and/or are demon-possessed, they may even have supernatural powers that go beyond their special abilities!

Preaching (though teaching is) is not a gift of the Holy Spirit, though it may be a talent. If someone is teaching without the gift of teaching, they need to pray for the gift. If God does not give them the gift then I agree, they should serve the church in another way, as there will always be some way to serve, and always at least one gift they will have as a Christian.

It seems conceivable to me that a person may not like to lead yet finds it necessary in the natural, since no one else has any capacity for governing. But it is inconceivable that a person would be given the gift of leading (governing), then dislike it! One should not become an elder unless they desire to be a leader and shepherd, as the Scripture records. Secondly, such a teaching elder would have to meet all the other requirements of elders (as listed in the Scriptures) before he would even be biblically entitled to become an elder or deacon. One can't decide he is going to lead God's people simply because he believes he has that gift. The gift must be tested and Scripture must be obeyed, "Lay hands suddenly on no man, neither be partaker of other men's sins: keep thyself pure" (1 Tim. 5:22).

❋   ❋   ❋

Question or Comment
Perhaps the full range of gifts (your list from Scripture) just does not exist in that particular fellowship.

Response
The Lord will not leave his people without a witness, and if there is a need in the body then that particular group of believers needs to pray that the need be filled. There is *no* record in the New Testament that lends support to the idea that any particular body of believers was left without the gifts of the Holy Spirit in operation. However, using your assumption that this may be the case, you still can't "invent" gifts or have "imaginary" gifts of the Holy Spirit, based upon a man-made temperament test being used simply to fulfill a perceived need. The church could still function without the gifts of the Holy Spirit, for the test is not whether there is a gift present, but rather that Jesus Christ is present. "For where two or three are gathered together in my name, there am I in the midst of them" (Matt. 18:20).

❋   ❋   ❋

Question or Comment
If the full range is not in a group it seems to contradict Romans 12 where I think it suggests that all the gifts will be present in the body. Can one suggest then, that such a group is not really a "body" and maybe shouldn't exist as a separate church or group?

Response
To which "group" are you referring? It is true that Romans 12, as do other passages, describe the church as a physical body, so that *all* are needed to work together, in that we can't dismember the body and have it still function. But the primary emphasis is the need for each person who is a Christian, not the gifts. This would seem to affirm that the church can't function without the gifts of the Holy Spirit;

however, nowhere in Scripture are we told that it is the gifts that make up the body of Christ. Rather, the true church is made up of his people . . . the living stones . . . gathering together in worship, prayer, and the reading of the Scriptures, who comprise the body with Christ as the Head. Yes, Romans 12 does make it appear as though the Lord desires to see all of the gifts in operation within the body of Christ. Yet, nowhere in the reading of Romans 12 are we told to limit the gifts to a particular building with four walls. For example, throughout the ages the gifts have been distributed over a large geographical region of many individual churches, ages, without them all being vested in one individual local congregation. After all, we are members of one body throughout the ages, not millions of bodies.

※   ※   ※

Question or Comment
Have you addressed the issue of what gifts have to be present in a group to allow it to function as a body? Maybe churches exist improperly because they are just too small and have insufficient gifts available.

Response
Does this mean that our Lord has made a mistake in calling the saved, putting them together in a particular church? Furthermore, Paul's writings are clear, and his key word is "some." Some . . . not *all* . . . have been given particular gifts. If a body of believers is gathered together in the Name of Christ, and if there are no apparent gifts of the Holy Spirit in operation within that gathering, then it is up to that group to pray and seek the Lord that He, by His Holy Spirit, would (1) empower some within that group to receive the gifts that are needed, or (2) that He, by His Holy Spirit, would send others to that group with the gifts that are needed. Either way, there is certainly no place in Scripture where we are to take it upon ourselves to determine our gifts by the use of a man-made test, nor is a group of believers forbidden to gather in worship of the Lord if no gifts are in existence. The very act of gathering in the Name of the Lord is in obedience to God's

Word, which can only come by the empowerment of the Holy Spirit indwelling each and every believer! And the very act of worship and praise is, indeed, a "gift" given to true believers by our Lord!

All that has to happen for the body to function is for two or more to be gathered in His Name. However, the gifts do enable the church to be edified, to be built up in the faith, and to do more works in the Lord. But it is not as though the body is defective without the gifts. (If Christ is present, who is perfect, the body can't be defective.)

Two or more gathered in His name can pray with *no* gifts present or being manifested. Is this body of Christ functioning? Absolutely yes! In one case the container is full, and in the other it is pressed down and running over. There is not one single scripture to support the contention that a church cannot function properly because it is too small. Even if this were true, who decides the exact size necessary to qualify the church as running properly or improperly? Scripture is silent on this point. If this were true, you might never know until someone comes along who has the gift of discernment to point this out, one way or the other. This may be ten years later. Does this mean that the church was defective for those ten years? But your point to some extent is academic, because every Christian already has at least one gift of the Holy Spirit, so there will never be *none* when two or more gather in His Name!

Who is there who can possibly and adequately decide that a local body is insufficient in its gifts? Conversely, what would sufficient mean? Sufficient to do what? To grow a church with a larger population? Since when does the size of the church equate to spirituality? Many martyrs of the faith, who loved not their lives unto death, died in their cells in solitary confinement. These are those of whom the Lord has said this world is not worthy of them. How big was the apostle John's church on the Isle of Patmos where he was exiled? It is very dangerous to suggest that growth in a church means God is blessing it. Narrow is the way and few it be that find it. Combine this with the great falling away in the end times, and it sounds more like the smaller the church, the greater God is blessing it!

❋   ❋   ❋

Question or Comment

Maybe the Church Growth Movement is what the fully function-ing church ought to be and it only stands out in contrast to the vast numbers of no growth churches who lack all the spiritual gifts?

Response

See commentary on the question above. It is inconceivable that true believers gathered in His Name would not possess at least some of the spiritual gifts of the Holy Spirit, but they may possess only what they might need for a particular mission that the Lord has for them. Or the gift may be possessed, but dormant until the need arises.

❀ ❀ ❀

Question or Comment

I heard once that a survey of pastors revealed that only 8 percent of them felt that evangelism was their gift (or gifts). Which means, clearly, doesn't it, that someone else in the body needs to provide that gift?

Response

No survey was taken for at least nineteen hundred years to see who thought they had a gift of evangelism and the church grew anyway. Where in the Bible does it say a survey is necessary? Do you remem-ber what happened to King David when he took a census? Don't you think it's presumptuous of Christians to take man-made surveys in an attempt to determine God's will and His ways? Where is the scrip-tural backing for this? Likewise Saul listened to the people instead of obeying the Lord when he was afraid of the people and offered a sacri-fice anyway to the Lord when he was supposed to have destroyed all of the Amalekites and every living thing belonging to them. Is it possible that what happened to Saul for listening to the people could happen to people today who listen and follow the Church Growth Movement today? The Lord lifted his blessing on Saul. Result? God removed Saul from being king and replaced him with David. Shouldn't we be wor-ried that the Lord will lift his blessing on the church if it also builds the church by listening to people rather than God? (See 1 Samuel 28 for the account of Saul.)

Every Christian is called to be an evangelist. *That is the Great Commission.* Now I will concede that evangelism is also listed as a distinct gift of the Holy Spirit. But even assuming such a survey is from the Lord, who then decides that 8 percent is the wrong percentage? And how do you know that the Lord has a larger percentage in mind? How do you know that the Lord may not have only 3 percent that should be evangelists? He may trim the percentage *down* not up, as he did with Gideon's army.

Therefore, are we to trust the results of the survey? Does one possess the gift simply because they "feel" like they have it? How about the "fact" that they have it? You state, "Which means, clearly, doesn't it, that someone else in the body needs to provide that gift?" No, it doesn't, and how do you know or determine what is "clearly"?

Do we now need take a poll to see if this gift should be provided? What percentage of church members then determines that this gift must be provided? A majority? A simple majority? Perhaps the elders should decide, which would be a minority. Do you cast lots and pick somebody? The disciples also did something similar by casting lots to see who should replace Judas, so that there would still be twelve disciples. But it was Christ alone who commissioned every disciple and apostle. Christ commissioned Paul to be the twelfth apostle. This can be confirmed in Revelation 21:14: "And the wall of the city had twelve foundations, and in them the names of the twelve apostles of the Lamb." So it was Paul who completed the twelve whom Jesus selected, not Mathias, whom the disciples selected.

Maybe someone with this gift of evangelism is not even in your local church, but if the Lord puts it on your heart, you could pray and the Lord might send you one from afar. Someone with the gift of evangelism might only visit from another local church, without that particular local church he or she visited ever having its own member with such a gift. What if the person never arrives? Is the church now crippled and unable to function properly? Of course not! They could simply pray and fast, give themselves to the public reading of the Scriptures as commanded by the apostle Peter, continue in their love for one another (by which all men will know them to be true believers) and still be perfectly within the will of God *without* a person with the gift of evangelism.

❈   ❈   ❈

Question or Comment

My first exposure to teaching on gifts came through Bill Gothard over thirty years ago. He believed that the Bible taught that a person can have at most one gift, and to think otherwise was arrogant. But he also had a whole section on how to discover ones spiritual gift.

Response

I have attended Bill Gothard's workshops, too. I also have his "Principles of Life" Advanced Seminar Workbook. It is hard to know where to begin when speaking of Bill Gothard's theology and teaching, except to say that a good place to start is: *Midwest Outreach Ministries* (*www.midwestoutreach.org/02-Information/02-OnlineReference/02-UnorthodoxyGuide/105-IKnowSomething/Gothard-IBLP/index.html*) and *www.rapidnet.com/~jbeard/bdm/exposes/gothard/* where you can find more extensive documentation on his teachings. Let me just say that his theology is fraught with difficulties and biblical problems. His whole approach to discovering your gift(s) of the Holy Spirit is purely theoretical and laced with the same theories found in psychology (though he maintains that they are not) and ecumenism. Show me the scripture(s) which says a Christian can only have one predominate gift.

Show me the scripture(s) that supports a person believing otherwise is arrogant. Show me the scripture(s) which support how you discover your one spiritual gift. They certainly are not in chapter four of his *Institute of Basic Life Principles* book. He does give scriptures, but they don't support his contention, and they couldn't because they don't exist!

Bill Gothard maintains that a Christian will have only one motivational gift, but at the same time many other gifts. But what scripture makes such a distinction? And Paul gave a further injunction to seek the higher gifts. We should be motivated to seek many of the gifts. Doesn't that sound like plural? Which gift are you going to select that a given individual would not be motivated to get?

Bill Gothard also makes a distinction of "motivational" gifts that the Bible does *not* make. He lists seven motivational gifts. They are: prophecy, serving, teaching, exhortation, giving, organizing, and mercy. If it is true—as Bill Gothard states—that a Christian can have only one motivational gift, then the apostle Paul would not agree with him, as he and other apostles ministered in *all seven* of these gifts.

And what about the qualifications of an elder? The scriptures clearly tell us that elders must be apt to serve, teach, exhort, give, organize, and be merciful. Additionally, we are told that in some cases the elders would also prophesy. Yet according to Bill Gothard's unfounded biblical theory, we now would have to consider all of the apostles and most of the elders as being arrogant because they not only believed they had more than one motivational gift, but they most certainly obeyed the Holy Spirit's leading in the actual use of all their gifts!

If Bill Gothard is right about every Christian having at least one gift of the Holy Spirit, then there is no such thing anyway as a body of believers in which the gifts do not exist. His unbiblical reasoning for only one motivational gift is found in Romans 12:6–8. However, there is nothing in that passage to suggest only one motivational gift. Bill Gothard then defines "motivation" as "the desire and power He puts within us to accomplish His will." But this should be the definition for every Christian, irrespective of the possession of *any* gift of the Holy Spirit.

Likewise, how would Gothard's faulty definition not also apply to the other two categories of gifts that he labels as ministry and manifestation gifts? (Besides this, no such definition even exists in the Bible.) He then proceeds to tell us that one of the ways we discover our motivational gift is to "identify what Christians do to irritate you." His defense of this method is invoking 1 John 3:16, but there is nothing in that passage even remotely connected with the gifts of the Holy Spirit. This passage is talking about all Christians and how they need to love and not harden their hearts when compassion is required.

Does a Christian need a gift of the Holy Spirit to do that? Certainly one could minister to a brother who lacks this world's goods with the gifts of giving and mercy. But again, every Christian should do this anyway!

A gift of the Holy Spirit is a distinct entity. It is something given to a Christian that they did not possess before. It is something supernatural, not a natural talent or gift that God simply improves, as Bill Gothard would argue when he states, "God takes these natural abilities and turns them into the means by which He can work through us supernaturally."

Bill Gothard then contradicts himself when he says: "Every Christian must know how to exercise all of the gifts." How can any Christian do this if they are supposed to have only one gift in the first place (according to Gothard)?

※　※　※

Question or Comment
Whatever the process of identifying a person's spiritual gift, would you say that every Christian has a gift or gifts and that a person knowing what his or her spiritual giftedness is, would be useful?

Response
I would use only the process given in the Bible to identify my spiritual gift. I would not go beyond what is written. The Bible does not give us a process, so we should not be implementing one with Scripture or by any other method, such as Rick Warren's SHAPE. Whatever gifts are given by the Holy Spirit are simply known, just like when the very first gifts were given at Pentecost. *Absolutely no process was used to identify gifts!*

So, no, any process to identify a person's spiritual gift would *not* be useful. Of course, if a gift were truly given by the Holy Spirit, it would in fact be useful, as the Scriptures say they will be useful to the Body of Christ.

※　※　※

Question or Comment
On your list below you represent your position as believing that a person has a single gift, am I reading that right?

Response
I believe that every Christian has a least one spiritual gift the moment they are saved, but it might not manifest itself until they mature. For example, the apostle Paul, who could have received some or all of the gifts when he was struck on the road to Damascus, did not immediately manifest his gifts, but rather at the direction of the Holy Spirit, went into the wilderness for three years, thus being unable to use any of the gifts in the church. Also, we have the example of the house of Cornelius manifesting gifts of the Holy Spirit immediately upon their conversion, because they were baptized in the Holy Spirit upon conversion, so would have had a least the gift of tongues upon conversion (see Acts 10). But the Bible does not specifically say every person has more than one gift of the Holy Spirit immediately upon conversion. Of course they would immediately have had more than one upon being baptized in the Holy Spirit. However, because the Lord puts such emphasis on the importance of the gift(s), they would soon be manifested in any church at some point.

❀   ❀   ❀

Question or Comment
On the list you seem to be arguing that very little detail was given about spiritual gifts in the New Testament, which is, I think, true. However, would you agree with the thought that the fact that anything was said about them at all is because God apparently thought there was some need to have them identified and discussed.

Response
Yes, I agree. We are to identify those individuals who have the gifts in order to see whom God has already approved. The church is to confirm what God has already done. There certainly would also be discussion in seeing who has gifts which might qualify them to be an elder, as well as discussion to ensure all things are done decently

and in order. However, what is said about them (the gifts) pertains to who *already* has them and how to administer their gift. This is a far, far cry from discussing how to "get a gift" or "how to discover a gift," using a man-made and/or pagan based methodology, one's life experiences or repressed memories, and at the very worse divination (see definition and scriptural reference) or hypnotism, so on and so forth. It is impossible to identify what God has not already given! For any church or individual believer to attempt to do so is an attempt to read God's mind, thus leaving the church (or Christian) to wander in a futile maze of frustration and guesswork, no matter how urgently a person or a church thinks they must have a particular gift of the Holy Spirit.

❉   ❉   ❉

Question or Comment
Doesn't the fact that the very raising of some issues in the Bible suggest that there were questions about the gifts and the proper use of gifts in those early fellowships?

Response
Absolutely, but the questions were over abuse of only certain gifts and over administrating the gifts (why deacons were created, for example). We cannot and dare not read more into the Scriptures than is given to us.

❉   ❉   ❉

Question or Comment
While you state that there isn't any scripture which instructs on how to find our spiritual gift, are there any scriptures which say that it is not necessary to be instructed on how to identify and find your spiritual gift? (And if so, what was Paul doing when he wrote about it?)

Response
Yes, Paul did write about the spiritual gifts, and even tells us that he does not want us ignorant about them. But show me one scripture

wherein he gives us a "process" to use by which we can identify our gift(s)?

※   ※   ※

Question or Comment
Isn't there only *one* spiritual gift of the Holy Spirit per Christian?

Response
No, there is not one scripture to support only one gift per Christian, though many Christians may have only one. There are, however, many passages describing the implementation of those gifts . . . from Pentecost, to miracles, to Paul's passages on church government. I think it is safe to say that signs and wonders follow them that believe by simply doing the work of the ministry. But we don't conjure up or guess at our gifts by using some sort of testing apparatus.

※   ※   ※

Question or Comment
What was Paul's one spiritual gift? Leadership, teaching, evangelism, discernment, faith, apostleship, healing? Didn't he do all of those?

Response
Yes, yes, yes, and again I say yes, Paul did do all of these!!!

※   ※   ※

Question or Comment
Don't you feel the Bible says very little about the day-to-day life of individual Christians who were members of churches?

Response
Yes, but the gifts of the Holy Spirit are supernatural and self–contained entities. Day-to-day New Testament life didn't contain anything we need to know today, such as Paul's laundry list. However, to exercise gifts of the Holy Spirit that you don't have—or simply just "feel" you have or wish you had—has led multitudes into error, false teaching, and ultimately a great falling away. But getting Paul's day-to-day life issues such as getting his laundry list wrong and publishing it is of little consequence to the Church.

✖   ✖   ✖

Question or Comment
Doesn't the Bible only focus on a few of the leaders of the early church, certainly not all of them? Does the Bible exhaust all the problems or questions that must have existed?

Response
That is the argument to integrate psychology into the church. But what does the Bible really say? God's Word speaks for itself (*ip sa loquitor*) because it says it contains everything we need for the perfecting of the saints, with regard to all questions on faith and morals. Consequently, if it is not in the Bible, regarding faith and morals, we don't need to know the answer. The Bible doesn't record all of the problems or questions that would come up long after the Holy Canon was written, but it does provide the blueprint and church government for how to resolve disputes.

> All scripture is given by inspiration of God, and is profitable for doctrine, for reproof, for correction, for instruction in righteousness: That the man of God may be perfect, throughly furnished unto all good works.
>
> —2 Timothy 3:16–17

Once again I must ask, what is lacking in "perfect?" What is lacking in being "thoroughly furnished?" And what needful question is not answered or problem not solved in "all good works"? You have to ask yourself how Paul and the early church managed to achieve this with only the Scriptures, while we in the twenty-first century must find a new method because "the times they are a changin' . . ."

. . . and . . .

> According as his divine power hath given unto us all things that pertain unto life and godliness, through the knowledge of him that hath called us to glory and virtue.
>
> —2 Peter 1:3

Isn't "all things," all things? Of course, the Bible doesn't tell us how to build a computer or automobile, but what we are talking about is all things unto godliness and the perfecting of the saints.

※ ※ ※

Question or Comment
Don't you think that God didn't intend the Bible to be that specific, but instead intended to allow those in the body to use their gifts to deal with situations as life changed?

Response
Nothing has changed which requires any different response than what Scripture has already given us. And the gifts of the Holy Spirit were not given to provide an alternative answer, but affirm what the Scripture already has told us to do in order to obey Him.

※ ※ ※

Question or Comment
Do you feel that the gifts required in the early church in what was a relatively simple society with few issues and few complexities compared to life today, are expressed in the same way then, as they are today?"

Response
Yes, I do believe the gifts as expressed in the early church are the same today, because Jesus Christ is the same yesterday, today, and forever. What issue or complexity that exists today would entitle us to provide a different or a better answer than what the Scriptures already give us? And who would be the one able to give us the answer which is absolutely true, and how would we know the answer to be true? Apart from God's Holy Writ—neither adding to it nor taking away from it—the church (and every individual Christian) cannot judge the truthfulness and rightness of any answers provided by any person, regardless of whether the person who is providing the answers is saved or unsaved.

The Gospels and the apostles Paul, John, Peter, and Jude devote a large percentage of the Scripture to the *same* problems the early church had as we have in the twenty-first century. In fact, they warn that the questions and problems of the last days would be the same ones as the early church had. Instead of addressing a question or problem the Scripture does not pose, why not first concentrate on the problems the Scriptures do present. Example: false teaching, and identifying and marking false teachers who would import psychology and personality theory into the church and into the gifts of the Holy Spirit. It is not knowledge of complexity in society new to the church in the twenty-first century which causes men to perish, but rather the lack of knowledge of the Scriptures *already* given which cause men to perish! Instead of tolerating new teaching in the church, the church needs to expose, warn, and be intolerant of false teaching.

❊ ❊ ❊

Question or Comment
Have you ever met Rick Warren or Bill Hybels; or do you know them personally? Have you ever been to Willow Creek or Saddleback Church?

Response
No, I have never met them personally. And I am not making an assessment on their personal lives. I am making an assessment on their public teaching. Rick Warren (and his wife) and Bill Hybels (and his wife), in their own books, in their own words, and by their actions, reveal their worrisome teachings and beliefs. Their books were endorsed by those involved in New Age beliefs, psychology, and psychiatry. They have incorporated ungodly beliefs in their teachings and books; e.g., Celebrate Recovery, Twelve-Step groups of all kinds, supporting AA, etc.

> For by thy words thou shalt be justified, and by thy words thou shalt be condemned.
>
> —Matthew 12:37

You seem to be suggesting that my not having been to Rick Warren's or Bill Hybel's churches or knowing them personally does not give me (or anyone) the right to disqualify him as a teacher. We don't need to meet him and know him personally in order to know that we should avoid his teaching at any and all costs.

> Now I beseech you, brethren, mark them which cause divisions and offences contrary to the doctrine which ye have learned; and avoid them. For they that are such serve not our Lord Jesus Christ, but their own belly; and by good words and fair speeches deceive the hearts of the simple.
>
> —Romans 16:17–18

> I marvel that ye are so soon removed from him that called you into the grace of Christ unto another gospel: Which is not another; but there be some that trouble you, and would pervert the gospel of Christ. But though we, or an angel from heaven, preach any other gospel unto you than that which we have preached unto you, let him be accursed. As we said before, so say I now again, If any man preach any other gospel unto you than that ye have received, let him be accursed.
>
> —Galatians 1:6–9

(Note: The Holy Spirit inspired Paul to repeat that any man preaching a contrary gospel is to be accursed! What more do we require in the way of instruction?)

❊ ❊ ❊

Question or Comment
There are thousands who attend Saddleback Church every week, and millions of Christians who attended Purpose Driven Life churches. There are over a thousand people who attend Willow Creek each week; there are thousands upon thousands of WCA churches. Therefore, the numbers alone should tell you that Willow Creek must be doing something right. Look how God is blessing this ministry with growth!

Response
Just because there are over a thousand in attendance there each week,

just because there are thousands of PDC and WCA churches, does not mean this is a work of our Lord! To use this argument to support Rick Warren and Hybel's "Willow Creekism," would mean that the Muslim faith must also be "of God," as there are over a billion adherents around the world, and the Muslim faith is growing by leaps and bounds. In fact, the Muslim religion is the largest and fastest growing in the world religion and one of the fastest in the U.S.!

❊   ❊   ❊

Question or Comment
Rick Warren and Bill Hybels are wonderful preachers/teachers. People are drawn to the truths they share.

Response
> There is a way which seemeth right unto a man, but the end thereof are the ways of death
> —Proverbs 14:12; 16:25

> Enter ye in at the strait gate: for wide is the gate, and broad is the way, that leadeth to destruction, and many there be which go in thereat: Because strait is the gate, and narrow is the way, which leadeth unto life, and few there be that find it.
> —Matthew 7:13–14

The issue is not the charismatic personality of an individual, but rather that the individual is preaching, teaching, and walking in obedience to the Word of God, as it is written.

Charisma of a founder means nothing! Over all of time many false teachers have been very charismatic. But we have the infallible, inherent Word of God as our plumb line, blueprint, guideline, for faith and practice, and we dare not veer away from God's Word.

Psychology vs. The Bible Chart

And Jesus asked him, saying, What is thy name? And he said, Legion: because many devils were entered into him.

—Luke 8:30

	Psychology	Bible
1	Psychology counsels no fear of the Lord at *anytime* in any of its therapies, let alone at the beginning.	The fear of the Lord is the beginning of wisdom.
2	Most Founding Fathers were atheists or humanists, including Freud, Jung, Rodgers, Maslow, James, and of course, Charles Darwin.	The fool has said in his heart there is no God.
3	Man's nature is comprised of body and soul or body, soul, and personality.	Man is made up of body, soul, and spirit: "And the very God of peace sanctify you wholly; and I pray God your whole **spirit** and **soul** and **body** be preserved blameless unto the coming of our Lord Jesus Christ" (1 Thess. 5:23).
4	Offers no hope for eternity	Teaches us about our eternal destiny.
5	Psychology doesn't even believe in the Holy Spirit.	The Bible teaches us that it is the Holy Spirit that will lead us in all truth and that it is sharper than a two-edged sword, dividing even the soul from the spirit.

	Psychology	**Bible**
6	Offers no concept of heaven to lay up your treasures for.	Teaches us to lay up for ourselves treasures in heaven.
7	Doesn't seek *first* the Kingdom of God; in fact, it *never* seeks the Kingdom of God.	Says, "Seek ye first the kingdom of God" and all these things (our needs) will be added unto us.
8	Tells us our help comes from one or more unproven theories and tens of thousands of psychotherapists whose ideas were drawn from paganism, divination, astrology, humanism, and evolution.	The Bible teaches that our help comes from the Lord.
9	Teaches that being lovers of selves is the solution	Teaches that being lovers of selves is mankind's problem.
10	Celebrate self.	Pick up the cross and deny yourself.
11	Charges for it and you still haven't received true living water.	Teaches that we can come freely to drink the waters of life.
12	Offers an improved or even damaged version of the old man.	Offers the opportunity of becoming a new man in Christ.
13	Come unto your psychotherapist and I will give you rest.	Come unto *me*, all you who are heavy laden and I will give you rest.
14	Psychology teaches us how to balance our strengths and weaknesses with personality profiles derived from paganism and divination.	Teaches that our strength is perfected in weakness and that in suffering, sin loses its power.
15	There is no such thing as demons to war against and certainly no such thing as demon-possession, so there is nothing to be delivered from.	Teaches that we war not against flesh and blood, but against principalities (i.e., demons).
16	Psychology doesn't even comprehend blessing, so it cannot offer anyone a blessing because it omits the person required to administer these blessings, that is Jesus Christ.	Tells us how to be blessed in the Beatitudes.

	Psychology	Bible
17	Attempts to bear this fruit by abiding in the teachings of such founders as Carl Jung and Sigmund Freud, who opposed Christianity!	Tells us we can't produce the fruit of the Spirit which is love, joy, peace, patience, kindness, goodness, faithfulness, gentleness, and self-control without abiding in the vine which is Jesus Christ himself. In fact, apart from Him we can do ***nothing***.
18	Can't offer salvation, sanctification, and is unable to and does not even pretend to offer the Great Commission in order that others might be saved and sanctified.	Teaches there are three things that are required of every Christian: (1) salvation, (2) sanctification, and (3) carry out the Great Commission so that others may receive.
19	Based on power of myths, fables, principles of this world's philosophies and theories.	Paul in his second epistle to Timothy said to turn aside from myths!
20	Calls its teaching "science."	Calls psychology (philosophy) "science falsely so called."
21	Everyone is a victim.	Everyone is a sinner.
22	Man's nature is rooted in evolution.	There is no such thing as evolution.
23	Christian psychologists integrate Bible with psychology theories.	You cannot serve two masters. Choose today whom you will follow–the Mighty Counselor.
24	Blame their ancestors for their problems.	Do not keep track of endless genealogies.
25	Recovery from addiction.	Repentance from addiction.
26	Cast your anxiety upon your psychotherapist.	Cast your cares and anxieties upon Him.
27	Take psychotropic drugs to get in the right mood.	Get sanctified by the Word of God, obey His Word, and allow the Holy Spirit and the Vine (Jesus Christ) to produce the fruit of the Spirit, which is the right mood.
28	Cleans one's path or way with a journal and documents every abuse that ever happened to him.	Cleans one's path by walking in paths of righteousness and taking heed according to His Word.

	Psychology	**Bible**
29	Use guided imagery to find your true self.	"**Casting down imaginations,** and every high thing that exalteth itself against the knowledge of God, and bringing into captivity every thought to the obedience of Christ" (2 Cor. 10:5).
30	Attempts to track down the archetype buried in your unconscious in man.	He heals the brokenhearted and binds up their wounds (Ps. 147:3).
31	Seek counsel from the ungodly.	Why seek ye the counsel among the ungodly?
32	Peace definition not found in either psychology dictionary or encyclopedia.	I will keep him in perfect peace whose mind is stayed on thee (Isa. 26:3).
33	Counseling is constantly changing.	God's counsel is unchanging (immutable): "Wherein God, willing more abundantly to shew unto the heirs of promise the **immutability of his counsel,** confirmed it by an oath" (Heb. 6:17).
34	"I have never believed that psychology could ever serve more than a **catalytic** role in a biblical view of human distress and Christ-dependent response." –Larry Crabb	Never mixes God's counsel with any other religion or philosophy of this world.
35	Integrationists (Christian psychologists who add psychology to the Bible)	*Sola Scriptura* is sufficient for counseling the soul: "For I have not shunned to declare unto you *all* **the counsel of God"** (Acts. 20:27).

The Church Growth Movement and Purpose Driven Church vs. The Bible

A Comparison Chart Created by James Sunduist

DISCLAIMER: Not every PDC/CGM church holds to every one of the positions on the chart, but rather the chart is a general guideline to equip and warn the saints. As an example, some churches may exclude non-believers from partaking in communion.

Position of the CGM & the Purpose Driven Church	Position of the Bible
Man adds to the church daily as should be saved through contemporary marketing methods. . . . Churches are taking surveys among unsaved and/or unchurched to determine what they do and do not like about the church, then applying the results and statistics to determine how the church should be run.	". . . And the Lord added to the church daily such as should be saved" (Acts 2:47). "But if we walk in the light, as he is in the light, we have fellowship one with another" (1 John 1:7). "Except the LORD build the house, they labour in vain that build it: except the LORD keep the city, the watchman waketh but in vain. It is vain for you to rise up early, to sit up late, to eat the bread of sorrows: for so he giveth his beloved sleep" (Ps. 127:1–2).

Position of the CGM & the Purpose Driven Church	Position of the Bible
The church needs a new purpose.	The Church already has a purpose since its beginning 2,000 years ago. The Great Commission: "Go ye into all the world, and preach the gospel to every creature. He that believeth and is baptized shall be saved; but he that believeth not shall be damned" (Mark 16:15–16). "Ye should earnestly contend for the faith which was once delivered unto the saints" (Jude 1:3). "
Conform the church to the image of the world and culture in order to make the church more palatable and comfortable for the unsaved.	"Know ye not that the friendship of the world is enmity with God?" (Jam. 4:4). "And be not conformed to this world" (Rom. 12:2). "The just shall live by faith. For the wrath of God is revealed from heaven against all ungodliness and un-righteousness of men, who hold the truth in unrighteousness" (Rom. 1:17–18).
Promote self-love.	"He that loveth his life shall lose it; and he that hateth his life in this world shall keep it unto life eternal" (John 12:25). "Loved their lives not unto the death" (Rev. 12:11).
The goal of the church is happiness and personal fulfillment.	The goal of the church is holiness. "Because it is written, Be ye holy; for I am holy" (1 Pet. 1:16).
Do not offend seekers with "religious" words.	"And a stone of stumbling, and a rock of offense, even to them which stumble at the word" (1 Pet. 2:8).
This generation is different from all past generations.	This generation is **identical** to all generations.
Remove the cross from the church.	Cling to the ole rugged cross. The cross was in plain view for all to see: ". . . and they shall look upon me whom they have pierced" (Zech. 12:10).

Position of the CGM & the Purpose Driven Church	Position of the Bible
Man-made twelve-step programs toward psychological healing and deliverance.	One-step deliverance program: Being born-again in Christ. "If the Son therefore shall make you free, ye shall be free indeed" (John 8:36). At the most, we could also acknowledge a second "step"– sanctification, which is the process of perfecting the saints until we are resurrected in our glorified bodies.
Scriptures are insufficient for perfecting the saints. Psychology and sociology help the church where the Bible seems to lack.	"All scripture is given by inspiration of God, and is profitable for doctrine, for reproof, for correction, for instruction in righteousness: That the man of God may be perfect, throughly furnished unto all good works" (2 Tim. 3:16–17).
Need to discover the key to Unchurched Harry's heart to reach him for Christ.	Condition of man's heart is already known: "And GOD saw that the wickedness of man was great in the earth, and that every imagination of the thoughts of **his heart was only evil continually"** (Gen. 6:5).
Christ's salvation is equal trade for worth of man and focus on unsaved Harry's worth.	Unequal trade: Man's worth is zero; Christ's salvation is worth infinite value. "All our righteousnesses are as filthy rags" (Isa. 64:6). Christ alone is our refuge and our worth!
Entertain the world into the Kingdom of God.	**Convict** the world unto salvation: "No man can say that Jesus is the Lord, but by the Holy Ghost" (1 Cor. 12:3).
Caters to the flesh.	Crucifies the flesh: "For if ye live after the flesh, ye shall die: but if ye through the Spirit do mortify the deeds of the body, ye shall live" (Rom. 8:13).
A growing church means God is blessing us.	Blessing and cursing is completely dependent on obedience to God's Word.

Position of the CGM & the Purpose Driven Church	Position of the Bible
Pleasers of men.	Pleasers of God: "We were allowed of God to be put in trust with the gospel, even so we speak; **not as pleasing men,** but God, which trieth our hearts" (1 Thess. 2:4).
The answer to low self-esteem is high self-esteem.	Concept of self-esteem is nonexistent in Scripture. "The sacrifices of God are a broken spirit: a broken and a contrite heart, O God, thou wilt not despise" (Ps. 51:17).
How to become an "influential Christian." –John C. Maxwell	"But he that is greatest among you shall be your servant" (Matt. 23:11). We are to be imitators of Christ who made himself of no reputation.
Nature of man: Man is a victim.	Nature of man: Man is a sinner: "For all have sinned, and come short of the glory of God" (Rom. 3:23). "They did not like to retain God in their knowledge" (Rom. 1:28).
Focus on self.	Focus on God, then others: "A new commandment I give unto you, That ye love one another; as I have loved you, that ye also love one another" (John 13:34).
Christians need to be pleasing savor to the world.	"For we are unto God a sweet savour of Christ, in them that are saved, and in them that perish: To the one we are the savour of death unto death; and to the other the savour of life unto life" (2 Cor. 2:15–16).
Unchurched have rejected church but not necessarily God.	All unsaved are in rebellion and have rejected God: "For the preaching of the cross is to them that perish foolishness; but unto us which are saved it is the power of God" 1 Corinthians 1:18.
Communion inclusive.	Communion exclusive to believers.

Position of the CGM & the Purpose Driven Church	Position of the Bible
Be loved by the world.	"Blessed are ye, when men shall hate you, and when they shall separate you from their company, and shall reproach you, and cast out your name as evil, for the Son of man's sake" (Luke 6:22). "Marvel not, my brethren, if the world hate you" (1 John 3:13).
Seek ye first the felt needs of the world and the Kingdom shall be added unto you.	"But seek ye first the kingdom of God, and his righteousness; and all these things shall be added unto you" (Matt. 6:33).
Different church services for "Churched Harry and Mary" vs. "Unchurched Harry and Mary."	Same church service and message for both church and unchurched at the Sermon on the Mount (Matt. 5:3–11). Same message of repentance to every tribe, tongue, and nation: "And he said unto them, Go ye into all the world, and preach the gospel to every creature" (Mark 16:15). (Same message throughout the Old Testament as well!)
Shine the salt of earth into a sparkling gem.	As the salt of the earth, we must be covered with the blood of the Lamb in order to retain savor, remove poison in the world, and preserve the Word: "Ye are the salt of the earth: but if the salt have lost his savour, wherewith shall it be salted? it is thenceforth good for nothing, but to be cast out, and to be trodden under foot of men" (Matt. 5:13.)
Self-centered.	Self-sacrifice.
"Unchurched Harry" will come to church via a good experience.	Harry will come to church only by God's sovereign work of grace: "For by grace are ye saved through faith; and that not of yourselves; it is the gift of God" (Eph. 2:8).

Position of the CGM & the Purpose Driven Church	Position of the Bible
Asks what we can require of God.	Asks what God requires of us.
Seeks personal fulfillment.	Seeks obedience to Christ.
Unconditional acceptance.	Requires repentance; God is not tolerant of evil. Sets in place elders in church discipline to judge and restore those in the church.
Jesus used as a "higher power" for deliverance from "disease" of abuse.	"Neither is there salvation in any other: for there is none other name under heaven given among men, whereby we must be saved" (Acts 4:12).
Integrates psychology with the Bible.	"O Timothy, keep that which is committed to thy trust, avoiding profane and vain babblings, and oppositions of science falsely so called" (1 Tim. 6:20). "To the law and to the testimony: if they speak not according to this word, it is because there is no light in them" (Isa. 8:20). "Beware lest any man spoil you through philosophy and vain deceit, after the tradition of men, after the rudiments of the world, and not after Christ" (Col. 2:8). "But there were false prophets also among the people, even as there shall be false teachers among you, who privily shall bring in damnable heresies" (2 Pet. 2:1).
You set boundaries.	God sets the boundaries.
Invites false teachers to pulpit, such as Muslim clerics; or presents false or contrary teachings in positive light from the pulpit.	Shepherds protect and guard the flock from wolves and wolves in sheep's clothing. "Take heed therefore unto yourselves, and to all the flock, over the which the Holy Ghost hath made you overseers, to feed the church of God, which he hath purchased with his own blood . . ." (Acts 20:28–31).

Position of the CGM & the Purpose Driven Church	Position of the Bible
Integrates personality theory and tests with the Bible, such as the Myer-Briggs test, SHAPE, Kiersey-Bates Temperament Sorter based on occultists and atheists Carl Jung and Sigmund Freud . . . much of which is based on astrological signs of the zodiac.	"Let now the astrologers, the stargazers, the monthly prognosticators, stand up, and save thee from these things that shall come upon thee. Behold, they shall be as stubble . . . " (Isa. 47:13–14). "Ye shall know them by their fruits. Do men gather grapes of thorns, or figs of thistles?" (Matt. 7:16). "Ye cannot drink the cup of the Lord, and the cup of devils: ye cannot be partakers of the Lord's table, and of the table of devils" (1 Cor. 10:21).
Supports Evangelical and Catholics Together (ECT) and other ecumenical endeavors.	"Wherefore come out from among them, and be ye separate, saith the Lord, and touch not the unclean thing; and I will receive you" (2 Cor. 6:17). "Now I beseech you, brethren, mark them which cause divisions and offences contrary to the doctrine which ye have learned; and avoid them" (Rom. 16:17). "Be ye not unequally yoked together with unbelievers: for what fellowship hath righteousness with unrighteousness? and what communion hath light with darkness?" (2 Cor. 6:14).
Stand in counsel of men who are not Christians to implement or finance their new church building plans.	"Blessed is the man that walketh not in the counsel of the ungodly, nor standeth in the way of sinners, nor sitteth in the seat of the scornful" (Ps. 1:1). "But if they had stood in my counsel, and had caused my people to hear my words, then they should have turned them from their evil ways, and from the evil of their doings" (Jer. 23:22).
Respecter of persons.	"Then Peter opened his mouth, and said, Of a truth I perceive that God is no respecter of persons" (Acts 10:34).

Position of the CGM & the Purpose Driven Church	Position of the Bible
Invokes imaginary Jesus (spirit) with help of spirit guide to search for past wounds, generational curses, and lost memories.	"Brethren, I count not myself to have apprehended: but this one thing I do, forgetting those things which are behind, and reaching forth unto those things with are before, I press toward the mark for the prize of the high calling of God in Christ Jesus" (Phil. 3:13–14).
Never criticize what God is "blessing."	"But though we, or an angel from heaven, preach any other gospel unto you than that which we have preached unto you, let him be accursed" (Gal. 1:8). "And have no fellowship with the unfruitful works of darkness, but rather reprove them" (Eph. 5:11). "Beloved, believe not every spirit, but try the spirits whether they are of God: because many false prophets are gone out into the world" (1 John 4:1).
Principle of pragmatism: If it works, it must be good!	Be faithful to the message: "Get thee to them of the captivity, unto the children of thy people, and speak unto them, and tell them, Thus saith the Lord GOD; whether they will hear, or whether they will forbear" (Ezek. 3:11).
All truth is God's truth.	"Howbeit when he, the Spirit of truth, is come, he will guide you into all truth" (John 16:13; see also John 14:17).
Catch people unaware.	"**Beware** lest any man spoil you through philosophy and vain deceit, after the tradition of men, after the rudiments of the world, and not after Christ" (Col. 2:8). "**Be sober, be vigilant;** because your adversary the devil, as a roaring lion, walketh about, seeking whom he may devour" (1 Pet. 5:8).

Position of the CGM & the Purpose Driven Church	Position of the Bible
Mandatory signed pledges and pyramid schemes.	"Again, ye have heard that it hath been said by them of old time, Thou shalt not forswear thyself, but shalt perform unto the Lord thine oaths: But I say unto you, Swear not at all; neither by heaven; for it is God's throne: Nor by the earth; for it is his footstool: neither by Jerusalem; for it is the city of the great King. Neither shalt thou swear by thy head, because thou canst not make one hair white or black. But let your communication be, Yea, yea; Nay, nay: for whatsoever is more than these cometh of evil" (Matt. 5:33–37).
Makes the highway to heaven as wide as possible.	"Because strait is the gate, and **narrow is the way,** which leadeth unto life, and few there be that find it" (Matt. 7:14).
Endorses or teaches Alpha Course.	Evidence of the presence of the Holy Spirit does not imitate demon possession.
Preach only "positive" messages from the pulpit.	Preach publicly the full counsel of God, which includes both the love of God and the wrath of God.
Thinks men seek after God.	"There is none that seeketh after God" (Rom. 3:11). God seeks after men: "So then faith cometh by hearing, and hearing by the word of God" (Rom. 10:17).
Promotion comes via completion of courses.	"Humble yourselves therefore under the mighty hand of God, that **he may exalt you in due time**" (1 Pet. 5:6). "For promotion cometh neither from the east, nor from the west, nor from the south. But God is the judge: he putteth down one, and setteth up another" (Ps. 75:6–7).

Position of the CGM & the Purpose Driven Church	Position of the Bible
Based on principles of this world and "universal truths."	Church governed by Word of God, based on nothing but the Person of Christ and Him crucified. "For I determined not to know any thing among you, save Jesus Christ, and him crucified" (1 Cor. 2:2).
Monitors required tithing or pledge money.	"But when thou doest alms, let not thy left hand know what thy right hand doeth" (Matt. 6:3).
Lower mind's resistance.	"Wherefore **gird up the loins of your mind,** be sober, and hope to the end for the grace that is to be brought unto you at the revelation of Jesus Christ" (1 Pet. 1:13).
No silence during church service.	"Be silent, O all flesh, before the LORD: for he is raised up out of his holy habitation" (Zech. 2:13). "The LORD is in his holy temple: let all the earth keep silence before him" (Hab. 2:20).
Man builds the church.	Jesus Christ builds His church: "And I say also unto thee, That thou art Peter, and upon this rock **I will build my church;** and the gates of hell shall not prevail against it" (Matt. 16:18).
My strength is made perfect in my "strengths", i.e. SHAPE (personality profiles, gift profiles, etc.).	"My strength is made perfect in **weakness**" (2 Cor. 12:9).
Fear of the Lord?: "I don't think fear, as a tactic, really moves people toward faith these days. So, tactically, I think there are better ways to interest the uninterested in the claims of Jesus Christ." –Pastor Bill Hybels, Willow Creek Community Church	"And the way of peace have they not known: **There is no fear of God before their eyes**" (Rom. 3:17–18).

History of Carl Jung's Infiltration Into the Church

Carl Jung, Neo-Gnosticism, & The (MBTI)

A report by Rev. Ed Hird, Past National Chair of ARM Canada
(revised March 18, 1998)

In 1991, I had the wonderful privilege of attending the Episcopal Renewal Ministries (ERM) Leadership Training Institute (LTI) in Evergreen, Colorado. Since then, I and others encouraged Anglican Renewal Ministries [ARM] Canada to endorse the LTI approach, reporting in the *ARM Canada* magazine with articles about our helpful LTI experiences. ARM Canada, through our LTI Director, Rev. Murray Henderson, has since run a number of very helpful Clergy and Lay LTIs across Canada, which have been well received and appreciated. Through listening to the tapes by Leanne Payne and Dr. Jeffrey Satinover from the 1995 Kelowna Prayer Conference, I came across some new data that challenged me to do some rethinking about the Jungian nature of the MBTI (Myers-Briggs Temperament Indicator) used in the current ARM Canada LTIs. Dr. Jeffrey Satinover's critique of Jungianism came with unique credibility, given his background as an eminent Jungian scholar, analyst, and past President of the C. G. Jung Foundation. I began to do some reading on Carl Jung, and mailed each ARM Board member a copy of the two audio tapes by Payne and Satinover. The ARM Board at our April 1996 meeting took an initial look at the Jungian nature of the MBTI, and whether we should continue to use the MBTI in our LTIs. Our ARM Board agreed to do some investigating on this topic and report back with some information to discuss at the November 1996 ARM Board meeting.

Currently approximately two and a half million people are "initiated" each year into the MBTI process.[1] According to Peter B. Myers, it is now the most extensively used personality instrument in history.[2] There is even a MBTI version for children, called the MMTIC (Murphy-Meisgeier Type Indicator for Children),[3] and a simplified adult MBTI-like tool for the general public, known as the Keirsey-Bates Indicator. A most helpful resource in analyzing the MBTI is the English Grove Booklet by Rev. Robert Innes, of St. John's College, Durham, entitled *Personality Indicators & the Spiritual Life.* Innes focused on "the two indicators most widely used by Christian groups—Myers-Briggs and the Enneagram."[4] One of the key questions for the ARM Board to settle is whether the MBTI is an integral part of Jungian neo-gnosticism, or alternately, that it may be a detachable benevolent portion of Jung's philosophy in an otherwise suspect context. To use a visual picture, is the MBTI the "marijuana," the low-level entry drug that potentially opens the door to the more hardcore Jungian involvement, or is it just a harmless sugar tablet? To get at this question, I have broken my analysis down into smaller, more concrete questions.

1. Is the MBTI actually connected with Carl Jung?

The Rev. Canon Charles Fulton, President of ERM, commented in a June 17th, 1996 letter that "We have certainly had some concerns over the MBTI over the years and its Jungian nature". Rev. Fred Goodwin, Rector of National Ministries for ERM, commented in a September 18th, 1996 letter that ". . . we [ERM] no longer use the MBTI in our teachings . . . we've not included it in the last couple of years—believing that there are many other models and issues that need to be discussed with clergy and lay leaders." In Isabel Briggs-Myers' book *Introduction To Type* (1983), she comments that the MBTI is "based on Jung's theory of psychological types."[5] In the book *People*

Types and Tiger Stripes written by Jungian practitioner Dr. Gordon Lawrence, he states that "The [MBTI] Indicator was developed specifically to carry Carl Jung's theory of type (Jung, 1921, 1971) into practical application."[6] In the Grove Book on personality indicators, Robert Innes comments that "Carl Jung's psychology lies behind . . . the MBTI."[7]

The Buros Mental Measurement YearBook (1989, 10th Edition) notes that the MBTI ". . . is a construct-oriented test that is inextricably linked with Jung's (1923) theory of psychological types."[8] As to the evidence of validity, Buros characterizes the stability of type classification over time as "somewhat disappointing."[9] The Jungian/MBTI stance, as expressed by Dr. Gordon Lawrence, former President of the Association for Psychological Types, is that MBTI "types are a fact," not a theory.[10] After reviewing the statistical evidence relating to the MBTI, however, Dr. Paul Kline, Professor of Psychometrics at Exeter University, commented that "There has been no clear support for the 8-fold categorization, despite the popularity of the MBTI."[11] Mario Bergner, a colleague of Leanne Payne in Pastoral Care Ministries, observed in a July 2nd, 1996 letter that "of all the different types of psychological testing, forced choice tests (such as the MBTI) are considered the least valid." More specifically, Bergner noted that "the validity of the MBTI is at zero because the test is based on a Jungian understanding of the soul which cannot be measured for good or bad." The official MBTI view, as expressed by Dr. Gordon Lawrence, is that MBTI personality designations are "as unchangeable as the stripes on a tiger."[12] Bergner, in contrast, does not believe that all of humanity can be unchangeably boxed into 16 temperament types, and is concerned about cases where people are being rejected for job applications, because they don't fit certain MBTI categories.

2. What is Carl Jung's Relation to Neo-Gnosticism?

Carl Jung is described by Merill Berger, a Jungian psychologist, as "the psychologist of the 21st century."[13] Dr. Satinover says "Because of his great influence in propagating gnostic philosophy and morals in churches & synagogues, Jung deserves a closer look. The moral relativism that released upon us the sexual revolution is rooted in an outlook of which [Jung] is the most brilliant contemporary expositor."[14] One could say without overstatement that Carl Jung is the Father of Neo-Gnosticism & the New Age Movement. That is why Satinover comments that "One of the most powerful modern forms of Gnosticism is without question Jungian psychology, both within or without the Church."[15] Carl Jung "explicitly identified depth psychology, especially his own, as heir to the apostolic tradition, especially in what he considered its superior handling of the problem of evil."[16] Jung claimed that "In the ancient world, the Gnostics, whose arguments were very much influenced by psychic experience, tackled the problem of evil on a broader basis than the Church Fathers."[17] Dr. Satinover notes that "Whatever the system, and however the different stages are purportedly marked, the ultimate aim, the innermost circle of all Gnostic systems, is a mystical vision of the union of good and evil."[18]

Jung, says Satinover, "devoted most of his adult life to a study of alchemy; he also explicated both antique hermeticism and the 'christian' gnostics; his earliest writings were about spiritualism . . ."[19] In his autobiography *Memories, Dreams, Reflections,* Jung claimed: "The possibility of a comparison with alchemy, and the uninterrupted intellectual chain back to Gnosticism, gave substance to my psychology."[20] Most people are not aware that Jung collected one of the largest amassing of spiritualistic writings found on the European continent.[21] Dr. James Hillman, the former director for the Jungian Institute in Zurich, commented, "[Jung] wrote the first introduction to Zen Buddhism, he . . . brought in [Greek Mythology], the gods and the goddesses, the myths, . . . he was interested in astrology. . . ."[22]

In 1929, Jung wrote a commentary on the *Secret of the Golden Flower,* which he said was "not only a Taoist text concerned with Chinese Yoga, but is also an alchemical treatise."[23] He comments that ". . . it was the text of the Golden Flower that first put me on the right track. For in medieval alchemy we have the long-sought connecting link between Gnosis (i.e. of the Gnostics) and the processes of the collective unconscious that can be observed in modern man. . . ."[24] Dr.

Richard Noll comments that "the divinatory methods of the I Ching, used often by Jung in the 1920s and 1930s, were a part of the initial training program of the C. G. Jung Institute of Zurich in 1948, and its use is widely advocated today in Jungian Analytic-Training Institutes throughout the world."[25]

During the hippie movement of the 1960s, the Rock Opera *Hair* boldly proclaimed the alleged dawning of the Age of Aquarius. Once again Carl Jung foreshadowed this emphasis in a 1940 letter to his former assistant, Godwin Baynes: "1940 is the year when we approach the meridian of the first star in Aquarius. It is the premonitory earthquake of the New Age."[26] In Jung's book *Aion*, he holds that ". . . the appearance of Christ coincided with the beginning of a new aeon, the age of the Fishes. A sychronicity exists between the life of Christ and the objective astronomical event, the entrance of the spring equinox into the sign of Pisces."[27] In a letter written by Jung to Sigmund Freud, he said: "My evenings are taken up very largely with astrology. I made horoscopic calculations in order to find a clue to the core of psychological truth . . . I dare say that we shall one day discover in astrology a good deal of knowledge which has been intuitively projected into the heavens."[28]

Jung's family had occult linkage on both sides, from his paternal Grandfather's Freemasonry involvement as Grandmaster of the Swiss Lodge[29], and his maternal family's long-term involvement with seances and ghosts. John Kerr, author of *A Most Dangerous Method*, comments that Jung was heavily involved for many years with his mother and two female cousins in hypnotically induced seances. Jung eventually wrote up the seances as his medical dissertation.[30] Jung acquired a spirit guide and guru named "Philemon" [who was described by Jung as "an old man with the horns of a bull . . . and the wings of a fisher"]. Before being Philemon, this creature appeared to Jung as "Elijah," and then finally mutated to "Ka," an Egyptian earth-soul that "came from below."[31] It may be worth reflecting upon why Jung designated his Bollingen Tower as the Shrine of Philemon.[32]

Carl Jung himself was the son of a Swiss Pastor caught in an intellectual faith crisis. When younger, he had a life-changing dream of a subterranean phallic god which reappeared "whenever anyone spoke too emphatically about Lord Jesus."[33] Jung commented that ". . . the 'man-eater' in general was symbolized by the phallus, so that the dark Lord Jesus, the Jesuit and the phallus were identical."[34] This "initiation into the realm of darkness"[35] radically shaped Jung's approach to Jesus: "Lord Jesus never became quite real for me, never quite acceptable, never quite lovable, for again and again I would think of his underground counterpart . . . Lord Jesus seemed to me in some ways a god of death. . . . Secretly, his love and kindness, which I always heard praised, appeared doubtful to me. . . ."[36] The next major spiritual breakthrough in his life was what Jung described as a "blasphemous vision"[37] of God dropping his dung on the local Cathedral. This vision, said Jung, gave him an intense "experience of divine grace."[38]

3. How serious is the Jungian Reconciliation of Good and Evil?

Leanne Payne says of Dr. Jeffrey Satinover that "like [C. S.] Lewis, he knows that we can never reconcile (synthesize) good and evil, and this synthesis is the greatest threat facing not only Christendom but all mankind today."[39] Dr. Satinover sees the temptation facing our generation that ". . . on a theological plane, we succumb to the dangerous fantasy that Good and Evil will be reunited in a higher oneness."[40]

One of Jung's key emphases was that the "dark side" of human nature needed to be "integrated" into a single, overarching "wholeness" in order to form a less strict and difficult definition of goodness.[41] "For Jung," says Satinover, "good and evil evolved into two equal, balanced, cosmic principles that belong together in one overarching synthesis. This relativization of good and evil by their reconciliation is the heart of the ancient doctrines of gnosticism, which also located spirituality, hence morality, within man himself. Hence 'the union of opposites'."[42]

Jung believed that "the Christ-symbol lacks wholeness in the modern psychological sense, since it does not include the dark side of things. . . ."[43] For Jung, it was regrettable that Christ in his goodness lacked a shadow side, and God the Father, who is the Light, lacked darkness.[44] He spoke of ". . . an archetype such as . . . the still pending answer to the Gnostic question as to the origin of evil, or, to put it another way, the incompleteness of the Christian God-image."[45] Jung sought a solution to this dilemma in the Holy Spirit who united the split in the moral opposites symbolized by Christ and Satan.[46] "Looked at from a quaternary standpoint," writes Jung, "the Holy Ghost is a reconciliation of opposites and hence the answer to the suffering in the Godhead which Christ personifies."[47] Thus for Jung, says John Dourley, the Spirit unites the exclusively spiritual reality of Christ with that which is identified with the devil, including "the dark world of nature-bound man," the chthonic side of nature excluded by Christianity from the Christ image.[48] In a similar vein, Jung saw the alchemical figure of Mercurius as a compensation for the one-sideness of the symbol of Christ.[49] That is why Jung believed that "It is possible for a man to attain totality, to become whole, only with the co-operation of the spirit of darkness. . . ."[50]

4. How Much Influence does Jungian Neo-Gnosticism have on the Church?

There are key individuals promoting the Jungian gospel to the Church, such as Morton Kelsey, John Sanford (not John & Paula Sandford), Thomas Moore, Joseph Campbell, and Bishop John Spong. Thomas Moore, a former Roman Catholic monk, is widely popular with a new generation of soulseekers, through his bestseller: *Care of the Soul*. John Sanford, the son of the late Agnes Sanford, is an Episcopal Priest and Jungian analyst, with several books promoting the Jungian way. Morton Kelsey is another Episcopal Priest who has subtly woven the Jungian gospel through virtually every one of his books, specially those aimed for the Charismatic renewal constituency. Satinover describes Kelsey as having "made a career of such compromise," noting that Kelsey has now proceeded in his latest book *Sacrament of Sexuality* to approve of the normalization of homosexuality.[51]

Joseph Campbell, cited by Satinover as a disciple of Jung, is famous for his public TV series on "The Power of Myth."[52] Bishop John Spong, who has written two books (*Resurrection: Myth or Reality* &

The Easter Moment) denying the physical resurrection of Jesus Christ, gives Joseph Campbell credit for shaping his views on Jesus' resurrection. "I was touched by Campbell's ability to seek the truth of myths while refusing to literalize the rational explanation of those myths . . . Campbell allowed me to appreciate such timeless themes as virgin births, incarnations, physical resurrections, and cosmic ascensions. . . . Slowly, ever so slowly, but equally ever so surely, a separation began to occur for me between the experience captured for us Christians in the word Easter and the interpretation of that experience found in both the Christian Scriptures and the developing Christian traditions. . . ."[53] Few people have realized that Bishop Spong's spiritual grandfather is none other than Carl Jung.

"Jung's direct and indirect impact on mainstream Christianity—and thus on Western culture," says Satinover, " has been incalculable. It is no exaggeration to say that the theological positions of most mainstream denominations in their approach to pastoral care, as well as in their doctrines and liturgy—have become more or less identical with Jung's psychological/symbolic theology."[54] It is not just the more 'liberal' groups, however, that are embracing the Jungian/MBTI approach. In a good number of Evangelical theological colleges, the MBTI is being imposed upon the student body as a basic course requirement, despite the official Jungian stance that "The client has the choice of taking the MBTI or not. Even subtle pressure should be avoided."[55]

While in theological school, I became aware of the strong influence of Dr. Paul Tillich on many modern clergy. In recently reading C. G. Jung & Paul Tillich [written by John Dourley, a Jungian analyst & Roman priest from Ottawa], I came to realize that Tillich and Jung are "theological twins." In a tribute given at a Memorial for Jung's death, Tillich gave to Jung's thought the status of an ontology because its depth and universality constituted a "doctrine of being"[56] It turns out that Tillich is heavily in debt in Jung for his view of God as the supposed "Ground of Being." As well, both Tillich and Jung, says Dourley, "understand the self to be that centering force within the psyche which brings together the opposites or polarities, whose dynamic interplay makes up life itself."[57] As a Jungian popularizer, Tillich saw life as "made up of the flow of energy between opposing poles or opposites."[58]

So many current theological emphases in today's church can be traced directly back to Carl Jung. For example, with the loss of confidence in the Missionary imperative, many mainline church administrators today sound remarkably like Jung when he said: "What we from our point of view call colonization, missions to the heathen, spread of civilization, etc, has another face—the face of a bird of prey seeking with cruel intentness for distant quarry—a face worthy of a race of pirates and highwaymen."[59] In speaking of Buddhism and Christianity, Jung taught the now familiar interfaith dialogue line, that "Both paths are right."[60] Jung spoke of Jesus, Mani, Buddha, and Lao-Tse as "pillars of the spirit," saying "I could give none preference over the other."[61] The English Theologian Don Cupitt says that Jung pioneered the multi-faith approach now widespread in the Church.[62]

For those of us who wonder why some Anglicans are mistakenly calling themselves "co-creators with God," the theological roots can again be traced back to Jung: ". . . man is indispensable for the completion of creation; that, in fact, he himself is the 2nd creator of the world, who alone has given to the world its objective existence. . . ."[63] In light of our current Canadian controversies around "Mother Goddess" hymnbooks, it is interesting to read in the MBTI source book, *Psychological Types* (Carl Jung, 1921) about the "Gnostic prototype, viz, Sophia, an immensely significant symbol for the Gnosis."[64] Carl Jung is indeed the Grandfather of much of our current theology.

5. What is the connection between "Archetypes," the Unconscious and the MBTI?

Keirsey and Bates are strong MBTI supporters who have identified the link between the MBTI psychological types and Jungian archetypes. In their book *Please Understand Me,* they state Jung's belief that ". . . all have the same multitude of instincts (i.e. archetypes) to drive them from within." Jung therefore "invented the 'function types' or 'psychological types'" to combine the uniformity of the archetypes with the diversity of human functioning.[65] In their best-selling MBTI book: *Gifts Differing,* Isabel Myers Briggs and Peter B. Myers speak openly about Jungian Archetypes as "those symbols, myths, and concepts that appear to be inborn and shared by members of a civilization."[66]

Dr. Richard Noll holds in his book *The Jung Cult* that such Jungian ideas as the "collective unconscious" and the theory of the archetypes come as much from late 19th century occultism, neopaganism, and social Darwinian teaching, as they do from natural science.[67] Jung's post-Freudian work (after 1912), especially his theories of the collective unconscious and the archetypes, could not have been constructed, says Noll, without the works of G. R. S. Mead on Gnosticism, Hermeticism, and the Mithraic Liturgy. Starting in 1911, Jung quoted Mead, a practicing Theosophist, regularly in his works through his entire life.[68] Richard Webster holds that "the Unconscious is not simply an occult entity for whose real existence there is no palpable evidence. It is an illusion produced by language—a kind of intellectual hallucination."[69]

Jung was a master at creating obscure, scientific-sounding concepts, usually adapted from occultic literature. Jung held that "the collective unconsciousness is the sediment of all the experience of the universe of all time, and is also the image of the universe that has been in process of formation from untold ages. In the course of time, certain features became prominent in this image, the so-called dominants (later called archetypes by Jung)."[70] [Much of Jung's teaching on archetypes is so obscure that I have placed the relevant data in the footnotes of this report, for the more motivated reader.]

In his phylogenetic racial theory, Jung assumes that acquired cultural attitudes, and hence Jungian archetypes, can actually be transmitted by genetic inheritance. Richard Webster, however, explodes Jung's phylogenetic theory as biologically untenable.[71] Peter B. Medawar, a distinguished biologist, wrote in the *New York Review of Books* (Jan. 23, 1975): "The opinion is gaining ground that doctrinaire psychoanalytic theory is the most stupendous intellectual confidence trick of the 20th century: and a terminal product as well—something akin to a dinosaur or zeppelin in the history of ideas, a vast structure of radically unsound design and with no posterity."

"This work *Psychological Types* (1921), said Jung, "sprung originally from my need to define the way in which my outlook differs from Freud's and Adler's. In attempting to answer this question, I came across the problem of types, for it is one's psychological type which from the outset determines and limits a person's judgment."[72] In words strangely reminiscent of L. Ron Hubbard's Scientology, Jung teaches in Psychological Types (PT) that "The unconscious, regarded as the historical background of the psyche, contains in a concentrated form the entire succession of engrams (imprints), which from time to time have determined the psychic structure as it now exists."[73]

Jung held in *PT* that "The magician . . . has access to the unconscious that is still pagan, where the opposites still lie together in their primeval naiveté, beyond the reach of 'sinfulness', but liable, when accepted into conscious life, to beget evil as well as good with the same primeval and therefore daemonic force."[74] Jung entitled an entire section in *PT:* "Concerning the Brahmanic Conception of the Reconciling Symbol". Jung notes: "Brahman therefore must signify the irrational union of the opposites—hence their final overcoming. . . . These quotations show that Brahman is the reconciliation and dissolution of the opposites—hence standing beyond them as an irrational factor."[75]

My recurring question is: "Do we in ARM Canada wish to be directly or indirectly sanctioning this kind of teaching?" Symbolically, the MBTI can be thought of as a "freeze-dried" version of Jung's *Psychological Types* (1921). Since *PT* teaches extensively about Jung's archetypes and collective unconscious, it seems clear to me that to endorse the "freeze-dried" MBTI is ultimately to endorse Jung's archetypal, occultic philosophy.

6. What is the Relationship between Neo-gnosticism and the MBTI?

Dr. Richard Noll of Harvard University comments that "We know that [Wilhelm] Ostwald was a significant influence on Jung in the formation of his theory of psychological types."[76] Jung mentioned Ostwald's division of men of genius into classics and romantics in his first public presentation on psychological types at the Psychoanalytic Congress in Munich in September 1913. The classics and the romantics corresponded, according to Jung, to the introverted type and the extraverted type. Long quotations from Ostwald appear in other of Jung's work between 1913 and 1921—precisely the period of Ostwald's most outspoken advocacy of eugenics, nature worship, and German imperialism through the Monistenbund, a Monistic Alliance led by Ostwald. An entire chapter of Jung's *Psychological Types* is devoted favorably to these same ideas of Ostwald."[77] Is any link, however, between Ostwald's Germanic anti-Semitism and Jung merely an exercise in "guilt-by-association"? The newly emerging hard data would suggest otherwise. The influence of Germanic anti-Semitism on Jungianism can now be seen in a secret quota clause designed to limit Jewish membership to 10% in the Analytical Psychology Club of Zurich. Jung's secret Jewish quota was in effect from 1916 to 1950, and only came to public light in 1989.[78]

"The book on types [*PT*]," says Jung, "yielded the view that every judgment made by an individual is conditioned by his personality type and that every point of view is necessarily relative. This raised the question of the unity which much compensate this diversity, and it led me directly to the Chinese concept of Tao."[79] Put simply, the MBTI conceptually leads to Taoism. Jung held that the central concept of his psychology was "the process of individuation." Interesting the subtitle of the *PT* book, which the MBTI claims to represent, is ". . . or The Psychology of Individuation." Philip Davis, Associate Professor of Religious Studies at the University of P.E.I. comments, "In this lengthy process of 'individuation', one learns that one's personality incorporates a series of polar opposites: rationality and irrationality, the 'animal' and the 'spiritual', 'masculinity' and 'femininity', and so on. The goal of the [Jungian] exercise is the reconciliation of the opposites, bringing them all into a harmony that results in 'self-actualization'."[80] Once again, it seems that aspect after aspect of this seemingly innocuous personality test leads back to Jung's fundamental philosophic and religious teachings.

Two of Jung's "most influential archetypes" are the anima & animus, described by Jung as "psychological bisexuality."[81] Jung teaches in *PT* that every man has a female soul (anima) and every woman has a male soul (animus).[82] Noll comments that "Jung's first encounter with the feminine entity he later called the anima seems to have begun with his use of mediumistic techniques. . . ."[83] Based on the recently discovered personal diary of Sabina Spielrein, John Kerr claims that Jung's so-called anima "the woman within" which he spoke to, was none other than his idealized image of his former mistress, patient, and fellow therapist, Sabina Spielrein.[84] After breaking with both Spielrein and Freud, Jung felt his own soul vanish as if it had flown away to the land of the dead. Shortly after, while his children were plagued by nightmares and the house was seemingly haunted, Jung heard a chorus of spirits cry out demanding: "We have come back from Jerusalem where we have not found what we sought."[85]

In response to these spirits, Jung wrote his *Seven Sermons to the Dead*. In these seven messages Jung "reveals," in agreement with the 2nd century Gnostic writer Basilides, the True and Ultimate God as Abraxas, who combines Jesus and Satan, good and evil all in one.[86] This is why Jung held that "Light is followed by shadow, the other side of the Creator."[87] Dr. Noll, a clinical psychologist and post-doctoral fellow at Harvard University, holds that "Jung was waging war against Christianity and its distant, absolute, unreachable God and was training his disciples to listen to the voice of the dead and to become gods themselves."[88]

7. What Does the MBTI Prototype Book *"Psychological Types"* teach about Opposites?

Consistently Jung teaches about reconciliation of opposites, even of good and evil. Jung comments in *MDR*: ". . . a large part of my life work has revolved around the problem of opposites and especially their alchemical symbolism. . . ."[89] Through experiencing Goethe's *Faust*, Jung came to believe in the "universal power" of evil and "its mysterious role it played in delivering man from darkness and suffering."[90] "Most of all," said Jung, "[Faust] awakened in me the problem of opposites, of good and evil, of mind and matter, of light and darkness."[91] Being influenced as well by the Yin-Yang of Taoism, Jung believed that "Everything requires for its existence its opposite, or it fades into nothingness."[92]

Dr. Gordon Lawrence, a strong Jungian/MBTI supporter, teaches that "In Jung's theory, the two kinds of perception—sensing and intuition—are polar opposites of each other. Similarly, thinking judgment and feeling judgment are polar opposites."[93] It seems to me that the setting up of the psychological polar opposites in *PT* functions as a useful prelude for gnostic reconciliation of all opposites. The MBTI helps condition our minds into thinking about the existence of polar opposites, and their alleged barriers to perfect wholeness. In the *PT* book, Jung comments that "One may be sure therefore, that, interwoven in the new symbol with its living beauty, there is also the element of evil, for, if not, it would lack the glow of life as well as beauty, since life and beauty are naturally indifferent to morality."[94] My question for the ARM Board is: "Do we accept Jung's 'polar opposites' view that there can be no life and beauty without evil?"

"We must beware," said Jung, "of thinking of good and evil as absolute opposites. . . . The criterion of ethical action can no longer consist in the simple view that good has the force of a categorical imperative, while so-called evil can resolutely be shunned. Recognition of the reality of evil necessarily relativizes the good, and the evil likewise, converting both into halves of a paradoxical whole."[95] Here is where Jung ties in his ethical relativism to the PT/MBTI worldview: "In practical terms, this means that good and evil are no longer so self-evident. We have to realize that each represents a judgment."[96]

Jung saw the reconciliation of opposites as a sign of great sophistication: "[Chinese philosophy] never failed to acknowledge the polarity and paradoxity of all life. The opposites always balanced one another—a sign of high culture. Onesideness, though it lends momentum, is a sign of barbarism."[97] It would not be too far off to describe Jung as a gnostic Taoist. In *PT,* Jung comments that "The Indian [Brahman-Atman teaching] conception teaches liberation from the opposites, by which every sort of affective style and emotional hold to the object is understood. . . . Yoga is a method by which the libido is systematically 'drawn in' and thereby released from the bondage of opposites."[98]

While in India in 1938, Jung says that he "was principally concerned with the question of the psychological nature of evil."[99] He was "impressed again and again by the fact that these people were able to integrate so-called 'evil' without 'losing face.' . . . To the oriental, good and evil are meaningfully contained in nature, and are merely varying degrees of the same thing. I saw that Indian spirituality contains as much of evil as of good . . . one does not really believe in evil, and one does not really believe in good."[100]

In a comment reminiscent of our 1990s relativistic culture, Jung said of Hindu thought: "Good or evil are then regarded at most as my good or my evil, as whatever seems to me good or evil."[101] To accept the eight polarities within the MBTI predisposes one to embrace Jung's teaching that the psyche "cannot set up any absolute truths, for its own polarity determines the relativity of its statements."[102] Jung was also a strong promoter of the occultic mandala, a circular picture with a sun or star usually at the centre. Sun worship, as personified in the mandala, is perhaps the key to fully understanding Jung.[103] Jung taught that the mandala [Sanskrit for "circle"] was "the simplest model of a concept of wholeness, and one which spontaneously arises in the mind as a representation of the struggle and reconciliation of opposites."[104]

In conclusion, to endorse the MBTI is to endorse Jung's book *Psychological Types*, since the MBTI proponents consistently say that the MBTI "was developed specifically to carry Carl Jung's theory of types (1921, 1971) into practical application."[105] Let us seek the Lord in unity as he reveals his heart for us in this matter.

—Rev. Ed Hird, Past National Chair, ARM Canada

[Note: ARM Canada decided in November 1997 after much prayer and reflection to no longer use the MBTI in the Clergy and Lay Leadership Training Institutes.]

Footnotes for "Carl Jung, Neo-Gnosticism, & The MBTI"

1. Isabel Briggs Myers with Peter B. Myers, *Gifts Differing* (Palo Alto, CA: Consulting Press, Inc., 1980) p. xvii. Many charismatics have a soft spot for this book, because it quotes portions of scripture from Romans 12 and 1 Corinthians 12. The actual link, however,

between those Bible passages, and the Jung/Myers-Briggs theories is rather questionable. In an October 29, 1996, letter from Rev. Fred Goodwin, rector of national ministries for ERM, Fred Goodwin commented: "I would suggest that in light of your concerns, you drop the MBTI and use some of the material out on small group ministry and discipling instead—which we find are desperate needs for leadership training in the church."

2. Ibid., p. 210; also Dr. Gordon Lawrence, *People Types and Tiger Stripes*, p. xi. A book, *Prayer and Temperament*, written by Msgr. Chester Michael and Marie Norrisey in 1984 has been very effective in winning Roman Catholics and Anglicans to the MBTI. The book claims that the MBTI designations will make you either oriented to Ignatian prayer (if you are SJ), Augustinian prayer (if you are NF), Franciscan prayer (if you are SP), or Thomistic prayer (if you are NT). In the MBTI, the four sets of types are Extravert (E) and Introvert (I), Sensate (S) and Intuitive (N), Thinking (T) and Feeling (F), and Judging (J) and Perceiving (P). None of these eight innocuous-sounding type names mean what they sound like. Instead each of the eight type names has unique and mysterious, perhaps even occultic, definitions given by Jung himself in a massive section at the back of *Psychological Types*.

3. Dr. Gordon Lawrence, *People Types and Tiger Stripes* (Gainesville, FL: Center for Applications of Psychological Types, 1979), p. 222 .

4. Robert Innes, *Personality Indicators and The Spiritual Life* (Grove Books Ltd., Cambridge, 1996), p. 3. The Ennegram is significantly occultic in nature and origin, coming from Sufi, numerology, and Arica New-Age sources. George Gurideff, Oscar Ichazo of Esalen Institute, and Claudio Naranjo are the prominent New Agers who have popularized it, and then introduced it, through Fr. Bob Oschs SJ, into the Christian church. For more information, I recommend Robert Innes' booklet and Mitchell Pacwa SJ article's "Tell Me Who I Am, O Ennegram," *Christian Research Journal*, Fall 1991, pp. 14ff.

5. Isabel Briggs Myers, *Introduction to Type* (Palo Alto, CA: Consulting Psychologists Press, 1983), p. 4.

6. Dr. Gordon Lawrence, *People Types and Tiger Stripes*, p. 6; also p. x .

7. Robert Innes, *Personality Indicators and The Spiritual Life*, p. 8.

8. *The Buros Mental Measurement Yearbook* (1989, 10th Edition), p. 93.

9. Ibid., p. 93 .

10. Dr. Gordon Lawrence, *People Types and Tiger Stripes*, p. 150.

11. Dr. Paul Kline, *Personality: The Psychometric View* (Routledge, 1993), p. 136.

12. Dr. Gordon Lawrence, *People Types and Tiger Stripes*, back cover.

13. Merill Berger and Stephen Segaller, *The Wisdom of the Dreams* (C. G. Jung Foundation, New York, NY, Shamballa Publications), front cover.

14. Dr. Jeffrey Satinover, *Homosexuality and the Politics of Truth* (Baker Book House Co., 1996), p. 238.

15. Jeffrey Satinover, *The Empty Self*, p. 27. Jung has "blended psychological reductionism with gnostic spirituality to produce a modern variant of mystical, pagan polytheism in which the multiple 'images of the instincts' (his 'archetypes') are worshipped as gods" (Satinover, *Homosexuality and the Politics of Truth*, p. 238).

16. Ibid., p. 238.

17. Dr. Carl Jung, *Aion: Collected Works*, Vol. 9, 2 (Princeton: Princeton University Press, 1959), p. 10.

18. Jeffrey Satinover, *The Empty Self*, p. 23.

19. Ibid., p. 27, Ft. 28.

20. Carl Jung and Aniela Jaffe, *Memories, Dreams, Reflections*, translated from the German by Richard and Clara Winston (Vintage Books/Random House, 1961/1989), p. 205.

21. Jeffrey Satinover, *The Empty Self*, p. 28.

22. *The Wisdom of the Dreams: Carl Gustav Jung: a Stephen Segaller Video*, Vol. 3, "A World of Dreams." Jung also wrote the first Western commentary on the Tibetan *Book of the Dead* (*Psychology and the East*, p. 60).

23. Carl Jung, *Psychology and the East* (London and New York: Ark Paper Back, 1978/1986), p. 3.

24. Ibid., p. 6.

25. Dr. Richard Noll, *The Jung Cult: Origins of a Charismatic Movement* (Princeton, New Jersey: Princeton University Press, 1994), p. 333.

26. Merill Berger and Stephen Segaller, *The Wisdom of the Dreams,* p. 162; Jung and Jaffe, *Memories, Dreams, Reflections,* p. 340.

27. Jung and Jaffe, *Memories, Dreams, Reflections,* p. 221.

28. Richard Webster, *Why Freud Was Wrong: Sin, Science, and Psychoanalysis* (Basic Books: Harper Collins, 1995), p. 385. Jung comments: "For instance, it appears that the signs of the zodiac are character pictures, in other words, libido symbols which depict the typical qualities of the libido at a given moment. . . ."

29. Jung and Jaffe, *Memories, Dreams, Reflections,* p. 232.

30. John Kerr, *A Most Dangerous Method: the Story of Jung, Freud, and Sabina Spielrein* (New York, Alfred Knopf Books, 1993). pp. 50, 54.

31. Satinover, *The Empty Self,* p. 37. The spirit guide Philemon/Elijah later mutated into Salome, who addressed Jung in a self-directed trance vision as Christ. Jung "saw" himself assume the posture of a victim of crucifixion, with a snake coiled around him, and his face transformed into that of a lion from the Mithraic mystery religion. (C. G. Jung, *Analytical Psychology* [Princeton University Press, 1989], pp. 96,98).

32. Jung and Jaffe, *Memories, Dreams, Reflections,* p. 223. "Shrine of Philemon: Repentance of Faust" was the inscription carved in stone by Jung over the entrance of the Bollingen Tower, where he lived and wrote.

33. Ibid., p. 12.

34. Ibid., p. 12.

35. Ibid., p. 15.

34. Ibid., p. 13.

35. Ibid., p. 15.

36. Ibid., p. 13.

37. Ibid., p. 58. Jung concluded from this "cathedral" experience that "God Himself can . . . condemn a person to blasphemy" (*Memories, Dreams, Reflections,* p. 74).

38. Ibid., p. 55.

39. Satinover, *The Empty Self,* p. 3.

40. Satinover, *Homosexuality and the Politics of Truth,* p. 238.

41. Ibid., p. 240.

42. Ibid., p. 240. Keirsey and Bates, authors of *Please Understand Me,* and creators of the more popularized Keirsey-Bates adaptation of the MBTI, teach openly in their book on the Jungian "shadow. . . . It's as if, in being attracted to our opposite, we grope around for that rejected, abandoned, or unlived half of ourselves. . . ." (p. 68).

43. Jung, *Aion: Collected Works,* p. 41.

44. John P. Dourley, C. G. Jung, and Paul Tillich: *The Psyche as Sacrament* (Inner City Books, 1981), p. 63. "[Jung] also feels that it is questionable in that [the Christ symbol] contains no trace of the shadow side of life." Fr. Dourley, a Jungian analyst, also comments on p. 63 about Jung's "criticism of the Christian conception of a God in who there is no darkness."

45. Jung and Jaffe, *Memories, Dreams, Reflections,* p. 318.

46. Dourley, Jung, and Tillich, p. 70.

47. Carl Jung, "A Psychological Approach to The Trinity," CW11, para. 260.

48. Ibid., para. 263.

49. Carl Jung, "The Spirit Mercurius," *Alchemical Studies,* CW13, para. 295. Jung comments, "As early as 1944, in *Psychology and Alchemy,* I had been able to demonstrate the parallel-

ism between the Christ figure and the central concept of the alchemists, the lapis or stone" (*Memories, Dreams, Reflections*, p. 210).

50. C. G. Jung, "The Phenomenology of the Spirit in Fairy Tales," CW9, para. 453.

51. Satinover, *Homosexuality and the Politics of Truth*, p. 241.

52. Satinover, *The Empty Self*, p. 9. Joseph Campbell in fact worked personally with Jung and published through the Jungian-controlled Bollingen Foundation (Philip Davis, "The Swiss Maharishi," *Touchstone*, Issue 92, Spring 1996, p. 11).

53. The Right Reverend John Spong, *Resurrection: Reality or Myth* (Harper, 1994), p. xi. His parallel book is *The Easter Moment*.

54. Satinover, *Homosexuality and the Politics of Truth*, p. 240. Satinover dryly comments that "in the United States, the Episcopal Church has more or less become a branch of Jungian psychology, theologically and liturgically" (*Empty Self*, p. 27, Ft. 27).

55. Dr. Gordon Lawrence, *People Types and Tiger Stripes*, p. 218.

56. A Memorial Meeting (New York, Analytical Psychology Club, 1962), p. 31.

57. Dourley, Jung, and Tillich, p. 17.

58. Ibid., p. 48. The persistent modern emphasis on the so-called "inner child" makes a lot more sense when seen as a spin-off from Jung's teaching that the symbol of the child is "that final goal that reconciles the opposites" (Dourley, p. 83).

59. Ibid., p. 248.

60. Ibid., p. 279.

61. Dourley, Jung, and Tillich, p. 65.

62. *The Wisdom of the Dream*, p. 99.

63. Jung and Jaffe, *Memories, Dreams, Reflections*, p. 256.

64. Carl Jung, *Psychological Types: or the Psychology of Individuation* [Princeton University Press, 1921/1971], p. 290. Dr. Jeffrey Satinover memorably comments as a former Jungian that "goddess worship" is not the cure for misogyny, but it is its precondition, whether overtly or unconsciously (*The Empty Self*, p. 9). Marija Bimbutas, the late professor of archeology at UCLA, included Jung and more than a half dozen of his noted disciples in the bibliographies to her books on the alleged matriarchies of the Balkans, *The Language of the Goddess* (1989) and *The Civilization of the Goddess* (1991) (Philip Davis, "The Swiss Maharishi," *Touchstone*, Spring 1996, p. 13).

65. David Keirsey and Marilyn Bates, *Please Understand Me* (Del Mar, CA: Promothean Books), p. 3.

66. Isabel Myers Briggs and Peter B. Myers, *Gifts Differing*, p. xiv.

67. Richard Noll, *The Jung Cult*, front cover.

68. Ibid., p. 69. Dr. Noll comments: "I therefore argue that the Jung cult and its present day movement is in fact a 'Nietzschean religion'" (p. 137). Frederick Nietzsche's stated view on Christianity is: "The Christian Church has left nothing untouched by its depravity; it has turned every value into worthlessness, and every truth into a lie" (*Canadian Atheist*, Issue 8, 1996, p. 1).

69. Richard Webster, *Why Freud Was Wrong*, p. 250.

70. Jung, *Collected Papers on Analytical Psychology*, "The Psychology of Unconscious Processes," p. 432. These dominants, said Jung, "are the ruling powers, the gods; that is, the representations resulting from dominating laws and principles, from average regularities in the issue of images that the brain has received as a consequence of secular processes." (p. 432).

71. Webster, *Why Freud Was Wrong*, p. 387.

72. Berger and Segaller, *Wisdom of the Dreams*, p. 103; *Memories, Dreams, Reflections*, p. 207.

73. Jung, *Psychological Types*, p. 211.

74. Ibid., p. 233. It would be interesting to research how much Jungian reading George Lucas did in preparing to produce his blockbuster *Star Wars* [i.e. "May the Force be with you"]. The

deity-like Force in *Stars Wars* was either good or evil, depending how you tapped into it.

75. Ibid., pp. 245–46.

76. Noll, *The Jung Cult,* p. 51.

77. Ibid., p. 69.

78. Ibid., p. 259.

79. Jung and Jaffe, *Memories, Dreams, Reflections,* p. 207; Carl Jung, *Psychology and the East,* p. 15. "The wise Chinese would say in the words of the I Ching: 'When yang has reached its greatest strength, the dark power of yin is born within its depths, for night begins at midday when yang breaks up and begins to change into yin."

80. Ibid., p. 209; Philip Davis, "The Swiss Maharishi," p.12.

81. Ibid., p. 391. Henri F. Ellenberger makes a strong case that Jung borrowed his matriarchy and anima/animus theories from Bachofen, an academic likened by some to the scientific credibility of Erik Von Daniken of *The Chariots of the Gods* and Maharishi Mahesh Yogi of TM and its yogic flying (Ellenberger, *The Discovery of the Unconscious* [Penguin Press, 1970], pp. 218–223; Philip Davis, "The Swiss Maharishi," p.13; Richard Noll, *The Jung Cult,* pp. 188–90).

82. Jung, *Psychological Types,* p. 595.

83. Noll, *The Jung Cult,* pp. 202–203. Philip Davis comments: "Jung's therapeutic technique of 'active imagination' is now revealed as a sanitized version of the sort of trance employed by spiritualistic mediums and Theosophical travelers, with whom Jung was personally familiar" (Philip Davis, "The Swiss Maharishi," p. 14).

84. John Kerr, *A Most Dangerous Method,* pp. 12, 49, 191. ". . . There [the Russian-born Spielrein] remained (in almost complete obscurity) until the publication of the Freud/Jung correspondence in 1974" (p. 498). After the collapse of the Spielrein affair, John Kerr notes that "Jung's condition had so deteriorated that his wife allowed Toni Wolff openly to become his mistress, and a sometime member of the household, simply because she was the only person who could calm him down" (pp. 502–503). Jung's stone bear carving in his Bollingen Tower specifically symbolized the anima (p. 507). Curiously the inscription said: "Russia gets the ball rolling." In a letter to Freud, Jung commented: "The prerequisite for a good marriage . . . is the license to be unfaithful" (*The Freud/Jung Letters,* trans. by R. Manheim and R. Hull [Cambridge, Mass.: Harvard University Press, 1988], p. 289).

85. Ibid., p. 503; *Memories, Dreams, Reflections,* p. 190.

86. Jung and Jaffe, *Memories, Dreams, Reflections,* p. 378.

87. Ibid., p. 328.

88. Noll, *The Jung Cult,* p. 224.

89. Jung and Jaffe, *Memories, Dreams, Reflections,* p. 233.

90. Ibid., p. 60.

91. Ibid., p. 235.

92. Jung, *Psychology and the East,* p. 184.

93. Lawrence, *People Types and Tiger Stripes,* p, 113.

94. Jung, *Psychological Types,* p. 235.

95. Jung and Jaffe, *Memories, Dreams, Reflections,* p. 329.

96. Ibid., p. 329.

97. Jung, *Psychology and The East,* p. 11.

98. Jung, *Psychological Types,* pp. 149–50.

99. Jung and Jaffe, *Memories, Dreams, Reflections,* p. 275.

100. Ibid., p. 275.

101. Ibid., p. 275.

102. Ibid., p.350.

103. Noll, *The Jung Cult,* p. 137.

104. Jung and Jaffe, *Memories, Dreams, Reflections,* p. 335.

105. Lawrence, *People Types and Tiger Stripes,* p. 6.

Rick Warren/Carl Jung
Personality Theory Chart

Rick Warren	"When you minister in a manner consistent with the personality God gave you, you experience fulfillment, satisfaction, and fruitfulness" (*The Purpose Driven Life*, p. 246)
	"... when you are forced to minister in a manner that is 'o u t of character' for your temperament, it creates tension and discomfort, requires extra effort and energy, and produces less than the best results. This is why mimicking someone else's ministry never works. You don't have their personality" (*PDL*, p. 245).
Carl Jung	"... the ultimate aim and strongest desire of all mankind is to develop that fulness (sic) of life which is called personality.... To the extent that a man is untrue to the law of his being and does not rise to personality, he has failed to realize his life's meaning" (The Development of Personality, Collected Works 17; from *The Essential Jung*, pp. 191, 207)
Biblical Response	There is absolutely no biblical precedent for this position. Personality typology has never been a criteria for God choosing someone for ministry, but is in great part grounded in Jungian psychology.
	"And he said unto me, My grace is sufficient for thee: for my strength is made perfect in weakness. Most gladly therefore will I rather glory in my infirmities, that the power of Christ may rest upon me. Therefore I take pleasure in infirmities, in reproaches, in necessities, in persecutions, in distresses for Christ's sake: for when I am weak, then am I strong" (2 Cor

12:9–10). (See also 1 Cor 1:27–29.)

By focusing on assessing and developing one's personality as the key to a successful life or ministry, Warren (and Jung) are promoting a reliance on one's inner self instead of on God's transcendent truth and the working of the Holy Spirit.

"All scripture is given by inspiration of God, and is profitable for doctrine, for reproof, for correction, for instruction in righteousness: That the man of God may be perfect, throughly furnished unto all good works" (2 Tim. 3:16–17). (See also 2 Pet. 1:3).

THEIR CONNECTION ON THE UNCONSCIOUS

Rick Warren | "You may be driven by a painful memory, a haunting fear, or an unconscious belief" (*PDL*, p. 27).

"[Guilt-driven people] often unconsciously punish themselves by sabotaging their own success" (*PDL*, pp. 27–28).

Carl Jung | "The unconscious . . . is the source of the instinctual forces of the psyche and of the forms or categories that regulate them, namely the archetypes" (*The Structure of the Psyche*, CW 8, par. 342).

"Constant observation pays the unconscious a tribute that more or less guarantees its cooperation. One of the most important tasks of psychic hygiene is to pay continual attention to the symptomatology of unconscious contents and processes" (*The Portable Jung*, New York: Penguin Books, 1986, p. 156).

Biblical Response | The "unconscious" is the foundational concept of both Freudian and Jungian psychology, and has no biblical basis whatsoever. By endorsing the idea of the unconscious, Warren is promoting the Jungian belief that people must analyze the forces of the unconscious to discover their life's purpose.

According to Scripture, any driving force outside of God's will is sin, no matter where it resides. Psychology, however, downplays our personal accountability for sin by making the "unconscious" the ultimate reservoir and bastion of unavoidable human instinct.

THEIR CONNECTION ON
UNCONSCIOUS METAPHORS AND IMAGES

Rick Warren | "If I asked how you picture life, what image would come to your mind? That image is your life metaphor. It's the view of life that you hold, consciously or unconsciously, in your mind" (*PDL,* pp. 41–42).

"Your unspoken life metaphor influences your life more than you realize. It determines your expectations, your values, your relationships, your goals, and your priorities" (*PDL,* p. 42).

Carl Jung | "An archetypal content expresses itself, first and foremost, in metaphors" ("The Psychology of the Child Archetype," CW 9i, par. 267).

Archetypes are not inborn ideas, but "typical forms of behaviour which, once they become conscious, naturally present themselves as ideas and images, like everything else that becomes a content of consciousness" (*Collected Works 8,* par. 435).

"Indeed, the fate of the individual is largely dependent on unconscious factors" ("Conscious, Unconscious, and Individuation" CW 9).

Biblical Response | The analysis of "metaphors" housed in the unconscious is a trademark concept of psychology, not of Scripture. The use of images, fantasies, and dreams to better understand our "unconscious" is a signature feature of Jungian psychotherapy that borders on the occult.

THEIR CONNECTION ON
USING JUNGIAN TERMINOLOGY

Rick Warren | "God made introverts and extroverts. . . . He made some people 'thinkers' and others 'feelers'" (*PDL,* p. 245).

"Your personality will affect how and where you use your spiritual gifts and abilities. For instance, two people may have the same gift of evangelism, but if one is introverted and other is extroverted, that gift will be expressed in different ways" (*PDL*, p. 245).

"Ask yourself questions: . . . Am I more introverted or extroverted? Am I more a thinker or a feeler?" (*PDL*, pp. 251–252).

Carl Jung | "Two types (of typical differences in human psychology) especially become clear to me; I have termed them the introverted and the extraverted types" ("Introduction," *Psychological Types*, CW 6 par. 1).

"I have found from experience that the basic psychological functions, this is, functions which are genuinely as well as essentially different from other functions, prove to be thinking, feeling, sensation, and intuition. If one of these functions habitually predominates, a corresponding type results. I therefore distinguish a thinking, a feeling, a sensation, and an intuitive type. Each of these types may moreover be either introverted or extraverted . . ." ("Introduction," *Psychological Types*, CW 6).

Biblical Response | Warren is explicitly using the specific terminology of the psychological typology theory originally conceived by Carl Jung. Despite the claims of his supporters, Warren has clearly based his personality theory (the "P" in his SHAPE teaching) on the unbiblical foundation of Jungian psychology.

"Beware lest any man spoil you through philosophy and vain deceit, after the tradition of men, after the rudiments of the world, and not after Christ" (Col. 2:8).

"Now we have received, not the spirit of the world, but the spirit which is of God; that we might know the things that are freely given to us of God. Which things also we speak, not in the words which man's wisdom teacheth, but which the Holy Ghost teacheth; comparing spiritual things with spiritual" (1 Cor 2:12–13).

THEIR CONNECTION ON THE FOUR TEMPERAMENTS

Rick Warren	"The Bible gives us plenty of proof that God uses all types of personalities. Peter was a sanguine. Paul was a choleric. Jeremiah was a melancholy. When you look at the personality differences in the twelve disciples, it's easy to see why they sometimes had interpersonal conflict" (*PDL*, p. 245). "There is no 'right' or 'wrong' temperament for ministry" (*PDL*, p. 245).
Carl Jung	". . . the physicians of ancient times . . . tried to reduce the bewildering diversity of mankind to orderly groups. . . . The very names of the Galenic temperaments betray their origin in the pathology of the four 'humours.' Melancholic denotes a preponderance of black bile, phlegmatic a preponderance of phlegm or mucus, sanguine a preponderance of blood, and choleric a preponderance of choler, or yellow bile" ("Psychological Typology," CW 6). "The whole make-up of the body, its constitution in the broadest sense, has in fact a very great deal to do with psychological temperament . . ." ("Psychological Typology," CW 6).
Biblical Response	Despite Warren's claim, the Bible never gives proof of the classification of personalities; it is a purely pagan concoction. The four temperaments, as conceived by Hippocrates and later developed by Galen, was a prevalent Greek philosophy during the time of Paul's apostolic ministry. Unlike Warren and Jung, however, Paul did not implement these Greek ideas into his teachings. In fact, he categorically rejected them and "determined not to know any thing among you, save Jesus Christ, and him crucified" (1 Cor 2:2). "O Timothy, keep that which is committed to thy trust, avoiding profane and vain babblings, and oppositions of science falsely so called" (1 Tim. 6:20). Worse yet, Warren is teaching that a person's "no right or wrong" personality is somehow unaffected by the fall and is always beneficial for ministry. How, we ask, does a "phlegmatic temperament" toward laziness and slothfulness serve God's purpose in ministry?

THEIR CONNECTION ON ENDORSING PSYCHOLOGY

Rick Warren	"Every behavior is motivated by a belief, and every action is prompted by an attitude. God revealed this thousands of years before psychologists understood it" (*PDL*, p. 181).
Carl Jung	"[Unconscious phenomena] manifest themselves in the individual's behaviour . . ." ("Conscious, Unconscious, and Individuation," CW 9). "Modern psychological development leads to a much better understanding as to what man really consists of" ("Psychology and Religion," CW 11).
Biblical Response	Warren is suggesting here that psychologists have the same understanding as God on the issue of human behavior, thus putting man's "wisdom" on equal footing with God's revelation. If Warren truly believes in the preeminence of God's revelation to understand man, then why does he rely so heavily on the "useless wisdom" of psychology instead of Scripture? "For the wisdom of this world is foolishness with God. For it is written, **He taketh the wise in their own craftiness.** And again, **The Lord knoweth the thoughts** of the wise, **that they are vain**" (1 Cor 3:19–20). "It is better to trust in the LORD than to put confidence in man" (Ps. 118:8).

THEIR CONNECTION ON
FINDING AND DEVELOPING PERSONALITY

Rick Warren	"The best use of your life is to serve God out of your shape. To do this you must discover your shape, learn to accept and enjoy it, and then develop it to its fullest potential" (*PDL*, p. 249). The SHAPE program states: "To discover your S.H.A.P.E. is to discover where God is calling you to do His work in the world."

Carl Jung	"Only the man who can consciously assent to the power of the inner voice becomes a personality" ("The Development of Personality," CW 17).
	"The achievement of personality means nothing less than the optimum development of the whole individual human being" ("The Development of Personality," CW 17).
	"In so far as every individual has the law of his life inborn in him, it is theoretically possible for any man to follow this law and to become a personality, this is, to achieve wholeness" ("The Development of Personality" CW 17).
Biblical Response	Finding your SHAPE has no biblical support. Warren's teaching that one must "discover his shape" is philosophically and systematically akin to Jung's teaching that a man must "consciously assent to the power of the inner voice" and be true to "the law of his being."
	While Warren has rightly acknowledged God's sovereign purpose in creating us, he has mistakenly made God's divine purpose synonymous with our so-called "shape" by advocating the Jungian idea of developing the personality to "achieve wholeness." This Jungian process, however, does not serve God, but serves the god within us.
	Scripture calls for an active, heartfelt obedience to God's will through the transforming power of the Spirit, not a misguided exploration of our natural psychological makeup to define our God-given purpose.
	"Trust in the LORD with all thine heart; and lean not unto thine own understanding. In all thy ways acknowledge him, and he shall direct thy paths" (Prov. 3:5–6).
	". . . your faith should not stand in the wisdom of men, but in the power of God" (1 Cor 2:5).

Appendix E

Other Excellent Resources, Reviews, and Exposés on *The Purpose Driven Life* and the Purpose Driven Church in General

Southwest Radio Church Ministries
The Prophetic Observer with Dr. Noah Hutchings and Dr. Larry Spargimino—*www.swrc.com/broadcasts/2004/april.htm*

Watchman on the Wall broadcast hosted by Dr. Larry Spargimino, with guest and author James Sundquist, addressing the issues raised in this book. It is an entire week devoted to commentary on *The Purpose Driven Life*—*www.swrc.com/broadcasts/2004/october.htm*

and

Watchman on the Wall with guest Dr. Robert Morey, addressing Rick Warren and Natural Theology—*www.swrc.com/broadcasts/2004/september.htm*

Radio Liberty
Guest Robert Klenck, M.D., addressing "Diaprax and the Church: Manipulating the Church into Globalism."
P.O. Box 969
Soquel, CA 95073
e-mail: *radiolib@aol.com*

Pastor Bob DeWaay, Pastor, Twin City Fellowship
Critical Issues Commentary
Twin City Fellowship
www.twincityfellowship.com/cic/articles/issue80.htm

Lighthouse Trails Publishing
www.lighthousetrailsresearch.com/Warren.htm

Gary Gilley
Southern View Chapel
Think On These Things articles
www.svchapel.org/resources/articles/read_articles.asp?id=50

Jewel Grewe
Discernment Ministries
www.discernment-ministries.com/Purpose_Driven.pdf

Warren Smith
Deceived on Purpose: The New Age Implications of the Purpose-Driven Church
Available at Discernment Ministries
www.zyworld.com/Discernment/Catalog.htm

Pied Pipers of Purpose
Lynn D. Leslie, Sarah H. Leslie, and Susan J. Conway
www.discernment-ministries.com/Purpose_Driven.pdf

Paul Proctor
News With Views
www.newswithviews.com/PaulProctor/proctor50.htm
Religious Relativism

Dr. John MacArthur
John MacArthur: Hard to Believe—The High Cost and Infinite Value of Following Jesus (Thomas Nelson: Nashville, 2003) and *Does the Truth Matter Anymore* video.

Hear Dr. MacArthur's interview and opinion of *Purpose Driven Life* on **Jan Markell's** radio show, *Prophetic News Behind the News*, May 22, 2004, seventeen minutes into the second hour. He specifically addresses *Purpose Driven Life* at twenty-seven minutes into the program. To hear his interview, go to:
www.olivetreeviews.org/radio_archives.shtml

Deception in the Church Ministries
www.deceptioninthechurch.com/profitdrivenchurch.html

Let Us Reason Ministries
www.letusreason.org/Popteac23.htm
          and
www.letusreason.org/BookR12.htm
This is a superb review and lists a host of other biblical errors which I have not mentioned, as my commentary is by no means exhaustive. This review also covers and confirms many of my own observations.

Fundamental Evangelistic Association
www.fundamentalbiblechurch.org/Foundation/fbcAnalysis.htm
An analysis of Rick Warren's *The Purpose-Driven® Life* by Matt Costella, *Foundation Magazine*

Berit Kjos Crossroad Ministry
www.crossroad.to/articles2/2003/1-purpose.htm
Extensive review of *The Purpose Driven Life* book.
Simplicity in Christ
www.simplicityinchrist.org

Despatch Magazine, Australia
www.despatch.cth.com.au/Transcripts/THEPURPOSE2.rtf

Purpose Driven Nightmare by **Wendy Howard**
Eastern Regional Watch
www.erwm.com/Church%20Growth%20Movement.htm

Media Spotlight
www.mediaspotlight.org
Al Dager has written an extensive documentary on both *The Purpose Driven Church* and *The Purpose Driven Life.*

Biblical Discernment Ministries
www.rapidnet.com/~jbeard/bdm/exposes/Rick Warren/

Berean Call
www.bereancall.org
Dave Hunt's Organization. Note particularly his article entitled "The Vanishing Gospel" (pub. date: 2/1/2004), which documents Rick Warren's affiliation and participation with **Robert Schuller's Institute for Successful Church Leadership.**

and

Dave Hunt & T.A. McMahon
Search the Scriptures Daily radio broadcast
"Psychology vs. Scripture, Parts I, II, and III"
*www.oneplace.com/ministries/search_the_scriptures_daily/
   Archives.asp*

More on Robert Schuller

Let Us Reason Ministries
www/letusreason.org/Poptea1.htm
and
Biblical Discernment Ministries
www.rapidnet.com/~jbeard/bdm/exposes/schuller/

Other Valuable Resources Addressing Purpose Driven Church and Church Growth Movement:

Cephas Ministry
www.cephasministry.com/index_purpose_driven_churches.html

Biblical Discernment Ministries
www.rapidnet.com/~jbeard/bdm/exposes/cho/general.htm

Christian Research Ministries
www.crmspokane.org/Philemon.htm

Diakrisis
Christian Occultism
www.diakrisis.org/Christianised_Occultism.htm

The Mission of Truth
Revealing the biblical truth about contemplative spirituality, mysticism, and other false religions through personal, firsthand Christian testimonies.
www.themissionoftruth.org/

Those who have endorsed *The Purpose Driven Life* on the back of Rick Warren's book include Billy Graham, Franklin Graham, Bruce Wilkinson (author of *The Prayer of Jabez*), Lee Strobel, and Max Lucado. Various websites listed above discuss the teachings of these individuals. Lee Strobel stated on the back of Rick Warren's book, "If you only read one book on what life is all about—make it this one!" He should have named the Bible instead!

Disclaimer: With respect to all of the websites and ministries referenced throughout this book, you will find many articles and links to sites that may be helpful to you in your search for the truth. We either know these ministries personally, or have verified the content of specifically referenced articles as they relate to the subjects in this book. Although we have linked to certain articles, we may not necessarily be in 100 percent agreement with every single statement on a particular website, nor have we verified every link that happens to appear on these websites, as this would be a virtually impossible task. Therefore, please be a good Berean and use discernment as you read through the materials, testing every teaching and every spirit to be sure they line up with Scripture.

About the Author

 **Mr. James Sundquist** is the founder of Rock Salt Publishing. He was the founder of another musical production company where he was the executive producer, composer, guitarist, and developer of health maintenance compliance software for such clients as Sony and Nordictrack. His innovative musical production work has been featured on "All Things Considered" on NPR, and Comcast Newsmakers, the *Washington Post,* and several hundred publications and networks around the world. He wrote and produced two documentaries on the history of hymns and Christmas carols (for which James was nominated for a Grammy for Best Album Notes) aired on National Public Radio, Calvary Satellite Network, Family Life Radio Network, Salem Broadcasting, and the Armed Forces Radio Network. James' first solo record album is entitled "Freedom Flight," on Lamb & Lion Records for Pat Boone Productions.

James was also a biblical commentator with astronomer Dr. Danny Faulkner and Dr. Kent Hovind on a video creation series entitled: "Age of the Earth" for Creation Science Evangelism. Most recently he released an article entitled: "Islamic Jesus vs. Biblical Jesus, Scriptural Reasons Why They Are Not the Same Jesus," featured on Andy Andersen Live, WMCA Radio in New York, Sharon Hughes' "Changing Worldviews," Moody Broadcasting Network, and recommended by *Calvary Contender* magazine and Berit Kjos, editor, *Christian Prophetic News Journal,* Dr. Larry Spargimino, Southwest Radio Church, Power of Prophecy, Prophecy Update, and Dr. Ted Baehr, director, Movieguide. He has been a frequent guest on "Crosstalk" VCY America, and now on "Watchman on the Wall" on Southwest Radio Church.

He also wrote and produced a documentary and video on creation and prophecy, entitled "CREATION & PROPHECY: Does God Expect Man to Be Able to Tell Time." James is a speaker and concert artist and has published other end-times articles on various current issues. James has written a number of documentaries exposing the Purpose Driven Church and Church Growth Movement teachings and practices; and the infiltration of Carl Jung and psychology into the church in which he demonstrates these to be a clear and present danger to the church. James is married and has a 23-year-old son.

Some of his articles may be accessed at:
http://www.abrahamic-faith.com/False-Teachers.html